"This book provides a guide to align personal expectations with the demands of a role in civilian life - making for a more satisfying and fulfilling experience. Highlighting the differences and the similarities between military life and a civilian career, Bill and Dave leverage their experience to provide insights and guidelines to help both veterans and employers yield the greatest results for both."

> *Roger J. Wood, former Co-CEO & President Tenneco Corporation; former Chairman & CEO Fallbrook Corporation; former CEO & President Dana Holding Corporation*

"Wow! This book is amazing. Not only is it a great resource and primer for veterans transitioning into the civilian sector, it has great application for many people. I found it very insightful as a recent government retiree. When I speak about service member transition, I touch on several of these points but you all did the true deep dive and prepared a great primer for how to fully transition and be successful!"

> *The Honorable Cheryl L. Mason, Former Chairman, Board of Veterans' Appeals, Department of Veterans Affairs*

"An essential read not just for service members and veterans, but for anyone undergoing a major life or career transition, "Veteran Career Journey- More Insights from the Employer Side of the Desk" provides critical insight into the conventions of the civilian workplace that has broad applicability for people from all walks of life. In a day and age in which young people are seeking help with "adulting" and adults are still adjusting to life in a post-pandemic world, Bill and Dave's advice—provided with the scrutinous eye of military veterans who have experienced pitfalls first hand—goes a long way towards demystifying the challenging process of forging a purposeful, fulfilling career in a complex world."

> *Dr. Alice Atalanta, Ph.D., CEO SOFxLE, Author, Consultant, Educator*

"Bill Kieffer and David White hit a walk-off grand slam with "Veteran Career Journey - More Insights from the Employer Side of the Desk". The 3Ps process outlined in Veteran Career Journey provides a clear understanding of the path to workplace success and fulfillment. Written with unabashed humility, Bill and Dave illustrate what is best about our military; two humble professionals willing to share their successes and failures to improve the career journey of their fellow Veterans. Well done."

> *Tony Mayne, U.S. Army Ranger veteran and Military Transition Career Counselor*

"Bill and Dave have written a must read with hundreds of nuggets for military to civilian career transition. Their approach to writing, where a military member can immediately apply their proven advice is one of a kind. This is a new and better approach to military transition which they have honed over the last many years. They have properly evolved this process, so much so that those who have transitioned within the last decade will gain much here. Well done!"

> *Joe Barnard, (ret) Lt Col; Former COO and Exec Dir; 33 year USAF Veteran*

"Through their book "Veteran Career Journey - More Insights from the Employer Side of the Desk", authors Bill Kieffer and David White provide invaluable insights for veterans seeking to transition into successful civilian careers. The book offers practical advice and real-world examples in a clear and concise manner. As a veteran, and business leader I highly recommend this book to both veterans and employers seeking to create a more effective and mutually beneficial transition process."

> *JC Glick, retired US Army Officer, Ranger, and leadership consultant*

"***Veteran Career Journey*** is a book for veterans who are seeking both a great new career and a rich life. The authors know the challenge well and have created a powerful yet practical guide to help you navigate this process and secure the right role in the right organization. This is essential reading for all veterans and the leaders who seek to hire them."

Brian Bowers, Visiting Professor, Ohio State University.

"Dave and Bill wrote a roadmap, using their 3P model, that helps veterans take control of their own transition and successfully land, integrate, and thrive and survive in the workplace. It puts you in the learning mindset and speaks directly to where the value is added."

Raye Perez, retired Army Ranger and VP of Strategy

VETERAN CAREER JOURNEY

More Insights from the Employer Side of the Desk

William E. "Bill" Kieffer

&

David White

Copyright © 2023 by William E. Kieffer; David White

All rights reserved. No part of this book may be reproduced or retransmitted in any form or by any means without the written permission of the publishers.

ISBN 978-1-7373714-2-7 (print)
ISBN 978-1-7373714-3-4 (ebook)

Bill Kieffer Contact Information:
bill@kieffer-associates.com
https://www.linkedin.com/in/williamkieffer/
419.205.7072

Dave White Contact Information:
Dave.ohio@hotmail.com
https://www.linkedin.com/in/davidmwhite1/
706.570.2491

Printed in the United States of America

We dedicate this book to all military servicemembers past, present, and future.

Blessed be the peacekeepers.

CONTENTS

Contents...ix
Foreword..xi
Acknowledgements xiii
Letter to our Readers..xv
Prologue..1
Starting Points..23

LANDING *(LANDING is about IDENTIFYING)*.............. 27

Introduction/General LANDING Insights....................29
The Three P's - *People, Process, and Product/Service* in
    LANDING..35
        People 35
        Process..44
        Product/Service...67

INTEGRATING *(INTEGRATING is about LEARNING)*.............. 83

Introduction/General INTEGRATING Insights............85
The Three P's - *People, Process, and Product/Service* in
    INTEGRATING..112
        People 112
        Process 130
        Product/Service 144

THRIVING & SURVIVING *(THRIVING & SURVIVING is about LEVERAGING)*.............. 155

Introduction/General THRIVING & SURVIVING Insights............157

The Three Ps - *People, Process, and Product/Service* in
    THRIVING & SURVIVING..195
        People...196
        Process 218
        Product/Service..255
Final Thoughts..266
Key Insight Summary...267
About the Authors...289

FOREWORD

My first real adult job came to a close at the end of my military enlistment in the mid 1980's. During that formative time, the army had shaped and disciplined my character, with indelible and positive impact to this day. For veterans steeped in a military culture, the move into civilian life can be daunting. For me, it was more like anti-climactic disillusionment. The civilian world just seemed comparatively concerned with superficial and petty issues. It felt passive and undisciplined, with a soft underbelly. (And that was before social media.) This new environment seemed a far cry from the "get 'er done," "lives depend upon it," "complete-the-mission" military posture. It took a long time for me, through college and into the civilian business world, to better understand the nature of civilian approaches to both life and work. As it turns out, this book details those civilians approaches to the very people, processes, and production outputs that veterans must come to understand if they are to survive and even thrive. It reveals the business world is no better or worse than the military world, just quite different: different environments, social structures, and drivers. This book is both the roadmap and the accelerator I wish I had to kick start my learning curve!

Fast forward through my career as a physician, lawyer, and health system executive. I have hired hundreds of highly skilled, educated medical professionals, including those transitioning out of the military. Unfortunately, many are often lost on how to succeed in very different matrix and siloed environments within business and corporate systems. What's worse is that onboarding, mentoring and personal development at businesses and corporations, remain woefully inadequate. This book is an ideal reference and formula for success, not just for veterans, but for anyone entering the corporate realm. Within these pages, Dave and Bill comprehensively guide the reader step by step through the entire employment life cycle. "So, you got the job…. Now what?"

Reading this book cover to cover creates a broad overview of the employment journey. Best of all, it serves as a facile and ongoing, ready reference to refresh and review key issues as they arise in real time. Three key features really standout: First, the authors' "Career and Life Journey Alignment" info-graphic is a quick reference that provides an easy visual framework showing how each step of the method fits together to guide your success. You should hang it on the wall! Second, they have divided the narrative into topical areas throughout the employment lifecycle and developed bite-sized gems of how-to wisdom. Finally, both Dave and Bill scatter countless, highly relevant examples from their lived experience, to reinforce how their guidance might apply to the veteran employee in real terms. This publication is a must-have for anyone starting in a new work environment. It is the perfect pocket mentor, at any time, for any situation, right at your fingertips!

—ADB James MD, JD, CPE

ACKNOWLEDGEMENTS

Bill

As with my first book "Military Career Transition: Insights From the Employer Side of the Desk," writing this book has been a labor of love, and a next step in my career and life journeys to make a positive impact on people and organizations. It has been fun, challenging, frustrating, and fulfilling.

This never would have happened without the love and support of my wife Nikki, who continues to encourage me, stand with me, and give me the honest feedback I need to keep driving on.

All my kids – Nate, Traci, Ben, Ryan and Jeremy – each in their own way, continue to inspire me to do better every day.

To my parents, Ed and Mary, who are now viewing the world from above, your lessons of discipline, tough love, manners, respect, and so much more keep me grounded on a solid foundation.

Dave – you sparked the fire for this extension of my first book. Joining forces and sharing these legs of our respective career and life journeys is a joy. I truly value our unique ability to converse, confer, collaborate, and create.

To the countless military leaders, business leaders, fellow soldiers, co-workers and colleagues, and the service members and veterans with whom I am privileged to work, I send my sincere "Thank You." Your individual and combined contributions to my journey and this book are invaluable.

Alice – thank you for your insightful perspective and your outstanding partnership. You smoothed out the rough edges to make this book infinitely more readable.

Dave

An eternal thanks to my wife, Libby, who graciously held down the fort while I was away and continues to support me through my labors. From raising our kids into the loving humans they are becoming, to standing by me through the hard times, I love you, and you will always be my rock.

To my kids, who give me purpose and inspire me to do better, thank you for being you.

A sincere thanks to my parents, who raised me with the values that have made me who I am today. I could never thank you enough for the sacrifices you made for me. Matt, thanks for being an inspiration. Your thoughtful kindness is something I try to model.

To the boys of 3C, 2B, BCO 3/75, Comanche Company and all of the Rangers and soldiers with whom I have served: you have molded me more than you know. Your dedication to our country and to your men is unparalleled, and I hope that the mark you left on me comes through in this book.

To the Special Operators Transition Foundation, Bill, Team 7 and C21, and all my mentors in the private sector, thank you for taking a chance on me. I hope to continue to use my experience to make an impact on our communities.

LETTER TO OUR READERS

We wrote this book for many reasons.

First, we believe in our methodology, and are certain that if well-executed, the guidance offered here will help veterans land on their feet, integrate well into the workplace, and ultimately thrive and survive in the civilian work world.

Yes, our focus is on helping veterans successfully make the career transition, but we are also acutely aware that work and career are only part of one's overall life journey.

At the core, we are offering our insights and experiences to help veterans achieve their best possible post-military lives – whatever that looks like for each individual veteran.

We know firsthand by our own experiences—and by the experiences we've shared with fellow veterans, combat buddies who chewed the same dirt, coaching clients, and incidental acquaintances—that life after the military is fraught with challenges that are new, unfamiliar, and sometimes downright scary. We've both struggled in our journeys. We've enjoyed wins and suffered losses. We've shared great days and dark days with our brothers and sisters.

We've lost too many who succumbed to the difficulties and taken their own lives.

Suicide among the veteran community is endemic. There are many reasons why some of the most resilient people in our country decide they can no longer cope with this thing we call life: lost sense of purpose, loss of community, loss of contributing to something larger than yourself, loss of identity, loss of income, loss of status, loss of familiar structure, exposure to a nearly unlimited new world of possibilities with no training on how to assess and deal with the variables, and the list goes on and on. Are PTSD and related injuries contributors? Absolutely. But based on our experiences—though, admittedly, neither of us is a psychologist—it is our belief that it is usually a complex combination of contributing factors.

It's been said that "Hope is not a plan, nor a method of execution." We get it. But we also know that hope is essential to success. We believe, as Viktor Frankl did, that hope can be found in even the darkest places.

We hope that this book can give veterans hope for the future. We hope that by sharing our experiences, we can make your experience better; that we can help you take a next step forward in your career and life journey, and that if needed, perhaps help you make one small step that backs you off the ledge.

It's tough out there, but you can do it.

You get to write your future, and you get to decide where you find your purpose. Whether you find it at your job, or with your family, in your community, or an amalgamation of them all, find it and live it.

You don't have to do it alone. The world is full of willing, capable people standing by to help. Reach out. Let them in. We've both done so. It makes a world of difference.

Be well my friends. Keep up the fire!	RLTW
Bill	Dave

PROLOGUE

Bill's prior book *Military Career Transition: Insights from the Employer Side of the Desk* focused on helping servicemembers with their "pre-deployment" into the civilian work world. It offered insights from the employer side of the desk—providing "intelligence preparation of the career battlefield"—and its mission was to support servicemembers and new veterans making that first jump from the military to the civilian work environment. To those of you who are readers of *Military Career Transition,* welcome back! We are excited to partner with you on this next leg of your military career transition journey. To those of you who are just meeting us, we invite you to join us as we provide an in-depth exploration of the next step in your transition journey.

Why the need for the second book? To put it simply, imagine your career transition from the military as you would a combat jump into a foreign land. The jump would be comprised of two primary elements: first, the jump itself and all its technicalities (everything from training for the jump to preparing your gear, packing your parachute, exiting the aircraft safely, maneuvering yourself through the air, and landing in one piece on the ground at your target location). This jump is your initial transition into the civilian world, and it is the subject matter of Bill's previous book.

The second element, and the subject matter of the book you now hold in your hands, is the equally important matter of what happens—the course you chart, and the path you take—once you've landed on the ground. Our focus at this stage of the game is to help you get your bearings in the dog-eat-dog climate of the civilian professional world, where your objective has now become to win the battle on the ground. That is why we focus in this book on expanding the discussion to consider one's broader career and life journey beyond the military. We offer insights to help readers look past the job they are in today—beyond finding a landing spot—to help you not only land well, but to integrate well once you've landed, and to thrive & survive over time.

In the vast world beyond the military, you are free to choose between nearly unlimited paths to take you from wherever you are today to wherever you want to be in the future. While this freedom is exhilarating, it can also be overwhelming and even burdensome. The good news is that we've been there, done that. We've enjoyed the freedom and endured the burdens. We've enjoyed success and have gotten our asses kicked. We've learned from it all, and we've got your back. We are excited to share our lessons learned, and insights gained.

So, let's begin!

DAVE STORY

"Who's Gonna Wipe Your Ass?"

In 2007, my best friend was killed near Balad, Iraq. I was supposed to escort him home, but was feeling an incredible amount of guilt about leaving my guys in Iraq while I went home. I thought there was no way that I could go home to the States while the guys were still risking their lives nightly. What if something happened to one of them while I was gone? I presented this to my boss at the time, and without missing a beat, he said, "Dave, the Army's not going to wipe your ass when you're eighty. Go home." This was a mantra I repeated throughout my career. Up to this point, I had never thought about envisioning my life more than a month ahead, let alone more than fifty years down the road. But look: if you don't want to be a passenger in your own life, it's prudent to

PROLOGUE

start to understand how decisions you make today will affect your life journey. His point was that I needed to take care of my family, who was in it for the long haul—if I wanted to keep that family.

What do you want your life to look like when you're eighty? Who will be there to wipe your ass? It's not going to be the military, and it won't be your new employer either. Will they play a role in how you get there? Absolutely! But you are in control, and how you navigate the journey will dictate whether you get to where you want to go in life.

BILL STORY

"What a long, strange trip it's been."

Jerry Garcia may have sung it best in the classic Grateful Dead song, "Truckin'," but it is also a perfect description of my career and life journey. My plan was to do a full career as a U.S. Army officer, retire, and then figure out the rest of it. My Army career was going great; all the right assignments, all the right opportunities, all the right connections, etc. I was about halfway to retirement when life happened. An unexpected divorce created a fork in the road. I was then forced to make a choice: did I continue with the career I planned (and that was going very well), or did I leave it to be closer to my three then-small kids? I chose to resign my commission and chart a whole new career course. I had no idea what I was doing, what my next career step would be (let alone my new career plan), or how to do any of it. I struggled, but I knew that my life journey was going in new, uncharted directions, and my career journey was going to have to shift to align with it.

Your career transition journey is only one part of your life journey, but in many ways, it can determine everything that comes afterwards. This is why it is critical to ask yourself: do you have a plan? Is reality lining up with your plan? Have you considered what you might do if the unexpected occurs? Our hope is to share what we've learned from our experiences so that you might be better armed, better informed, and better prepared for your life journey, your career journey, and for those unexpected speed bumps that just may pop up along the way.

As we mentioned before in the analogy of the combat jump, getting to the objective—jumping out of that plane, or transitioning out of the military and into civilian life is one thing. It takes planning, coordination, decisive action, and multiple other thoughts and actions across a wide spectrum of topics and disciplines. All that simply to get there—to land safely in that new space!

Having arrived at the objective, however, you're not done. In fact, your real work is just beginning. You are now in uncharted territory, as a member of the civilian workforce, and you need to forge a path ahead.

Now it's about performing. Your mission has changed, and you need to change with it. You may have spent days, weeks, months or longer preparing for and making the journey to your target.

But did you really plan for what you'd do on arrival? Or after the first day? Week? Month? Quarter? Year?

This book is about preparing for success once you've landed and succeeding in that new landing place. It's about making entry to the new world, making a great first impression, learning the ropes, navigating a new work environment and culture, winning the early innings, and setting yourself up for long-term success. But this is more easily said than done; what does it actually look like in practice for a newly minted veteran navigating the civilian work world?

We have walked this walk. We both made tough transitions, had some early wins, and fumbled some easy passes. We're both "statistics." We have changed jobs/careers within the first year of separating from the military. We've both changed again after the first year. We've both felt the thrill of career victory, and the agony of defeat.

Think of us as your ADVON – the team that went in early, gained real-world intel and experience, and are now here to share that first-hand knowledge and experience with you so you are prepared for success upon landing, and beyond.

The reason that this book is desperately needed is because, sadly, our experiences were not unique. In fact, far too many veterans struggle with their careers after transition, which the statistics show.

- ★ Multiple studies over multiple years from Syracuse University and the Veterans Administration have consistently found that 40 -50% of military veterans leave their first post-military jobs within a year. Upwards of 80% leave within two years. This level of churn is an unacceptable problem for both veterans and employers.
- ★ Other studies from the Department of Labor consistently reveal that roughly 1/3 of veterans are underemployed. This means that highly capable, top-quality talent is being employed below their level of experience and capability... sometimes *far* below. This reality in and of itself is concerning. It reveals that great potential is not being realized. Top talent goes unutilized, and organizations that need top talent miss great opportunities to bring veterans to the table.
- ★ The cost of employee turnover is significant at all pay levels. The Society of Human Resource Management (SHRM) has calculated the cost of turnover for entry level jobs at $4,125. As you might expect, the costs rise substantially as the pay level increases.

These are real problems for both veterans and employers. With this book we offer insights, real-life stories, and action steps that will help solve multiple, relevant disconnects between veterans and employers, enabling each to leverage prior experience and new learning in order to:

- ★ Enhance veterans' career and life journeys.
- ★ Improve veteran under-employment.
- ★ Reduce veteran turnover and turnover associated costs.
- ★ Improve workplace satisfaction, workplace culture, and veteran employee productivity, thus positively impacting business results.

Why are we the right people to talk about it?

- ★ Bill is a military veteran who, despite a tough transition, built a highly successful career leading human resource and talent management functions for large and complex global companies. In 2018, he became an entrepreneur, starting an independent coaching/advisory firm focused on helping military veterans make a successful transition, and helping employers optimize their veteran hiring and employment practices. Since then, he has helped hundreds of veterans find success in the civilian sector.
- ★ Dave is a former Army Ranger with 18 years in the special operations community who struggled through his transition. Trying to find his footing in the workforce after separating from the Army, he held three different jobs in three different industries over the course of his first two years in the civilian workforce. Why? Because of the changed landscape and unexpected realities he encountered, which we will discuss in this book. However, through lessons learned the hard

way, he graduated with his executive MBA, obtained his black belt in Lean Six Sigma, and has begun a meaningful career in something that gives him purpose.

Who is this book for?

- ★ Veterans who are transitioning and those who have landed and want to optimize their initial and long-term performance/success, improve their current workplace satisfaction, or who are considering another career move.
- ★ Employers who are considering having military veterans join their team and/or have already invested in hiring veteran talent.

What can you expect to come away with after reading this?

- ★ Veterans can expect a practical guide to achieving success in the workplace with a high level of intrinsic satisfaction and organizational impact that enhances their career and life journeys in both the short and long term.
- ★ Employers can expect valuable insights to better understand their role in helping military veteran employees land well, integrate fully, and thrive & survive throughout their career journey.

How this book is structured:

Having experienced career transition's ups, downs, challenges, and opportunities, we have written this book in three sections in order to address what we have identified as being the three major phases to success after transition: LANDING, INTEGRATING, and THRIVING & SURVIVING.

- ★ **Section 1: LANDING,** which covers the period from job acceptance through the completion of onboarding activities. This includes the first days and the basics of successfully joining your new team.
- ★ **Section 2: INTEGRATING,** which includes the period after onboarding through the first ~180 days. It takes you from "Where's the coffee pot and the latrine/head?" to becoming a productive, value-adding, and accepted member of your new team.
- ★ **Section 3: THRIVING & SURVIVING,** which addresses topics related to success after your first ~180 days on the job, focusing on how to thrive in your newly obtained role, and how to survive and be successful in the long run (e.g., career planning, networking on the job and other similar topics that will help you define how to get from where you are today, to where you want to go in your career).

CAREER PHASES

Remember the metaphor — your transition is like a combat jump: you're in an unfamiliar foreign land and facing new threats—some anticipated, seen, and planned for, but others unforeseen which will require maximum adaptability accompanied by peak performance and sound judgment.

COMBAT JUMP METAPHOR

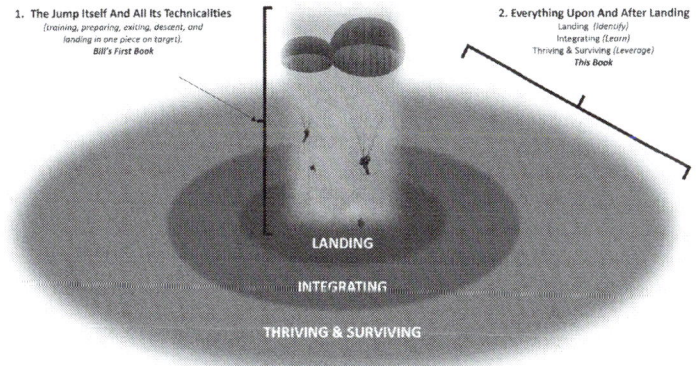

In short: this is what nearly every veteran faces post-transition. You now find yourself in an unfamiliar new landscape where you desire to thrive & survive—but how? Which of the skillsets and abilities that you developed in the military will be an asset to you in this new environment—and which may become a hindrance? And how can you best align yourself from the very beginning to successfully achieve your ultimate goal?

Now imagine that, before making the jump, you could sit down and talk to someone who had made that same jump into that same environment before, and had already coached hundreds of other jumpers to do the same. They would have deep expertise to share that could make your journey a whole lot easier—and that, in short, describes the authors of this book, Bill and Dave.

Bill made the jump a while ago, and has gone on to successfully thrive & survive in the civilian work world for years. He works with hundreds of servicemembers and veterans who are making the jump and creating their own post-transition successes. Dave is an Army Ranger that made the jump more recently, and has gone on to lead an organization that has earned international recognition for the impact it has made in the public sector. Dave and Bill connected not long ago because Dave was in transition and Bill was the experienced sage purveyor of wisdom, who had gone through it successfully himself. As they built their personal and professional relationship, they both came to the realization that their combined experiences could perhaps prepare others for what lies ahead, after the jump is made.

Because, as you know, getting to the battlefield is only the beginning of the mission.

Additionally, we present thoughts regarding the three key areas upon which business leaders typically focus their attention: People, Process, and Product/Service (The 3Ps).

THE 3 Ps of Business

- ★ **People** - No job exists in a vacuum. People are involved to varying degrees in every job there is. No matter what others do or how you interact, you will always have to be mindful of the people aspects of your work experience.
- ★ **Process** - How the work gets done within and across internal groups and external organizations. Identifying relevant processes, learning about them, and leveraging them for individual and organizational success is critical.
- ★ **Product/Service** - This is the output of your business' efforts – the products or services you provide to consumers

PROLOGUE

(or other businesses). Knowing and understanding these is paramount to understanding how you fit, where your growth opportunities may be, and how you can best add value today and tomorrow.

These "3Ps" are relevant in all three phases of your success after transition. They impact and are impacted by you, your role, and other factors.

- ★ When LANDING, simply identifying the "Whos" and "Whats" is your priority.
- ★ While INTEGRATING, learning about People, Processes, and Products/Services is key. Understanding what each does, the value they add, how they play together, and how they impact/are impacted by your role should be a priority.
- ★ Later, as you focus on THRIVING & SURVIVING, leveraging all you've learned about the 3Ps for individual and organizational success today and tomorrow becomes a valuable capability.

THE 3Ps APPLY ACROSS ALL CAREER PHASES

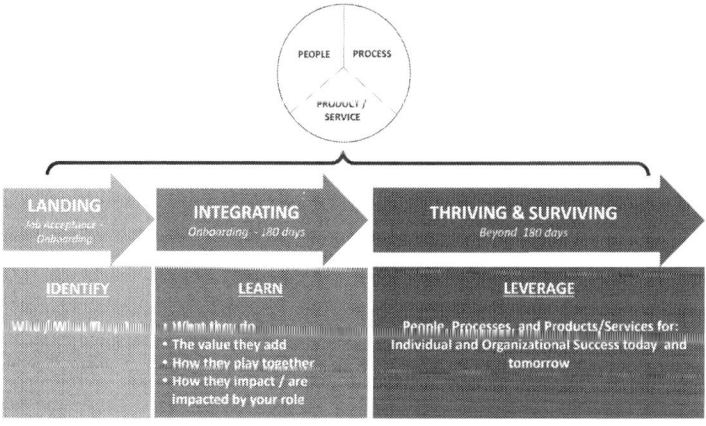

For each aspect of the 3Ps, we dive even deeper, identifying the critical bits that are commonly relevant to success after transition.

DETAILS – THE 3P MODEL

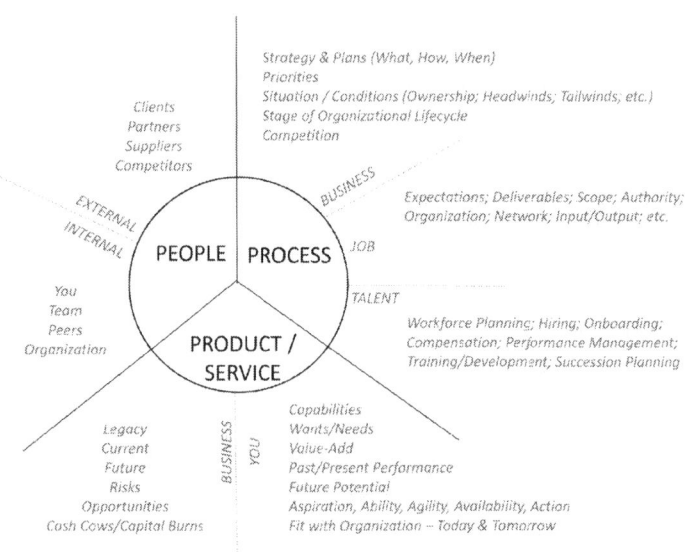

In each section of this book, we will address all three areas, focusing on key items that are most appropriate for that section.

Our goal is to present information in a clear, organized manner to the maximum extent possible. Toward that end, we will endeavor throughout the book to provide the "What," "So What," and "Now What" for all content. Some will be formatted this way explicitly and some will have a different format, but in all cases possible, we will address all three.

★ "What" (*Key Learning Points*): Insights, observations, and lessons learned from our journeys and experiences.

- ★ "So What" *(Content and Stories):* Comments and content to help bring home the point(s) in a way that helps readers connect with them and clarify their experience and make plans/decisions that are best for them.
- ★ "Now What" *(Take Aways):* to help readers easily understand the topics, relate to them, and have useful takeaways.

In every possible instance, insights will be offered to add value for veterans and employers, so that all readers gain familiarity with both sides of the topic and are better able to appreciate and deal with concerns as they may arise.

You'll notice that we offer stories throughout to help drive home key points by sharing narratives of our actual experiences. We both have extensive career and life journey experience, and we've included these stories to share some of what we've seen, done, and endured to help drive home relevant learning points.

We also include a summary of key insights that serves as a quick reference for your use when a quick refresher is needed.

While the overall focus of this book is on employment and career success, it is important to remember that work is simply a part of life, and it must well align with your overall life journey.

So, what does a life journey look like?

Life is a journey, and if you want to get to where you're going, it behooves you to have a plan. As an integral part of this journey, your career should be interlaced in this plan. Think of your career as a lane on one of the roads that will take you to your destination. At this point of your life (military career transition), you are most likely ready to get back on the road after a brief rest stop. You are setting out on a different road that you have never been on before, and whether this was planned or an unexpected detour, there are some tips that will help you ensure your journey is still successful. Before we describe the phases of the remainder of your trip (LANDING, INTEGRATING, and THRIVING & SURVIVING), here are some tips that the "wise guy at the gas pump on life's journey" shared that will help you on your way.

★ *Know your why.*

You don't go on a trip without a reason; whether your goal is to relax on vacation or to learn at a conference, when you plan your trip, it usually starts with your answer to the question, "Why?" Why are you going? And what do you hope to achieve once you get there?

We bet if we asked you why you joined the military, you would be able to tell us pretty easily. For Dave, he was a junior in high school when 9/11 happened. Like most people his age, he remembers exactly where he was when he learned what had happened. It created a deep sense of patriotism and sense of duty. He wanted to ensure something like that never happened again. That was his purpose, and it did not change for eighteen years.

When he retired, he had a complete lack of direction because he thought his "why" no longer applied. What was his purpose? It took a couple of whiffs on the career front to figure it out, because Dave couldn't define it at first. He started in insurance, but didn't feel like he was making an impact. But through this experience, he found out that if he wasn't making a tangible impact, he felt like he lacked purpose. Dave then transitioned to work in a VA hospital because he was sure that he would feel like he was making an impact. Surprise, surprise…bureaucracy is deeply entrenched in the VA system, and he felt like he had zero autonomy to build something and facilitate change.

And there it finally was: his purpose. Through this process of trial and error, Dave discovered that he needed to positively impact his community while having the autonomy to build something. Only then, armed with this knowledge, could he seek employment that would provide the intrinsic motivation that he needed to keep him professionally fulfilled.

★ *Write your legacy.*

Once you have figured out why you're going somewhere (i.e. your purpose), you still need to decide where you're going! This is where writing your legacy comes in.

When Dave was going through his executive MBA program at Ohio State University, his C-suite experience professor (who was an incredible mentor) had him write his legacy. The premise of this assignment was to write a living document that started with where you wanted to be at the end of your life and how you wanted to be remembered, and then planning backwards to get there.

What do you want your family life to look like? What does your work life balance need to be in order to realize that? What are your defining values? How much money do you need to make? What are some things that you want to accomplish in your life? It was an extremely powerful experience which forced Dave to really think about what he wanted his life to look like. Your career is an integral part of your legacy, but you won't be able to pinpoint the ideal career for you until you've looked at your life's long game and determined which career is going to get you to where you want to be.

★ *Build your own personal board of directors.*

It is hard not to like hearing that our ideas are good ones; that's why it feels so good to be surrounded by hype men and women who tell us we are doing a good job. It gives us confidence and makes us feel like winners. But is only surrounding yourself with this crowd really going to make you the best you can be?

When Dave co-founded Gold Star Scholars (a nonprofit

that supports gold star family members through school), he was focused on raising capital. His biggest fear was that he would make the commitment to put someone through college, only to find himself in a position financially where he would be unable to follow through. He was so concerned with this that he didn't focus on anything else.

Over time, his board became less and less engaged. When Dave sat down with them to have the hard conversation about why this was the case, the board shared their concern: "We joined Gold Star Scholars to help gold star family members and so far, we haven't helped anyone. Raising money is important, but we need to start making an impact or we're gone."

This stung, but there was no denying that it was true. It's not easy to hear the truth sometimes, but it's necessary for success. Dave wrote a check and donated it to the first scholar the very next day. The lesson to be learned here is that it is important to have a trusted group of people who will support you no matter what, but at the same time are also not afraid to tell you the hard truth. These are the people who are integral to your success. They are the people who will steer you back onto the right path when you are lost. They are your own personal board of directors.

★ *Be deliberate.*

There was a worry towards the tail end of one of Dave's deployments that preventable injuries were increasing due to what was deemed "complacency." Naturally, the fix was for leaders to reiterate to the guys to not be complacent. This approach was sure to change human behavior, right?

Wrong. It didn't change a thing, and it's not surprising. What does telling people "Don't be complacent" actually achieve, and how can you even quantify it? It wasn't until leaders did a root cause analysis and implemented specific and deliberate counter measures that they actually influenced the outcomes.

For example, guys were undoubtedly sleep deprived. The good news was that they could influence the amount of sleep they got. Rehearsals were too short, and not intentional enough. Again, they could fix that. They could ensure they were just as detailed in their route planning as they were at the beginning of the deployment, and so-on. The root cause analysis was key here, as it enabled the team to deliberately counteract each of the contributing factors to the team's nebulous "complacency."

The lesson here is that in order to move the needle in the direction you want to go, you must be deliberate in your actions to get there, and you need to identify some quantitative component to measure whether it is working or not. If you want to become the COO of a large healthcare system, wishing it into fruition is probably not going to happen. There are certain gates that you will need to hit in order to get there, and being deliberate about it will be critical.

★ *Take risks.*

THE RISK SPECTRUM

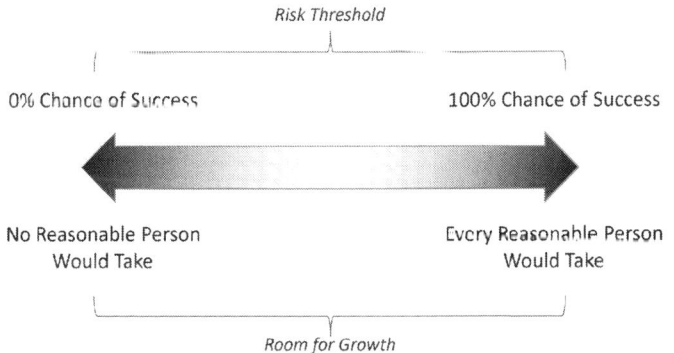

> ### BILL STORY
>
> *"Risky Business"*
>
> *I've made multiple career transitions along my life journey. Each had unknowns. Each had potential upsides. Each brought risk. Leaving the military was risky. It was not what I had planned. But my life situation had changed, and I decided that for the greater good of my life journey, I needed to change careers. It was risky; the military was the only career I had ever known. I had no idea of what to do or how to do it. My lack of knowledge and preparation created more risk. But I did it. I took the risk. I changed careers. Many of my colleagues thought I was nuts. It wasn't easy. It wasn't quick. But over time, I learned. I got good at life in this new situation, and the risk level subsided. My career wasn't what I thought it was going to be, but If I hadn't taken the risk, my life journey would not be as good as it has been.*

Growth requires risk because there is always a chance of failure. During your career and life journey, there will be times when it may be easy to say, "It's too risky." During these times, you need to challenge yourself by asking "What is the risk if I don't do it?" There will be times when your answer doesn't change, but there will be other times when perhaps a different perspective will shift your thought process to "How can I mitigate risk to get to yes?"

★ *Be a lifelong learner.*

This adage has been repeated in thousands of books, in most management curricula, and it has been a recurring theme for many thought leaders throughout history. We think it is worth repeating here because, although by no means a groundbreaking theory, it is not always easy to practice. Learning the right things at the right time in order to amplify your knowledge base and ability to problem solve are skills requiring deliberate effort. As Albert Einstein wisely once said, "Intellectual growth should start at birth and cease only at death."

As you write your legacy, plan and execute deliberately, take risk, consult your personal board of directors, all in pursuit of your "why," and think about what your lifelong learning journey looks like for you (what came first, how did that help you learn more, and what you still seek to learn). While we're not saying everyone should go to Harvard, or even college if it doesn't align with your plan; what is critical for success is a thirst for knowledge and self-improvement that will keep your brain sharp and your feet moving forward.

★ *Remember your why.*

DAVE STORY

"Lost and Found."

I grew up playing soccer, so I was always a runner. However, I was not always very fast. I loved to run, though, and ran often just to clear my head. When I joined the Ranger Regiment, my ultra-competitive side came out. I ran so that I could become faster than my peers. The more I ran, the faster I got, and the faster I got, the more I ran. I started competing in endurance events. I competed in triathlons and marathons outside of the Army, and events like the Best Ranger Competition inside the Army. I even signed up for a 50k the night before, with no training, all because of a bet.

Here's the thing, though. After all that, I started to not like running anymore. I still loved to compete, but the running itself was becoming less and less enjoyable. Instead of running for the joy of running, I only ran so I could get faster, because I wanted to be more competitive.

In 2018, while deployed to Afghanistan, I had a career-ending injury. It took me a long time to run again after that—much longer than it probably should have. In my mind, if I couldn't run an eight-minute mile, I was not ready to run. I don't know why I came up with that as the line in the sand pace. Maybe because that was the slowest pace you could run and still pass the Ranger standard five-mile test. I would start to run, realize that I couldn't run an eight-minute mile, and then throw in the towel.

After about three years of this, I finally ran a mile at the magical pace, but again in about mile two, when I couldn't maintain that pace, I figured I wasn't ready to run again, and would stop—again. I was embarrassed that I couldn't run fast anymore, so I didn't run. I thought that my body would magically be ready to run again. In fact, I signed up for an Olympic distance triathlon and attempted it before I could even run two miles. It may come as a shocker to you, but it didn't go well.

One morning around that time, I was attempting to run and getting frustrated by my speed (as usual), so I stopped running and began walking home. I was upset at myself for recovering so slowly, feeling sorry for myself, and generally cursing running. It was morning time, and I was walking over a river that connects to Lake Erie. The sun was coming up over the water painting the sky a deep red and bright orange. As I stopped to look at the beauty that was my new hometown, an overwhelming sense of calm overtook my frustration. Why was I upset over a made up, self-imposed barrier?

I was looking at something pretty cool, was up walking and alive when 1/10th of an inch the other way when I was shot could have changed the calculus significantly. Why did I start running in the first place? Because I used to love it. It didn't have anything to do with racing, being fast, etc. I loved to get out on the road and be alone with my thoughts. I loved

PROLOGUE

> *pushing myself for the sake of pushing myself. What if I could press reset and just run because I could?*
>
> *So that's exactly what I did. I started running without a watch. I ran as fast or as slow as my body wanted to go that day. I started to heal faster, had less pain, and guess what? It turned out that I could run longer and (probably) faster. In the summer of 2022, I completed my first Ironman 70.3 since before I was hurt. I wasn't fast, but I did it, and even enjoyed it (which I rarely did previously unless I won my age group). It was, by far, my greatest physical accomplishment. Greater than finishing the Best Ranger Competition, any ultra I ever ran, or even winning first place overall in several races.*
>
> *What's my point, and how does this have anything to do with your career and life journey? Look, most of us joined and stayed in the military because we loved the job. Most of us are starting our second careers for similar reasons. Whether it's because we love leading teams, building things, or taking care of people, we are excited to do it. Don't lose sight of the why during the grind, long hours, ups and downs with co-workers, projects that didn't turn out like you wanted, etc. Reset if you need to. Leaders who know their "why" are more engaged, innovative, and ultimately more effective. I forgot why I started running in the first place, and it had a significant impact on my performance, passion, and ultimately my overall well-being.*

Your career transition journey and your life journey are inextricably linked. As you move from landing in your new gig and identifying who's who and what's what, to integrating and learning more about how all the people, processes and products/services operate and interact, and then thriving & surviving in the long run, leveraging everything around you for individual and organizational success, it's important to remember that all the "career stuff" fits inside your LIFE! Keep things in perspective. Do the hard work.

Learn. Grow. Make great things happen over time. But be mindful that what you do today impacts your tomorrow, and that no matter what you've done, what you are doing, or what you plan to do, life is full of uncontrollables that can and will impact you (for better or for worse).

CAREER AND LIFE JOURNEY ALIGNMENT

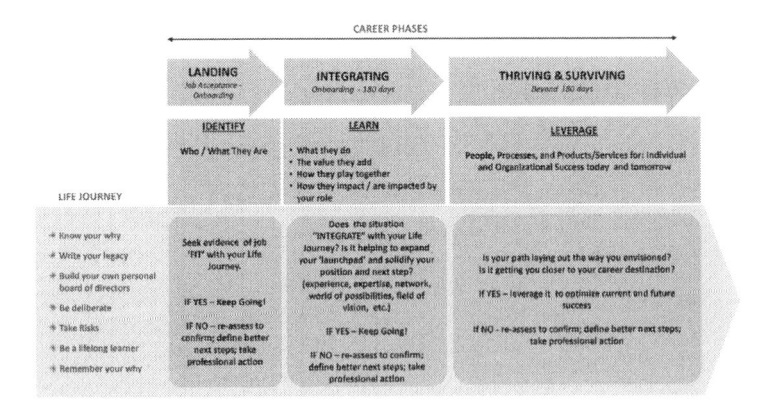

CAREER PHASES

	LANDING Job Acceptance - Onboarding	INTEGRATING Onboarding - 180 days	THRIVING & SURVIVING Beyond 180 days
	IDENTIFY Who / What They Are	**LEARN** • What they do • The value they add • How they play together • How they impact / are impacted by your role	**LEVERAGE** People, Processes, and Products/Services for: Individual and Organizational Success today and tomorrow

LIFE JOURNEY
- Know your why
- Write your legacy
- Build your own personal board of directors
- Be deliberate
- Take Risks
- Be a lifelong learner
- Remember your why

| Seek evidence of job "FIT" with your Life Journey.

IF YES – Keep Going!

IF NO – re-assess to confirm; define better next steps; take professional action | Does the situation "INTEGRATE" with your Life Journey? Is it helping to expand your 'launchpad' and solidify your position and next step? (experience, expertise, network, world of possibilities, field of vision, etc.)

IF YES – Keep Going!

IF NO – re-assess to confirm; define better next steps; take professional action | Is your path laying out the way you envisioned? Is it getting you closer to your career destination?

IF YES – leverage it to optimize current and future success

IF NO – re-assess to confirm; define better next steps; take professional action |

CAREER AND LIFE JOURNEY ALIGNMENT - ACTION ITEMS

	LAND	INTEGRATE	THRIVE & SURVIVE
Know your why	Vet reality against your WHY to optimize happiness and success	Don't let new influences sway you unintentionally	Stay true to yourself; let WHY evolve if appropriate.
Write your legacy	First impressions matter	How you integrate with others impacts your legacy	Remember – your legacy is the result of what you do over time; don't get the cart before the horse.
Build your own personal board of directors	Identify potential PBOD candidates	Build relationships with PBOD candidates and listen to their counsel	Review PBOD members for relevance over time; change members as s needed.
Be deliberate	Have a plan to land well; work the plan diligently	Work with others to understand how everything fits	Take intentional actions to optimize current success and future opportunities that align with your life plan.
Take Risks	Reasonable risks – don't stumble out of the starting blocks	Eagerly seek out others; introduce yourself; make connections; build relationships	Boldly seek and exploit opportunities to spread your wings, add more value, and expand your scope.
Be a lifelong learner	Identify the "Who's Who" and the What's What" of the new job	LEARN • What they do • The value they add • How they play together • How they impact / are impacted by your role	LEVERAGE People, Processes, and Products/Services for: Individual and Organizational Success today and tomorrow
Remember your why	To avoid being drawn off course in your new position	Share your unique value	To vet situations and evolving conditions for alignment with your overall life journey plan.

STARTING POINTS

DAVE STORY

"Coming Out of Your Bubble."

I spent my entire adult life, up until I was 36 years old, in the Special Operations Command. Some call it a bubble within a bubble. Thoughts of a post-military career were conceptual. I knew one day I would get out of the Army, but that day was not today, so why waste time thinking about it? My plan was to spend twenty-five years or so living the Army life, retire, kick my feet up and then think about what I wanted to do when I grew up.

Unfortunately (or fortunately), that was not what life had in store for me. On my thirteenth deployment, I was shot in the hip while on a special operations raid in the mountains of Afghanistan. I tried to recover, and even deployed again, but ultimately, I decided that after eighteen years of service, it was time to hang up the hat.

Suddenly, I found myself in this big scary thing called "the real world" and I needed to decide really quickly what I was going to do and how I was going to do it. Fortunately, I had a lot of great people in my corner to help me navigate the process.

Along the way, I met Bill, who became a mentor and a friend. Between my experience in the military and my journey through executive education and into the workforce, and Bill's experience as a veteran and executive leader for multiple global companies, we decided to write this book for both veterans and employers—a collection of insights and strategies for maximizing military experience in order to achieve individual career growth and success, and achieve desired business outcomes.

From starting as a nineteen-year-old kid, through 18 years of the Global War on Terror, I grew up in the U.S. Army's 75th Ranger Regiment. From learning to buy a house and a new car to the way I learned how to solve complex problems and lead in an ever-changing environment, these all occurred for me through the lens of the military. The military, the U.S. Army, the 75th Ranger Regiment were my framework for everything I knew and all that was familiar to me. They were my center point. They were my source of learning for nearly two decades. Throughout my transition and beyond, it became extremely important for me to understand and embrace this.

BILL STORY

"Your Career Is Not Your Life."

Early on, I focused on my career journey – the military. I thought little about my overall life journey. I figured that if I focused well and worked hard on my career, life would fall into place. As I noted in the prologue, that's not at all how things worked out. As I reflect from today's perch, having traveled my "long strange trip," I see how inverted my early focus was. Career journeys are but a part of life journeys, and having these out of order is not a recipe for success. Further, I realize today that despite what life events may arise on your journey, having eyes and ears open to possibilities, keeping a pragmatic perspective that is grounded in reality, and having some vision for what you want your life journey to look like can lead to amazing success.

Leveraging your experience as a veteran is about utilizing the skills gained from years of working and leading teams in ambiguous and complicated environments, and applying those skills towards a different problem set. It means knowing what you need to learn and learning it, knowing what relationships you need to create and creating them, and knowing the career path you want and building it. Sounds easy right? Well, that's what we thought at first, too. Conceptually, we were right but here in "the real world," we quickly found that knowledge, understanding, and application are significantly different animals.

There are approximately 9 million veterans in today's labor market. There are over 6 million employers. The U.S. Department of Labor consistently reports that one third of all veterans are underemployed. This means that there are three million highly capable, talented veterans that are being employed below their level of experience and capability. The labor market over the last couple of years has been extremely tight. There is a talent war going on out there, and the veteran population is a highly talented and vetted group. However, veterans represent only about 5% of the labor force. This means that it is a niche market in which employers need to not only understand how to attract veterans, but how to retain them once they land.

Veterans, this means that there is a strong likelihood that the business that you land with may not fully understand your previous experience and the unique skillset that you bring to the table. It also means that it is very likely that the systems that are well established in the private sector may differ from what you are used to. This book will help guide both employers and veterans through the employment life cycle and give tips to maximize the positive impact of differing experiences to create the most value for both employers and employees.

The military has likely shaped veterans' expectations for what the labor force experience will look like when their service is over. This can be problematic for both veterans and employers. Most companies in both the private and public sector will not, and should not, look or operate like the military. However, it is imperative that some of the misperceptions of both employers and new veteran hires are dispelled. The better veterans understand their new operating environment, and the more employers understand their military veteran employees, the more likely engagement, retention, and productivity will increase.

Bill's first book, *Military Career Transition: Insights from the Employer Side of the Desk,* lays out the dos and don'ts of getting hired. This book discusses strategies for success *after* you have successfully landed the job. There is no finish line to military transition. You will use different lessons learned from your time in the military at different points of your life. The military will always be a part of who you are, but to be successful in the corporate world, it can't be all of who you are.

We are firm believers in sharing our experiences—what went right, and what did not go so right—so that we can learn from each other. In this book, we will discuss both. We will discuss why veterans and employers may view onboarding differently, when and how to leverage your veteran experience, leader expectations of both, and more.

SECTION 1

LANDING

CAREER AND LIFE JOURNEY ALIGNMENT – LANDING

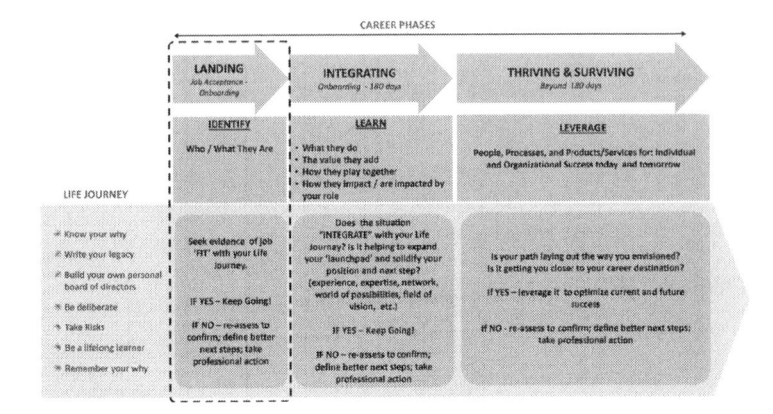

CAREER PHASES

LANDING	INTEGRATING	THRIVING & SURVIVING
Job Acceptance – Onboarding	Onboarding – 180 days	Beyond 180 days
IDENTIFY — Who / What They Are	**LEARN** — • What they do • The value they add • How they play together • How they impact / are impacted by your role	**LEVERAGE** — People, Processes, and Products/Services for: Individual and Organizational Success today and tomorrow
Seek evidence of job "FIT" with your Life Journey. IF YES – Keep Going! IF NO – re-assess to confirm; define better next steps; take professional action	Does the situation "INTEGRATE" with your Life Journey? Is it helping to expand your "launchpad" and solidify your position and next step? (experience, expertise, network, world of possibilities, field of vision, etc.) IF YES – Keep Going! IF NO – re-assess to confirm; define better next steps; take professional action	Is your path laying out the way you envisioned? Is it getting you closer to your career destination? IF YES – leverage it to optimize current and future success. IF NO – re-assess to confirm; define better next steps; take professional action

LIFE JOURNEY
- Know your why
- Write your legacy
- Build your own personal board of directors
- Be deliberate
- Take Risks
- Be a lifelong learner
- Remember your why

CAREER AND LIFE JOURNEY ALIGNMENT – LANDING ACTION ITEMS

	LAND	INTEGRATE	THRIVE & SURVIVE
Know your why	Vet reality against your WHY to optimize happiness and success	Don't let new influences sway you unintentionally	Stay true to yourself; let WHY evolve if appropriate.
Write your legacy	First impressions matter	How you integrate with others impacts your legacy	Remember – your legacy is the result of what you do over time; don't get the cart before the horse.
Build your own personal board of directors	Identify potential PBOD candidates	Build relationships with PBOD candidates and listen to their counsel	Review PBOD members for relevance over time; change members as is needed.
Be deliberate	Have a plan to land well; work the plan diligently	Work with others to understand how everything fits	Take intentional actions to optimize current success and future opportunities that align with your life plan.
Take Risks	Reasonable risks – don't stumble out of the starting blocks	Eagerly seek out others; introduce yourself; make connections; build relationships	Boldly seek and exploit opportunities to spread your wings, add more value, and expand your scope.
Be a lifelong learner	Identify the "Who's Who" and the What's What" of the new job	LEARN • What they do • The value they add • How they play together • How they impact / are impacted by your role	LEVERAGE People, Processes, and Products/Services for: Individual and Organizational Success today and tomorrow
Remember your why	To avoid being drawn off course in your new position	Share your unique value	To vet situations and evolving conditions for alignment with your overall life journey plan.

Introduction/General LANDING Insights

Doing the hard work to land a job that meets your needs merely gets you to the starting line. That's it. Welcome to the game. Think of all the training, practice and work you did to successfully join the military. Consider all the work that goes into making it to the professional level of any sport. Huge effort, great dedication, and all that does is get you to the unit or onto the playing field. It simply puts you in the arena.

Once you are there, you've got to get off to the right start! Think of a sprinter. They have trained hard, prepared well, and are now approaching the starting blocks. Foot position in the blocks is important; lean/crouch/stance is important; hand position is important; and the ability to hear the starting gun is important. The small things matter, and they must use every bit of their training and experience to get up out of those blocks and start their race strong.

Once you've accepted the offer, you enter those sprinter's blocks. What are the important things you need to know and be able to do? What are the things you should expect? What should you watch and listen for?

Well, keep reading! We've been through this multiple times and are excited to share our experiences and insights so that you might be able to pop out of the blocks strong.

BILL STORY

"The Landing Zone"

I remember Day 1 of my first post-transition job as Deputy Director, Economic Development for the county I lived in. The entire organization was three people. Me, the Director, and an admin. We had a large board of directors that included elected officials and prominent business leaders from throughout the county. I was used to onboarding from the U.S. Army...basic training, sponsors at every change of station, rigorous in-processing, etc. This three-person team had nothing of the sort. There was no structured plan, and there was no complex sequence of events to get me up to speed (but on the upside, there was no CIF either). My boss was tied up running the show. Our admin was occupied taking care of the dailies. Our board was not in the business of managing operations, let alone onboarding the new guy. I was mostly on my own to figure out how things worked, how business got done, what my duties really were, and how I could best add value.

Now, don't get me wrong, these were all great people, and the organization had a real mission. I just didn't know what I didn't know, and their onboarding process was totally foreign to me.

I had spent well over a decade in the U.S. Army—a large, established organization that had the experience, expertise, and resources to deliver robust onboarding at every turn. On top of that, I had spent the better part of a year focusing (at least somewhat) on transition – finding and landing a job.

BUT – now I wasn't in transition anymore. I landed! Got a job that filled the bill! I quickly realized that I had no idea what to do next. The paradigms were gone. Familiar systems evaporated. My expectations were so far off from the organization's that I wondered if I had made a huge mistake. There were no SOPs. No SITREPS. No OPORDS. No IPB. No installation management to check in with. Just three good folks doing their level best to fulfill the organization's charter—business attraction and retention.

I quickly realized that my perspective was VERY different from damn near everyone I dealt with.

I figured I'd be meeting with power players, noodling over big, strategic issues, and making significant impact for both the near and long-term.

Instead, I found myself doing the work the group needed to have done – figuring out how to build and maintain an inventory of available properties, defining a way to catalogue clients and prospective clients, building SOPs, etc. (think Microsoft Word, Excel and PowerPoint, Post-It notes, calendars, and the like).

I had no idea how I was adding real value, and quite frankly, I was disappointed that I wasn't doing sexier, bigger stuff.

But that was MY problem. The organization needed me doing what I was doing. I was helping build a foundation from which it could grow and achieve its mission to attract and retain businesses to our county. Shame on me. I got in my own way, made my life harder than it needed to be, and missed opportunities to make a bigger impact.

Side note – I must have done something right, because after just a few months when the director left for a fantastic new job, the board named me as the new director. That said, timing can sometimes be an interesting thing. You see, I had continued to network after I landed. One of those networking efforts unexpectedly produced a very attractive opportunity in a different industry, with a 3x salary increase. Imagine telling your board of directors you are leaving just a few short days after the newspaper and other media outlets announced you were taking over as the new top dog. Yep, this was not an easy discussion.

DAVE STORY

"Landing Again and Again."

Week one in my first two jobs out of the military varied widely. My first experience in the work force outside of the military was in a large, publicly traded insurance firm where I had just been hired as an employee benefits consultant. The recruiting process was very detailed and involved, so naturally, I believed the onboarding process would also be pretty deliberate. It wasn't. I was given a computer and a badge, given a list of people I should meet with to learn from, and was told to go get my insurance license. I had three months to do so.

I was done in three weeks. I asked my supervisor where I should focus my efforts now that I was licensed. His answer? "Go build a book of business." Wait...what? I knew how to spell "insurance," but that was about the extent of my expertise at the time; I still had no idea how to build a client base or talk to an HR Director or CFO (Chief Financial Officer) about comprehensive benefit plans that could both help their bottom line while still increasing benefits for their employees. I mean, this was some pretty complex stuff. I had expected to learn the craft before I was talking to senior level leaders and advertising myself as the subject matter expert. I wanted to get integrated into the culture and team. However, the employer hired me to increase their revenue by attracting and retaining clients. They wanted me to add value to the team as quickly as I could. After all, that's what they hired me to do. Build the book of business, and then we'll think about the "soft stuff."

For many reasons that Bill and I will discuss in this book, I soon left that position to accept a role working in a major VA healthcare system. This was a government entity, so I assumed

> *that the onboarding process would be a little closer to what I was looking for. They hired me into one of their fast-track leadership programs, with the intent to train me for mid- to senior level management. The catch was that there was no plan for me while I wasn't training...and this was the majority of the time. I wanted to add value, so I sought out projects that I could help with or lead. However, because I didn't have any credibility (I had capability; we will talk about the important difference later), I had a hard time pushing anything through. I asked and asked to be assigned somewhere. I was bored to tears. I wanted to work at the VA to make an impact, and expected to do so right away. After all, I was a veteran that had spent a lot of time in the healthcare system. Sadly, the culture I found on the job there was not what I had expected.*
>
> *These two drastically different experiences highlight some fairly normal onboarding practices for companies. However, as a newly transitioned veteran, I had some expectations that may not have been realistic.*

It's important to note that onboarding is just the start. There is a typical employment life cycle people experience. We will cover this in detail later in the book, but for now, keep in mind that starting strong is often a key to having the best possible experience.

As our stories show, there is a notable disconnect between veteran and employer experience and expectations. This is especially apparent in the case of onboarding–the initial introduction to the organization. It impacts everyone involved, and it can have a long-term impact on your overall career and life journeys. For that reason, we will discuss onboarding in detail later in this book.

As it relates to your life journey, the LANDING phase of your career transition is all about situational awareness and ensuring your situation aligns with your overall life plan. As the graphic above notes, there are several key action items you can employ to optimize your landing:

- ★ Know Your Why - Vet reality against your WHY to optimize happiness and success.
- ★ Write Your Legacy – First impressions matter.
- ★ Build Your Own Personal Board of Directors (PBOD) - Identify potential PBOD candidates.
- ★ Be Deliberate - Have a plan to land well; work the plan diligently.
- ★ Take Risks - Reasonable risks; don't stumble out of the starting blocks.
- ★ Be a Lifelong Learner – Identify the "Who's Who" and the "What's What" of the new job.
- ★ Remember Your Why - Avoid being drawn off course in your new position.

LANDING is about IDENTIFYING People, Processes and Products/Services relevant to you and your job.

The Three P's - *People, Process, and Product/Service* in LANDING

So how do you start off strong? Where should you prioritize your efforts? After all, starting a new job can be overwhelming, especially if you don't have a plan of approach. Building this plan can help establish focus areas to make order out of a pretty daunting thing.

For this purpose, we have broken down business into three components, its people, the processes it uses (both internal and external), and the product it sells or the service it provides. By organizing it this way, you will be able to construct your strategy within the key components most organizations focus on to ensure your landing is successful.

People

Introduction

If you asked the vast majority of employers what their most valuable asset is, they would likely say it is without question their employees. As one of their newest assets, it is important to them that you land on your feet, but no one is successful alone, and thus getting to know who's who in the zoo is incredibly important when landing in a new role. Who are the decision makers, the influencers, the talkers, and the doers? The only way you can find this out is by interacting with the new team. Be deliberate about introducing yourself, setting a time and place to discuss your role and how you can best support the team (if appropriate), and ensuring you identify names and faces. This could be by building a checklist or creating a calendar task with an invite for co-workers. Regardless of the method, it is important to have one, because after all, this is your new squad/platoon/team/squadron. If social hours are a part of the company culture, show up. Don't just focus on the professional aspects of your job. Do your new teammates have dogs? Kids? Do they like to golf? Or fish? The sooner you connect with your coworkers, the faster you will get out of the "new guy" phase and into the teammate phase.

Both of us have seen and participated in some successful landings and some not so successful ones. We are glad to share experience-based insights and stories to highlight some of the people related challenges during this important phase of your professional journey.

THE 3P MODEL – PEOPLE

Strategy & Plans (What, How, When)
Priorities
Situation / Conditions (Ownership; Headwinds; Tailwinds; etc.)
Stage of Organizational Lifecycle
Competition

Clients
Partners
Suppliers
Competitors

EXTERNAL
INTERNAL

PEOPLE | PROCESS

BUSINESS

JOB

Expectations; Deliverables; Scope; Authority;
Organization; Network; Input/Output; etc.

TALENT

You
Team
Peers
Organization

PRODUCT / SERVICE

Workforce Planning, Hiring; Onboarding;
Compensation; Performance Management;
Training/Development; Succession Planning

Legacy
Current
Future
Risks
Opportunities
Cash Cows/Capital Burns

BUSINESS
YOU

Capabilities
Wants/Needs
Value-Add
Past/Present Performance
Future Potential
Aspiration, Ability, Agility, Availability, Action
Fit with Organization – Today & Tomorrow

When landing, identifying "Who's who" and "What's what" is key. Identifying people relevant to you/your role is a great place to start.

There's much to do when landing. Don't overcomplicate things. Pay attention to people. Identify who's who. Get some idea of how they fit. You can continue to round out your knowledge as you continue your journey.

General *People* Insights When LANDING

Employers don't speak "mil-speak" or "veteran-ese."

As you discovered during your job search, most folks don't have a military background. They haven't walked your walk. And they certainly don't speak your language. Guess what? That is not their problem to fix. It is yours. You have entered their world.

Just like your entry into the military, you have to learn a new language–the language of the civilian work world and the dialect of the company/market/industry you joined. Further, you likely have to do it on your own, picking up terms and phrases on the fly, as you are trying to land well, find the restroom, the coffee pot, your workspace, and so much more. Linguist training via the Defense Language Institute, and similarly robust language resources likely won't exist in your new world.

To help land well, remember you have two ears, two eyes, and one mouth. Listen and watch more than you speak. Pay attention to conversations; hear what's being said and how. Read everything, consider the content and message, and consider the words that are being used and the style in which they are assembled. You don't have to forget your "mil-speak" or forever put aside your "veteran-ese" skills, but don't lean on them. Consider this your opportunity to become multi-lingual!

There may be biases or pre-conceived notions.

We can't tell you how many times we've heard, and continue to hear, "I bet it's difficult to go from such a regimented environment to one that is much more ambiguous." Veterans can be perceived as rigid conformists, who take action based on orders from superior officers rather than having the ability to solve complex problems in a small team environment. Many employers see movies of basic training, where everyone is marching in synch or an officer is barking orders to someone who yells at the top of their lungs "YES SIR!" and then promptly runs off to execute said order. People only know what they've been exposed to, and this is often the picture that is painted of the military.

Why does it matter? It matters because it isn't reality. This is not the case with most veterans. Most veterans have considerable experience working in small teams with little more than a stated objective with broad left and right parameters. The "how" is often solved at the small team level closest to the issue/situation/problem/opportunity. Whether military or corporate, good leaders empower their people and teams to make decisions. In fact, military leaders at all levels are used to making critical decisions in a fast paced, complex environment. Often, waiting for orders is too slow and puts people and progress at unnecessary risk. This means that not only are veterans likely comfortable with making decisions on their own, but they are also used to articulating direction with clear outcomes, in a concise manner, and with defined parameters in which to operate. On top of all that, veterans are used to training others to operate in the same way!

Employers utilize their employees' skillsets to get the work done with the highest quality at the lowest cost, to develop and execute projects for growth, to enhance organizational culture, and so on. Because employers always want to optimize productivity and efficiency, it's critically important they understand the capabilities of all team members. Wouldn't it be shame if a highly competent employee who was used to making tough decisions when it counted, was stuck in a box because of the impression that they could "only follow orders," were "too rigid," or "dangerous because of their military experience" (all of which are far-too-common biases)?

Imagine the value if the full range of veterans' capabilities were

SECTION 1: LANDING 39

unlocked by simply redefining and overcoming biases and preconceived notions. The opportunity cost of believing that all military members are rigid conformists who just follow orders is staggering. Veterans aren't robots, mindlessly following orders; they bring broad, deep, relevant capabilities that can add real value to any business or organization.

How can these biases and preconceived notions be overcome?

- ★ Employers - Don't get trapped by biases and misperceptions about military veterans or any other population. Look at each individual candidate with open eyes and ears, to hear their stories and learn their value.
- ★ Veterans – Seek opportunities to showcase your abilities and fit well on the team. Over time, leadership teams, peers, and others will recognize your positive impact and potential. Biases will begin to erode, and you will be more fully integrated into the organization. This takes hard work. You have to build credibility. Learn the job. Learn the business. Build relationships. Demonstrate thought leadership. Leverage your experience and then bring your unique perspective to the conversation. Biases are broken by positive action and results. You've done hard work before. Go get it!

No one wears their resume on their chest.

In the military, even if you are brand new to the team, it is relatively easy to figure out who's in charge, tell the logistician from the operations manager, and discern who is qualified in what domains/functions. Just look at your co-worker's chest, and you can deduce how long they have been in the military and what their general responsibilities are by their rank. You can even tell the depth of their knowledge in certain fields. For example, if you look at someone's airborne wings, you know if they have a little knowledge (basic wings), deeper understanding (senior wings), or are an expert in airborne operations (master wings). This means that you can walk into a meeting, take a few seconds to scan the room, and know the general landscape of the population within it.

Knowing skillsets, experience levels, and who the decision makers are is incredibly valuable because it can help frame the conversation, determine your approach, and provide context. Although it is not as easy in the civilian sector, understanding the landscape of both your co-worker population and external stakeholders is still doable. It may just take a little background work. Looking at someone's LinkedIn profile before a meeting can give some insight into experiences, skillsets, and (if they are active enough) what may be important to them and what's on their mind. Talk to your peers about clients, vendors, or partners to learn about their motivators. If you put in enough effort doing the background work, you may find that you can enter the environment armed with even more information than when you were in the military; you just have to look a little harder.

Detailed *People* Insights When LANDING

As the previous graphic displays, there are two general populations for you to learn about:

- ★ **Internal** – This includes **you**, **your team**, **peers**, and **other organizational members** that may influence/impact you/your success.
- ★ **External** – This includes **clients** (the folks that are buying/consuming your products/services), **partners** (people/organizations outside your company that have established partnership agreements beneficial to them and your company), **suppliers** (those people/organizations from whom you/your company purchases the goods/services that enable your business to operate), and **competitors** (people/

SECTION 1: LANDING 41

organizations in the same market space with either a similar product/service, a replacement product/service, or a product/service that eliminates the need for your product/service. Said another way, competitors are others who want your customers).

Let's first look internally:

- ★ **You –** You have likely heard the notion that first impressions matter. This isn't necessarily groundbreaking stuff, but there are some steps that you can take to ensure that you're putting your best foot forward early. Be on time. Dress appropriately. Be attentive. Listen actively. Speak clearly. Engage eagerly. Be open to learning. Identify how you and your position fit in the bigger picture and how you might best interact with others.
- ★ **Your Team –** At most jobs, you will be part of a team. Some may be individual contributors with no direct reports, but by and large, every position depends on others to successfully complete the overall mission. For example, *all* sports teams are teams—and this includes the so-called "individual sports." In a classic "team sport," each person plays a certain position that performs certain functions or covers certain areas of the playing field. Still, more individual sports like wrestling are conducted as parts of a team. The wrestler wins his match, but the points go to the team, and teammates train together to sharpen one another in pursuit of their collective goal of victory. Business is a different situation, but the team dynamic still exists in almost every industry. Engineers play a certain role. As do finance, IT, marketing, sales, HR, supply chain, and all others. Identify what positions exist on your team, what they do, and how they fit. Just as importantly, see yourself as a part of that team, and identify where you fit in, as well. You'll be glad you did.

- ★ **Peers** – When you land in your new gig, you're likely to find that other positions exist across different divisions, departments, and functions that are on the same level as yours. For example, if you are an operations manager, you'll likely find that there are sales managers, IT managers, procurement managers, HR managers and so on, that are similarly situated to you. These peer positions can be great resources for you when you land. Since you are peers, there may be some level of built-in familiarity or camaraderie that makes your landing easier, smoother, and more productive. If there are peers within the same function, you may also find that some level of competitive pressure exists. This competitive pressure can be a very helpful, positive thing, encouraging better performance across the board, but it can also be a toxic, negative situation that creates unnecessary, unproductive divides. Identify who your peers are. Explore the nature of their relationships. Discover points of positive potential and discern negative possibilities.
- ★ **Organization** – In every role, there will be other people from across the organization with whom you will interact, and that you will impact or be impacted by. There's no realistic way for you to identify who all these folks are upon landing, but it's worth your time and effort to have your eyes and ears open to see who they might be. Look at the scope of your role, think broadly about which positions from which parts of the organization may be upstream, downstream, or next to you. Reach out. Make contact. Begin to develop connections and relationships.

Externally, there are many folks with whom you may interact. Identifying them when you land can be a valuable use of your time. There are four general categories most of these external people will fall into.

SECTION 1: LANDING 43

- ★ **Clients** – Said simply, these are the folks who purchase, use, and/or consume the products/services you and your company produce.
- ★ **Partners** - Partners are those people and organizations outside your company with which you work, who bring certain knowledge, expertise, capability, or connections that better enable you and your company to achieve success, and that derive some manner of success for themselves. Identifying partners upon landing may or may not be a priority task. If the nature of your role inherently includes working successfully with external partners, it will be important for you to identify them forthwith. Check with your boss to see what, if any, external partners should be on your early radar screens.
- ★ **Suppliers** - Suppliers are individuals or companies that provide a product or service, for a fee, that you need to successfully complete your mission. They are sometimes referred to as vendors. Nearly every company in existence uses suppliers to some degree. Individual "solo-preneurs" use suppliers to obtain their raw materials, supplies and equipment. Larger companies use suppliers for everything from office paper, staplers, and pens; to the raw materials necessary for their products; to the machines and equipment that produce their products, and more. Suppliers may also provide services rather than products. These may include IT services, training services, repair services, training, coaching, auditing, or others. Regardless of the nature of the product or service, suppliers are key external resources that organizations need to thrive & survive. Identifying who your suppliers are when you land, can be helpful to getting off to a solid start.
- ★ **Competitors** – Competitors are entities that are competing in the same market space with either a similar product/service, a replacement product/service, or a product/service that eliminates the need for your product/service. Said another

way, competitors are others that want your customers. Many times, for them to be successful, you have to be less successful. Although it isn't personal (usually), it may feel like it. There are several reasons why it is important to identify who your competitors are and what their business strategy is. Discerning their strengths and weaknesses will allow you to identify what your competitive advantage is, will help minimize risk, and potentially help avoid making costly mistakes.

Process

Introduction

Every company does things a little differently, so identifying overall business processes, the processes related to your job, and the talent-related processes is essential. What are the key processes and what's your role in them?

When landing, it's not critical that you understand all of these in detail. It's only important that you begin to identify which ones are in play in your organization and most relevant to success for your role and your career. Later, when you're integrating, you can learn more about these. Beyond that, when you are thriving & surviving, the more in-depth knowledge and awareness you have of these key processes (how they operate, their levels of effectiveness, etc.), the more likely it will be for you to be successful.

Being deliberate in this effort will help you hit the ground running. Identifying existing process maps can be very helpful. You may not have been exposed to process maps in the military, but no worries! As you land and begin to identify key processes, ask folks to

SECTION 1: LANDING 45

share a copy of the process maps. Where they exist, you'll likely find them valuable, because they help you to visualize processes and see the big picture of how they are used across the organization. Process maps are also easy to refer to when you can't quite remember how the process works. You need to identify where you fit in these processes, who else is involved, why they are part of them, where the decision points are, and who makes them. At this point in your journey, identifying and cataloging these processes should be your focus.

If you start to catch yourself saying, "But this is what we did in the military," STOP! Organizations' processes likely have been in place long before your time at the company. They may not be perfect. They may benefit from process improvement. However, the fastest way to "be that guy" is to start pumping in suggestions before understanding how all of the pieces interact with each other.

THE 3P MODEL – PROCESS

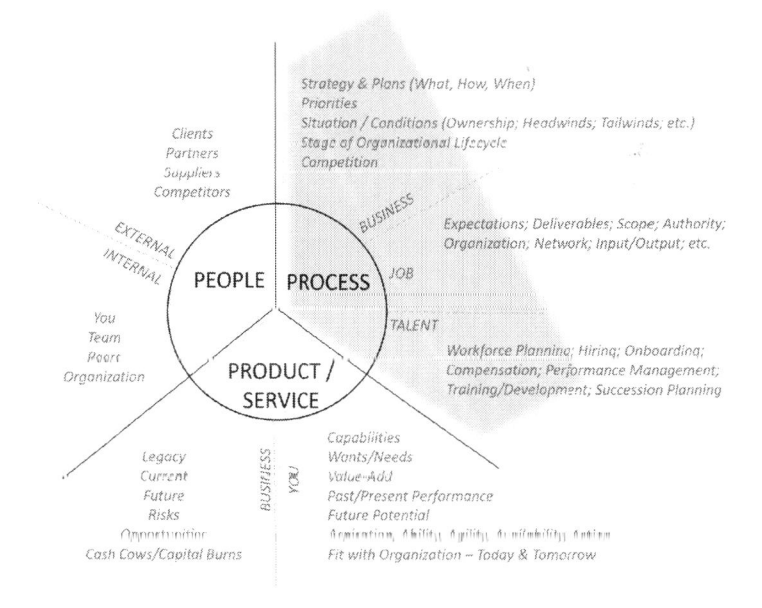

Strategy & Plans (What, How, When)
Priorities
Situation / Conditions (Ownership; Headwinds; Tailwinds; etc.)
Stage of Organizational Lifecycle
Competition

Clients
Partners
Suppliers
Competitors

EXTERNAL
INTERNAL

PEOPLE | PROCESS
PRODUCT / SERVICE

BUSINESS
JOB
TALENT
YOU

Expectations; Deliverables; Scope; Authority;
Organization; Network; Input/Output; etc.

Workforce Planning; Hiring; Onboarding;
Compensation; Performance Management;
Training/Development; Succession Planning

You
Team
Peers
Organization

Legacy
Current
Future
Risks
Opportunities
Cash Cows/Capital Burns

Capabilities
Wants/Needs
Value-Add
Past/Present Performance
Future Potential
Aspiration; Ability; Agility; Adaptability; Action
Fit with Organization – Today & Tomorrow

General *Process* Insights When LANDING

No time or training cycle.

The military has an operating cycle that typically includes three phases: Train, Deploy, Refit (then repeat). This is vastly different than most civilian companies, who are "deployed" - on production—all the time! Standing down for any reason takes away from revenue potential, and thus is not often a preferred approach.

This has a real impact on newly hired veterans. The absence of a training cycle and the notable diminished focus on training in general can lead to some serious disconnects, disappointment, and uncertainty about what you've gotten yourself into. I mean really? It naturally leaves you thinking, "You expect me to go crush this gig without training me? And how in the world do you expect me to get developed for future, larger roles without some sort of intentional developmental training?"

MILITARY VERSUS CIVILIAN OPERATING CYCLES

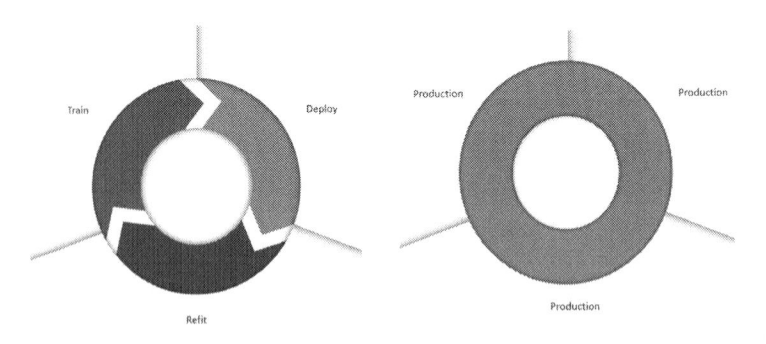

We have both seen and lived this. In Bill's case, part of his job in multiple companies was focused on establishing/improving the organizations' strategy and practices related to training/development that improve current company performance, readiness for future business needs, employee engagement, and attractiveness of the company to the employment market.

SECTION 1: LANDING

While the details of each company's experience vary, training was always viewed VERY differently inside civilian organizations than it is in the military. To a degree, it makes sense given that training is frequently viewed as a cost rather than an investment, and costs are not good for the bottom line.

If you join an organization that falls short of your expectations for training, you have to carefully assess the impact of this difference on you, your ability to perform your current role, and on the longer-term effects on your job satisfaction and career trajectory. By carefully assess, we mean, you need to seriously consider your situation and the alternatives. As we've noted earlier, MOST organizations don't approach training like the military. This means that it's unlikely that the grass will be greener at another company in this regard.

When in career transition/job search, you likely heard that you have to be the master of your career, and your own "Chief Marketing Officer." That same logic applies once you've landed.

Learning about an organization's training/development perspective and practices may or may not be an indicator that the company is not for you. On the other hand, it may provide an opportunity for you to leverage your great experience to help improve things!

If the company's take on training/development is concerning to you, make a level-headed assessment of how much this challenge really means to you.

★ Look at the overall situation (e.g., is everything else at this company pretty great, or is this just one more unexpected negative?).
★ Consider your circumstances outside the job (Do you have other opportunities at the ready? Can you afford to jump ship and start a new search?).
★ Seek counsel from your significant other, your mentors, and other trusted confidantes who know you well, and then make a decision to either continue this opportunity and leverage your great experience to create success, or to take a different course.

There may be some ambiguity when you first join a new company, and there may not be a field manual for everything (or anything!). But even in the absence of policy (SOPs), there likely will be common practices. Discover what these are, so you can begin to conduct business in a manner similar to what the organization is familiar with and expects. If you have a better way, pick the right time, then professionally suggest it. But be wary that you're not being overly critical or dismissive of their norms—don't call their baby ugly!

- ★ Yes, employers have work to do.
- ★ Yes, employers need people who fit in & add value to their team.
- ★ Yes, job openings exist because employers have unfilled business needs.
- ★ Yes, employers (usually) do their homework before posting a job opening.
- ★ BUT - they may not know exactly what they need done in every case.

Can you handle the ambiguity?

Detailed *Process* Insights When LANDING

As we noted earlier, when landing, identifying the "Who's who" and "What's what" is key – this includes identifying what processes are relevant to you.

As the previous graphic displays, there are three general process areas for you to consider:

Business – Processes related to strategy, plans, priorities, situation/conditions, stage of organization's life cycle, competition, and other topics impacting the enterprise.

Job-specific - Processes related to your job, such as expectations, deliverables, scope, authority, organization, network, and input/output.

Talent-related – Processes related to how the organization's talent is planned and managed: workforce planning, hiring, onboarding, compensation, performance management, training/development, succession planning, etc.

Why are these three process areas important? Because they encompass the broad areas in which you will exist and by which your career will be impacted. There are innumerable additional details inside each of these areas, but the topics we note herein are the ones that are broadly applicable.

Business Processes

- ★ **Strategy, Plans & Priorities –** It may have been hard to ascertain some (or any) of this during the interview process. Now that you have landed, if you haven't already done so, it will be important to identify what your company's strategic plan is and how your role fits within this strategy. It will also be important to become familiar with how the company defines its priorities. Knowing if your company is prioritizing growth, cash flow, new product development, cost avoidance, or other, will help you make decisions that align with the company's priorities. This knowledge will help you define what you should or should not be doing in support of your company's objectives.
- ★ **Situation/Conditions -** Much like global affairs had a significant impact on your life in the military, the impact of social conditions, business landscape, competitive pressures, internal company situations, and other factors all will likely influence your day-to-day job in the civilian work world. Figuring out what these indicators are, and the processes by which they are tracked, analyzed, and used for decision-making, will

help you predict and navigate changes in the market. For example, if you are in the ball bearing business, then you are probably paying attention to commodity prices of steel, import tariffs, shipping and transportation conditions, and other market-related factors that impact the availability, price, and quality of steel. Just like you paid attention to what was happening in China, the Middle East, or other areas while in uniform, it's time to identify what early indicators are relevant to your new role, and the processes related to tracking them.

★ **Stage of organization's life cycle** – Businesses tend to follow a life cycle from Launch/Startup to Growth/Expansion, then Shakeout/Stability, Maturity, and Decline. Businesses have different priorities in each stage of their life cycle, and because of this, your role will likely change depending on where your company falls on this path. Again, you are in the LANDING phase, so simply identifying roughly where the organization is in its life cycle is sufficient. How do you figure this out? Sales history and projections, product development and upcoming launches, share price, etc. can all be good indicators of where the business is and where they are going. Identifying this will give you context for understanding why decisions are being made and some of the factors impacting strategy, priorities, culture and more.

★ **Competition –** In the military, you had some infrastructure and resources available to help you develop knowledge of your competition. The military's collection and analysis of intelligence of our military competitors is a trillion-dollar endeavor that drives how and when we deploy, how and in what environment we train, and who and what we prioritize. The need to identify your competition also exists in the business world. Identifying them, understanding what their value proposition is, figuring out where they are positioned in the market, and learning what their growth plan is are all relevant to your company, and therefore should be relevant to you.

Discerning all this, and the processes by which they come to life will help drive your interactions with competitors and result in achieving competitive advantage rather than losing it.

Job Specific Processes

* ★ **Expectations –** One of the most important early tasks you can partake in is to get clear on the expectations for your role. Seek out your boss, your team members, your clients and others to get their perspectives. What were you hired for? What does your management team expect of you? What do your colleagues expect of you? Explore the simple stuff: are you on the clock, or is your schedule flexible as long as you get the work done? Dig into the details. Understand that the expectations may be far more ambiguous than you are used to, which may be especially true for higher level positions. If you find that the expectations are vague, refer to your understanding of the business strategy and look for how different processes interact. You'll likely be able to identify expectations with some clarity.

    Knowing what the initial expectations of you are may not be as obvious as it was in the military. Whether these are to increase production capacity, sales, conduct critical business functions, or other, it would be prudent to understand what the expectations are. What is the ROI (return on investment) requirement? What are the timing standards? Productivity levels? Quality levels? Cost parameters? Revenue targets? The better you understand where you fit in the business wheel, the sooner you will be able to add the value your employer needs. Do the work you were hired to do, demonstrate capability, build credibility, and your opportunities to do different and more things will grow.

    If you don't understand what the expectations are, it's going to be difficult to achieve them. Nobody wants a swing and a miss right out of the gate, and we all know that first impressions matter. You may be the most earnest, hardest working employee on the team, but if you're working hard on things that don't matter, you're missing the boat.

From the moment you accept the offer, make every effort to get as clear as possible about what the expectations are for you and for the position you fill. Talk to your manager, pay attention during your onboarding, listen closely to what's being said when you meet new people. Look for clear statements, nuances, confirmations, and contradictions. Check in with your manager on a recurring basis to continually refine your understanding.

★ **Deliverables** - Understanding what your expected output is seems obvious, but identifying this can be more complex than it appears on the surface. How often are you supposed to produce this output? To what level of quality? For which customer populations? Under what constraints? What are the reporting procedures? How do these deliverables interact with each other? Do some compliment others? Do they create impossible conflicts? What products or processes depend on your deliverables and what products and processes do you depend on? Identifying these deliverables early is an important step in your ability to deliver top notch results.

★ **Scope & Authority –** Identifying who owns the decision-making authority for decisions that impact your position and discerning the left and right limits for your position are important steps in the LANDING phase. Decision trees, information flow, lead times, and other conventions will all likely look different in every organization. These are topics that should be addressed as early as possible when landing. Identifying your scope and authority not only benefits you; it also benefits your team members, peers, and other internal and external folks.

SECTION 1: LANDING 53

★ **Organization** – Organizational architecture was usually fairly obvious when you were in the military. There was a clear chain of command that looked similar regardless of whether you were stationed at Fort Benning, Fort Bragg, Norfolk, San Diego, Barksdale, Gulfport, or anywhere else in the world. This architecture will look different in your new role, but how different it will actually be depends largely on your specific firm. The military (usually) has a very centralized hierarchy with a well-defined chain of command. Decisions are made by individuals or command teams depending on scope and authority at the appropriate level in that structure. However, in the civilian work world, organizations may be broken down by functional areas (marketing, operations, finance, sales, engineering and so forth). Global companies will likely have divisions based on geography, such as North America, South America, Europe and Asia. The organizational architecture may be broken down by product line or project. It may also be structured around customers. Making this all even more confusing, it may integrate two or more of these structures and operate as a matrix. Whatever the structure is, you should know what the organizational architecture looks like and how different internal departments, divisions, or teams interact with each other.

COMMON BUSINESS STRUCTURES/ORGANIZATIONS

Similar to the military, companies organize as needed to best position themselves for success ...

Product	grouped based on the product worked on (e.g. beverage, flexibles, specialty plastics)
Region	grouped based on the geographic area supported (e.g. NA, SA, EMEA, APAC)
Customer	grouped based on the customers supported (e.g. Ford, General Motors, Jaguar, Navistar)
Function	grouped by the main tasks they're responsible for (e.g. Operations, Sales, Finance, Engineering)
Matrix	Two+ models combined based on company initiatives (e.g. functional, product and regional)

- *"Centralized" versus "Decentralized" operations are also a consideration that may be applied to any/all of these.*
- *Structures become more complex as organizations grow, requiring ever-more skilled talent in positions of authority.*

- ★ **Network –** You probably networked your butt off to get introduced to the opportunity that resulted in your hire. That's great, and building that network is important, not only for getting the job but also for doing the job. Don't stop networking just because you got hired, though. Who in the company do you need to know? What external stakeholders will influence your ability to be effective in your role? Continue to network throughout your career, it was important to your transition, it is important to landing well, and it will be important to integrating, and thriving & surviving as long as you are in the workforce.
- ★ **Input/Output** – Identifying the inputs to and outputs from your role and the processes by which they flow is important. This knowledge provides you with valuable intelligence about where weak points might be improved, where reliable/dependable/repeatable processes may be replicated, and provides you with a general sense of the direction of your workflows.

Talent Related Processes

Before we get into the typical talent related processes worthy of your attention when landing, it's important to understand that there is a **typical employment life cycle** that we all are likely to experience. Getting hired is just the start of your journey with an organization. Your first days are truly the first steps on a path. While everyone's workforce journey is a bit different, there are always consistent features to the typical employment life cycle that you should understand.

TYPICAL EMPLOYMENT LIFE CYCLE

ATTRACTION → RECRUITMENT → ONBOARDING → DEVELOPMENT → RETENTION → SEPARATION

SECTION 1: LANDING

This cycle represents the typical stages by which organizations tend to arrange their people-related efforts. Certainly, there are many practices, processes, tools, and techniques used in each of these stages to optimize the experience for both employees and the organization.

- ★ **Attraction & Recruitment** - The efforts related to making the opportunity known to the employment market, causing great people to be interested in that opportunity, and taking all actions to get to know interested people and vet them to determine those that are the best fit. If you currently have accepted a job offer and are starting that new gig, congratulations! You've made it through this phase of the employment life cycle.
- ★ **Onboarding** - Once an individual has accepted the employment offer, onboarding includes all actions related to easing the new employee's entry to the organization, setting the foundation for them to quickly become an engaged, effective, and value-adding member of the team.
- ★ **Development and Retention** – Occurring throughout the employee's time with the organization, there are many components to effective employee development and retention work. All of these are focused on helping employees perform better in their current role, get prepared for potential future roles, remain positive, productive, engaged team members, and continue to thrive & survive as the organization evolves.
- ★ **Separation -** The final phase in the employment life cycle. Whether expected, unexpected, intended, or unintended, everyone leaves every organization someday.

Execution of this general employment life cycle will look very different from company to company. Larger companies may look more similar to what you experienced in the military, while smaller, or newer companies may have abbreviated approaches to each step. Regardless of these differences, it's important for you to understand how your new organization approaches talent related processes.

While Bill's first book addressed attraction and recruitment, this book's present section (LANDING) addresses the onboarding phase. The remaining sections of this book (INTEGRATING, THRIVING & SURVIVING) will touch on subsequent life cycle phases.

TYPICAL EMPLOYMENT CYCLE RELATED TO LANDING

Now for the details of talent-related processes.

- ★ **Workforce Planning –** During the LANDING phase, determining how the company manages its workforce planning will be a good indicator of its overall talent strategy and culture. Is your firm deliberately adding capacity in certain areas to scale certain product lines or services? Is your company consolidating tasks to streamline processes and gain efficiency? Are they adding talent to build a pipeline of future leaders for top spots? Do they have a deliberate plan, or do they seem to be winging it? These, and many more alternatives, are all distinct possibilities, and identifying them can help you understand both short-term and long-term strategic talent planning in your business—as well as how that might impact your ability to land well and perform successfully.
- ★ **Hiring** – Knowing the hiring process will help give you insight into your organization's overall talent and business

strategies. Are they increasing capacity in a certain area? If so, understanding the need to increase that capacity, what business problem your company is trying to solve, what opportunity is it trying to seize, and how/why your skillset fits and adds value is important. Are you replacing someone who retired, got promoted, fired, or moved on? Is the firm hiring you to do the same thing that the previous person in your role used to do, or do they want you to fundamentally change the way this position has functioned in the past? Again, all this is information that will help you understand where to prioritize your efforts and determine how you can add value right out of the gate in order to set yourself up for future success.

★ **Compensation** – Assuming that you aren't working for free, this is something that we hope you discussed/negotiated and understood during your hiring process. If you did, make time to reinforce and build upon that understanding. If you didn't, do yourself a favor and figure out what's up ASAP. Beyond the pay level and cycle, what is the salary increase process and strategy? Is there a bonus structure? Is it based on individual or company performance? What is the timing and frequency of pay, and how is it determined? What does the benefits package look like? More and more, companies are getting innovative with how they structure benefits. Some are offering more paid time off, while others may be offering childcare assistance or tuition reimbursement. Think "total compensation" and not just what goes directly into your bank account in the form of a paycheck.

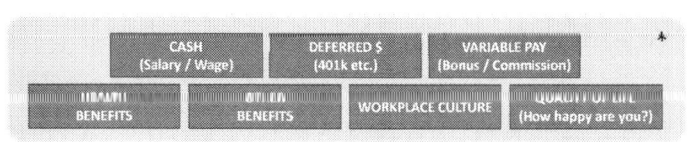

CASH (Salary / Wage)	DEFERRED $ (401k etc.)	VARIABLE PAY (Bonus / Commission)	★
HEALTH BENEFITS	OTHER BENEFITS	WORKPLACE CULTURE	QUALITY OF LIFE (How happy are you?)

* - Typical components. Many details & variations in each.

Important points to know about compensation and benefits when you land:

★ Know what your healthcare benefits cover, the costs to you, and any gaps that might exist. For example, do your employer-provided benefits cover dental and vision for you and your family? If not, how are you going to ensure that the coverage exists?
★ Understand your employer's deferred compensation plans (401k or similar) and be sure you're not throwing away opportunities to save money.
★ Understand the variable compensation plans – they are often based on individual, team and/or organizational performance – and do your job well in order to maximize your bonus potential.
★ Remember that quality of life is a HUGE piece of total compensation. If you aren't having fun, consider what your options are.

> **NOTE**
>
> *Some may say you should have known all this before you started the job, but let's be realistic—there's a lot going on here, and these details are all new. If you're not crystal clear on all the details when you start, make an effort to get clear when you land. You'll be glad you did.*

★ **Performance Management** – Does your company have a system for performance management? How are goals set and communicated? What, if anything, are they tied to? What should you expect for feedback? How are evaluations completed? What is the rating scale? What do the ratings really mean, and how are they determined? Are the ratings heavily focused on performance (like military OER/NCOER/JEPES/FITREP reports), or are they primarily focused on potential? What are evaluation results used for? If you happen to be in a position of authority, responsible for others, this is a critical part of your duties and responsibilities. Some companies have performance management software in which there is an expectation to contribute to your own evaluation. Some don't have any system in place, and there is an opportunity to influence the creation of one. At this phase, however, knowing what is being used and what your expectations are in the process will be adequate.

★ **Training/Development -** In the LANDING phase, figuring out what deficiencies exist in either your foundation of knowledge or skillset, and what opportunities exist both internally and externally to address these deficiencies, will be sufficient. In some instances, you will be required to get certified or licensed before you can perform your job. In any case, the oversight and training/development plan that you are used to from the military will look vastly different. Most likely, your training opportunities will be more decentralized and self-driven than you are used to. This can be great news if you are proactive and look for opportunities to improve. However, it can also be bad news if you don't advocate for your own development. You are your own biggest advocate, and no one will care more about your career than you do.

★ **Succession Planning** – When you are landing, succession planning may not be at the top of your priority list – after all, you're pretty focused on the more immediate basics, like, where's my workspace, what's my login, and who do I report to. We're not suggesting you put the cart before the horse here, but we do recommend you keep your eyes and ears open to get a basic level of awareness about how succession planning is addressed in your new organization. Coming from the military, you've experienced arguably the most well-developed, rigorous, and effective succession planning processes in the world. That experience, at the very least, created a level of familiarity, and it likely also created some strong expectations about how these things should work. When landing, identify what you can about how succession planning is handled, so you might have at least an initial impression about how this process might impact you later.

The most prevalent process that you are likely to experience during the LANDING phase is onboarding, and so we will dig into this topic in detail here. We hope to offer you a few insights that will broaden/deepen your awareness of the overall context surrounding your onboarding experience so that you can make the best of it.

Onboarding

Your first day(s) on the job are critical. How you enter your new organization, and how they receive you, can both make a huge impact on how your short and long-term career journey will look.

Your onboarding experience can be pivotal. Various studies from the Department of Labor and the Society of Human Resource Management indicate:

- ★ ~20% of employee turnover occurs within 45 days of hiring.
- ★ ~90% of new employees decide whether or not to stay in the company during their first six months after joining.

At its root, onboarding exists to help get employees up to speed and fully productive as fast as possible, at the least possible cost to the organization.

For military veterans, it may be the first blast of two core realities in the civilian work world —*speed* and *cost.* These realities will be a recurring theme throughout your civilian career. The variables impacting them are nearly innumerable, and sometimes one will overtake the other, but in the end, speed and cost are two primal business imperatives that savvy employees at all levels eventually must learn to handle.

Civilian Onboarding is Rarely as Rigorous as the Military.

The military has one of the most robust onboarding processes of any professional organization. New hires go through a weeks- to months-long onboarding where they learn about organizational culture, language, expectations, job skills and more. When they arrive at their new job site, they are assigned a sponsor to help them assimilate well.

Most civilian companies don't have time for that. They are hiring to fill a business need, full stop. Typically, the business need is urgent and ongoing. Perhaps the recruiting effort took longer than expected; perhaps business conditions changed, and you need to make an immediate impact. Regardless of the situation, onboarding is rarely anything close to the military's robust, extended, all-inclusive process.

These differences are understandable. BUT – the differences in expectations between employers and veterans about what the onboarding process should look like can create a disconnect that can misrepresent both parties, and lead to significant hurdles right out of the gate.

- ★ Imagine how disappointed/underwhelmed a veteran might be, having experienced the military's robust onboarding, when he or she joins a new company where onboarding is little more than administrative compliance work, after which they are cut loose to go produce!
- ★ Imagine also the employer's perspective. Their organization has worked long and hard to find a top-notch person who

has convinced them that they are the best person to do the work they need done and fit well/add value to the team. Their offer is made and accepted and everyone is excited to get together and get to work. Given their hiring diligence, they expect this great new talent is ready to hit the ground running, so their onboarding process focuses on the basics. Perhaps business exigencies even bastardize the process. If the veteran new-hire (who's likely disappointed by the process) balks, (or even worse, calls their baby ugly), the employer is now in an uncomfortable position. Their great new hire is not happy, not positively impressed, and may even be wondering what the hell they got into. Not a great situation to be in.

Onboarding experiences and expectations are often very different.

In the military, with a few notable exceptions, people are assigned to organizations, teams and jobs. This "assignment" model continues throughout a service member's career. Veteran new hires to civilian organizations are used to this and probably expect it (or at least something similar). First line supervisors, mid-level managers, and even senior leaders often meet the new hire for the first time AFTER they have already joined the team.

This works well for the military, but it sets expectations for veterans that may not be met in the civilian work world.

Vastly different than most military assignment processes, civilian organizations interview people before hiring. First line supervisors, mid-level managers, and even senior leaders often meet the new hire BEFORE they join the team. Understanding the candidate's capabilities, potential to do the work, and likelihood of fitting well with the culture are all part of a typical interview process. Big difference here from most military hiring/assignment processes.

DAVE STORY

"The Disconnect of Onboarding."

I talked before about my first job out of the military. I worked as an Employee Benefits Consultant for a large, publicly traded insurance brokerage firm. Now, this company generates over $8B in annual revenue, so they are well established in their market and have proven success when it comes to providing a service to their clients. Although I didn't have any experience in the insurance industry, I was hired because I had a demonstrated history of learning new skillsets, getting results, and leading change. However, up to this point, my entire adult life had been spent in the military, with all of the robust onboarding processes we have previously discussed.

Going into this job, I knew that my top priorities needed to be getting my insurance license, networking, and figuring out how to add value to the organization as quickly as possible. On my first day, I got my computer, met some of my colleagues, picked up my badge, and was told get your insurance license in the next sixty days and start getting ready to make cold calls. Three weeks later, I had my license and was ready to get on the phones but there was a problem. How was I supposed to sell myself as the subject matter expert, ready to help CFO's increase their bottom line by reducing cost and increasing retention, with only three weeks of experience? I trained for almost a year before I was even close to entering the operational environment in the military, and now I found myself talking to executives within three weeks of being in an entirely new industry. I felt completely under-prepared, and it left a pretty sour taste in my mouth.

Is this the norm in many civilian businesses and industries? Absolutely! Is a fortune 500 company going to change

> *their entire onboarding process just for me to accommodate the things that I'm used to? Absolutely not! However, had I understood what I was walking into, I would have set my expectations accordingly and changed the way I prepared myself. Knowing what this firm's onboarding process was like would have drastically changed my first impression, and it would have likely resulted in better outcomes for both me and my employer. I ended up leaving that firm after about three months for reasons I will discuss in more detail later, but the disconnect in onboarding expectations certainly played a role in my early discomfort with what I was getting into.*

Employer Onboarding Expectations – While onboarding processes vary wildly and may look nothing like your military experience, they commonly share similar objectives:

- ★ Facilitate the new employee's ability to contribute in the new role.
- ★ Increase the new employee's comfort level in the new role.
- ★ Reinforce his/her decision to join the organization.
- ★ Enhance productivity.
- ★ Encourage commitment and employee engagement.

Employers often have to focus on the most direct, cost-efficient paths to achieving their objectives, so onboarding processes may seem quite truncated to military veterans. They often focus heavily on "keep you out of jail stuff" (payroll, benefits, retirement enrollment, legal forms, and the like) and other administrative topics related to your job (access to relevant systems, access cards/ID badges, etc.). The broader topics like organizational culture, language, expectations, job skills and more may not receive the attention you're used to.

Employers expect new hires to come well prepared, ready to work, and poised to make a positive impact. This expectation is amplified the higher up you go in any organization. Entry level jobs may get more robust onboarding, as employers' expectations for quick impact may be a bit lower since folks in this employment realm typically have less work experience. (Onboarding for more senior level roles is often less detailed, focusing on broader topics rather than job details, since more senior new-hires are generally expected to come with robust relevant experience.) As a military veteran, you have experience. You've had rigorous training (which may/not directly translate to your current job). You've been in high performance organizations and know how to work as part of a team. Most of you are not seeking entry level, first-line gigs.

SO, here we are. The employer has their way of doing onboarding. You may get fed with a fire hose. You may be bored to tears. You as a veteran have your expectations of what onboarding should look like. The employer's typical approach to onboarding likely will be drastically different than what you experienced throughout your career. Few employers are likely to overhaul their onboarding process just for you. This difference often leaves newly hired veterans wondering "Is that it? What about (Insert any number of topics here)? When do I get the detailed job training I'm used to? Who's going to cover the heraldry and history, culture, social norms, and expectations? It also leaves employers wondering why newly hired veterans are so damn demanding right out of the gate.

And as a veteran, you're going to have to adjust (just like you had to adjust when you went through your military onboarding). Use that great agility and adaptability veterans are known for as you navigate these uncharted waters.

Two thoughts can be helpful when adjusting to this new onboarding experience:

1. Live the "3 Problems" mantra:
   a. I have no problems.
   b. I cause no problems.
   c. I'm here to solve your problems.
2. Don't be a critical jerk, denigrating everything you see, or calling their baby ugly.

Be present for the experience. Look beyond the surface when things aren't what you expected. Remember that the gaps you experience may only be gaps from your perspective. There are likely history, background, context and constraints of which you are not aware. When asked, offer positive feedback that might help improve the onboarding process. Be part of the solution, not the cause of headaches right out of the gate.

If your onboarding experience wasn't especially robust, here are some topics, you may want to explore when you land:

COMMON ONBOARDING COMPONENTS

NEW-EMPLOYEE PAPERWORK
W-4 and state tax forms; I-9 form; Employee handbook

ADMINISTRATIVE PROCEDURES
Office/desk/workstation; Computer username and password; E-mail; Keys/access card; ID badge; Mail (incoming and outgoing); Business cards; Purchase requests; Telephones; Conference rooms; Expense reports

KEY POLICY REVIEW
Anti-harassment / discrimination; Vacation and sick leave; FMLA/leaves of absence; Overtime; Dress code; Personal conduct standards; Progressive discipline; Security; Confidentiality; Safety; Injury reporting; Emergency procedures; E-mail and Internet usage

BENEFITS AND COMPENSATION
Health, life, disability insurance; Retirement benefits; Dependent care FSA; Educational assistance; Employee assistance program; Pay procedures; Salary increase / performance review process; Incentive/bonus programs; Paid and unpaid leave

INTRODUCTION TO THE COMPANY
Organization overview; Corporate culture; Company mission; Corporate literature/video; Organizational chart; internal and external stakeholders. (i.e. clients, suppliers, colleagues, managers, etc.)

INTRODUCTIONS AND TOURS
Department staff and key personnel; Tour of facility, including: Restrooms; Mailroom; Copy centers, printers, fax machines; Bulletin board; Parking; Office supplies; Break rooms; Coffee/vending machines; Watercoolers; Emergency exits

Identifying the processes that are relevant to your role, and those that impact or are impacted by your efforts is an important bit of work that you will be well served to do when you land. You don't have to learn every detail but identifying them is a great start.

Product/Service

Introduction

When first landing, it's important to start identifying your business' products and services. After all, your job exists to help deliver the best possible product/service at the least possible cost.

It's also important for you to remember that YOU are a product that provides services to the employer, and you need to ensure your ability to do so is well-maintained and developed. You worked your ass off to network, and market yourself into this new opportunity. Having landed, you need to remember that you are bringing value to the company, and YOU need to continue to be your own best advocate.

These are not mutually exclusive propositions. By growing your capability, your credibility, and your brand, you can grow your ability to help the company deliver their products and services. Similarly, as the company evolves, offering new/different products/services, it may generate new opportunities for you to learn, grow, and become a more capable person. Be conscious to keep a solid balance, not focusing so much on the business that you lose track of YOU, but also being mindful not to swing too far in the opposite direction by focusing so much on you that you become a self-absorbed prick who no longer supports the business.

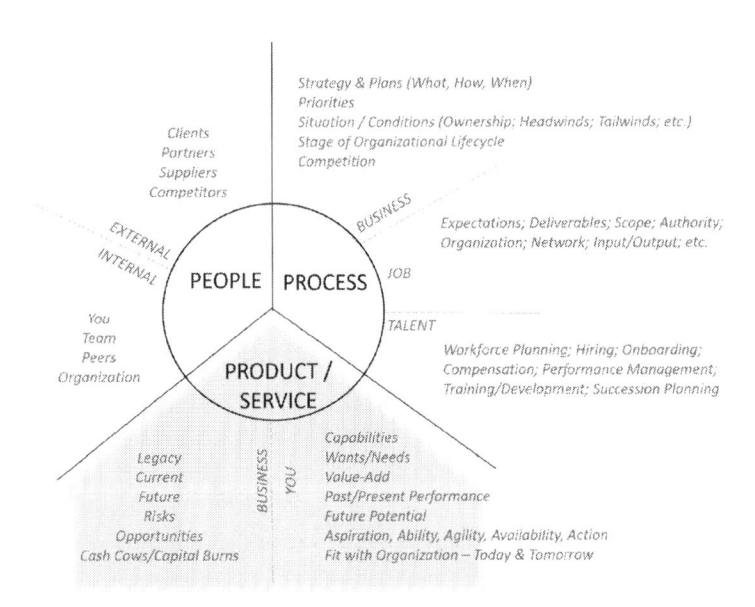

THE 3P MODEL – PRODUCT/SERVICE

Strategy & Plans (What, How, When)
Priorities
Situation / Conditions (Ownership; Headwinds; Tailwinds; etc.)
Stage of Organizational Lifecycle
Competition

Clients
Partners
Suppliers
Competitors

EXTERNAL / INTERNAL

PEOPLE | PROCESS

JOB

Expectations; Deliverables; Scope; Authority; Organization; Network; Input/Output; etc.

You
Team
Peers
Organization

PRODUCT / SERVICE

TALENT

Workforce Planning; Hiring; Onboarding; Compensation; Performance Management; Training/Development; Succession Planning

Legacy
Current
Future
Risks
Opportunities
Cash Cows/Capital Burns

BUSINESS / YOU

Capabilities
Wants/Needs
Value-Add
Past/Present Performance
Future Potential
Aspiration, Ability, Agility, Availability, Action
Fit with Organization – Today & Tomorrow

General *Product/Service* Insights when LANDING

Employers' business mission is as important to them as your military mission was to you.

An employer's mission is their mission. You may not yet be familiar with it. You may not find it to be quite as sexy or exciting as your military mission, but it is their mission and generally they are darn fond of it. Further, the employer's methods likely will be different than what you are used to.

Landing in a new environment can be challenging. Having come from the military, your frame of reference is unique in society. The Census Bureau states that only about 7% of American society has ever served in uniform and only ~1% of current eligible Americans volunteer for military service. The experiences veterans have are vastly different than damn near everyone around them. They've operated in long-established, large, rigorous, high-performing organizations with missions that have significant impact around the world. *(Note: We acknowledge that not everything in the military is perfect, that some roles seem less-than-sexy, and that some units are soup sandwiches, but overall, the military is definitely a high-performing organization with huge global impact).*

BILL STORY

"All We're Doing Is Kicking Boxes."

When I landed my first real corporate gig, as a training manager for an 1100-person air freight hub, I was a bit underwhelmed. On average, we moved approximately three million pounds of freight nightly via dozens of aircraft and trucks. Most nights, things moved like clockwork. Sometimes weather or other variables jumped up and got in the way, but overall, we had an efficient, effective operation. One evening, I was standing on the mezzanine viewing the operation when the thought hit me: "This ain't very exciting; all we're doing is kicking boxes." I was thoroughly underwhelmed with how seemingly blah the operation was. Pick up box. Move box. Deliver box. Whew! Sexy stuff...not.

As I stood there, our general manager stopped by to chat. He asked how things were going, and I shared my thoughts. Fortunately, he took no offense (which he surely could have done, since I was basically calling his baby ugly). He replied that while he could see my perspective, there were things I wasn't considering. We were enabling trade, helping suppliers get their goods to their customers, helping businesses get their product to end customers, enabling medical research (we moved lots of lab rats and other animals), providing wages and benefits to many people, and providing training and

> *development that helped people grow...the list went on and on. When he finished, I had a new perspective. I had been looking at the company's mission through the lens of my military experience. I didn't see or appreciate the richness and value of the mission. Totally my bad.*

If your landing leaves you disappointed or unfulfilled, get over it. Fast. When you joined the military, you had to adjust to military life ASAP. From the minute you stepped off that bus, you were in a whole new world that wasn't about to change just because you weren't used to it. Same thing here. Your employer has their mission and methods. They exist for a reason. They may need to evolve and improve, but don't come in calling their baby ugly, criticizing everything they do. Take the journey. Make some notes. Establish yourself, understand what's going on, and then offer up suggestions for improvement.

If on the other hand, your landing was truly unacceptable, and made such a negative impression that you know, without a doubt, that you are in the wrong place, you may have a tough decision to make. If so, be pragmatic, consider the totality of your situation, the impact of staying, the impact of leaving and so forth, then move forward purposefully and professionally.

DAVE STORY

"Aligning Employment and Purpose."

I was fortunate to work with an executive coach as I was transitioning from the military. She was pivotal in helping me determine both my why and how. I knew that I wanted to have the autonomy to build something new, and to have a positive impact in my community. I loved the people at the insurance firm, but along with some frustrations over some of the disconnects we have and will discuss, I also did not feel like I was making a positive impact in my community. I knew,

> *however, that I could find purpose using my experience to positively impact the veteran community, so I went to work at the Veterans Healthcare Administration.*
>
> *As a veteran, senior leader, and Executive MBA candidate who has experienced the VA healthcare system more than most, I felt like I was perfectly postured to make that impact. What I found when I got there was disturbing, to say the least. There was zero onboarding process, the executive leadership team told me that I probably wouldn't be busy until I had been there for six months, so I tried to grin and bear it, adding value where I could and making work for myself. Still, the organization was so incredibly limited by bureaucratic red tape that it was evident early on that I would have no autonomy, and my ability to add value would be severely limited until I climbed the prescriptive and lengthy General Schedule government rank structure. After witnessing the VA's completely inadequate response to the Afghanistan withdrawal, I knew that I was in the wrong organization, and this was the final straw for me.*
>
> *A key to long term happiness is finding employment that aligns with your purpose—finding the "what" to your "how" and "why." In a perfect world, you figure this out in the application/interview process. Like Bill stated previously, just because your "what" doesn't at first look exactly how you pictured it, does not mean that it is not or will never be there; give it some time. However, once you've had a chance to learn the lay of the land, if it looks like a duck and quacks like a duck...be prepared to move on as needed. I have found that life is too short to spend time in an organization that doesn't scratch that itch.*

Many businesses run lean. You were hired as an integral member of this lean team to fill a critical business need. Sometimes, this means that you are the only expert in the field. Here's an example: I may have hired you as a controller because I just lost my only finance expert. I need you to fix my account receivables because I am strapped for cash. I can tell you what the problem is, but I need your expert advice to help find the best solution. After all, I am an expert in making widgets; not a finance guru like you. What a great opportunity to step in, step up, execute well, and make a real, positive impact!

You may find yourself in a position where you have little clear and concise guidance. You may start your new job just to be given nothing more than a desired direction or a challenge that needs to be addressed. Remember, when facing this uncertainty, that this used to be the environment you operated in all the time. The enemy always gets a vote, the terrain always looks different on the ground, and your orders may come in the form of a "what" without a "how" (e.g., "Take that hill!"). The principles of patrolling apply here, too.

- *Plan* from what you know now, and identify what you don't know.
- Conduct *Reconnaissance* to fill in the gaps (what's the market, what are the risks, who are your customers, etc.)
- Pull *Security* by identifying challenges and obstacles and constructing solutions to overcome them or mitigation measures to minimize them.
- Maintain *Control* by ensuring that the organizational architecture, responsibilities, and risks are understood by all, and finally...
- Use *Common Sense*.

BILL STORY

"Ambiguity."

At one point in my career, I joined a Fortune 500 manufacturing firm that had recently emerged from bankruptcy. (Note – NETWORKING got me there). As you might expect, business conditions were challenging. There was a new leadership team, private equity held majority ownership, the organization was going through significant reorganization, and on top of all that, the economy was tanking in a manner not seen in decades. I was hired to establish a global talent management function that would support and enable achievement of the go-forward business strategy. There was a job description, which was written appropriately for the high level of the role. It included directional focus areas, high-level deliverables, and similar content. I basically had a clean slate with broad parameters. My charge included a cardinal direction and very broad, potentially mobile fences. (e.g., "Go north, do no harm, and build something that will work."). Fortunately, I had done similar work in a prior civilian role (but not with nearly this vague, broad operational window), so I felt well prepared for success. Had I, by some strange chance, landed in this role straight out of the military, I likely wouldn't have been nearly as capable of driving success.

Early in the hiring process, I found out just how vague and challenging things can be. I interviewed with multiple top-level leaders from across the global organization. Each of them shared their priorities, their interest in the role, and their preferred approaches. They all probed me on their various individual interests - talk about ambiguity and confusion! These were all highly placed, highly experienced, highly capable people with years of experience in their respective career fields. They all knew just how challenging the business conditions were. They were all under tremendous pressure to perform. Quite frankly, the company's success and the success of their own careers were on the line.

The situation was the very definition of ambiguity. I could have let it get to me. I could have walked away, but I didn't. Instead, I chose to double down. I took it all in, considered it all against my definition of success and the decision criteria I held dear, and I accepted the challenge. I dove in, made a plan, built my network, and started making things happen. Was it easy? Not often. Was it fun? Sometimes. Did I find it rewarding? Absolutely!

How did onboarding go? Well, given that I stayed with the company for eight years, I guess it went OK, but in all candor, there was no process beyond the administrative "keep you out of jail" compliance stuff. Given the organizational turmoil, there was little focus on history, structure, mission, vision, values, and other topics that are so commonly part of onboarding in the military. Getting familiar with the company, the people, and the culture was on me. I had to take the bull by the horns and make things happen!

Is this typical? Not exactly. Not every company you will experience is emerging from bankruptcy and facing similarly extreme levels of change, volatility, and ambiguity. BUT – change, volatility, and ambiguity exist in every organization. Be ready for it as you onboard. Understand that the clarity and rigor you experienced in military onboarding likely won't be what you experience in the civilian world. Gauge your comfort level for the ambiguity, decide if you are in the right place, consider whether or not you are willing and able to do the work that needs to be done, and ask yourself if you fit well and add value to the team. Be very thoughtful when you do this work. Don't let current discomfort or a lack of familiarity dissuade you. Be pragmatic and practical, but in the end, if you know it just ain't right, enact your PACE plan and make your move.

DAVE STORY

"A Journey of Ups and Downs."

After leaving the VA, I was introduced to an opportunity to lead a startup organization that had the potential to have a

> *serious impact in the region. This hit both components I had determined I was looking for in the perfect career. First, it would allow me the autonomy to build something, and second, that work would have a positive impact in my community. When I was hired, the board charged me with a couple of things; connect high school graduates to work, lower regional unemployment, and reduce regional turnover. Sounds easy, right? Well, it turns out that there's no step-by-step directions for any of those components, nor was the board going to hold my hand as I developed a plan. After all, that's what they hired me for.*
>
> *Talk about ambiguous...but also talk about an opportunity! I rolled up my sleeves and got to work. The team and I started to try new things, we noted what worked and what didn't, and then we adjusted accordingly. We implemented new programming, developed new software solutions, began consulting with employers, and more. Within a year, we had made a significant impact in the region in all of the components identified, and even won the top award for talent development and retention by the International Economic Development Council. After all, that's what we as veterans do: provide comprehensive solutions to complex problems.*

Bottom line – employers have work to do and need people who fit well on their team.

Onboarding processes are the way they are for a reason. There are likely many variables that contributed to the existing process. Being new to the team, you won't have this frame of reference. Yes, your experience is valid also, and most employers are always looking to improve, but before you make improvement suggestions, complaints, or the like, take your time. Unless they are somehow doing something illegal, immoral, or unethical, hold your tongue until you have experienced the entire process. Focus on getting up to speed fast and being a great add to the team – you'll have plenty of time to help them improve later.

Sometimes business conditions change.

The hiring process can take weeks, months, or longer. From first identifying the need, to clarifying and documenting the job description, to obtaining all the relevant approvals to post the job, to loading it in whatever systems and sources the company uses to get the word out, to receiving and screening applications, reviewing resumes, selecting top candidates for interviews, conducting various interviews, selecting the preferred person, preparing and sending an offer, to that candidate's acceptance, there are many moving parts impacting how long this process takes. We're walking you through all this to show that this cycle can take much longer than anyone prefers.

While all this is going on, business conditions can change in an instant. Perhaps a key customer changes their order. Maybe a key supplier has an interruption in their ability to service you. The economy might shift in an unexpected way. A competitor may announce a breakthrough new product/service, or perhaps they unexpectedly crash and burn. Maybe new legislation is approved that significantly impacts your market. Whatever the case, the variables are nearly endless. No matter the shift(s), they may impact business conditions to such a degree that the job you decided to accept is 1) no longer available or 2) substantially changed.

It's important to remember that in most cases, the employer has the right to rescind an offer, and/or terminate anyone with or without cause. It happens. I've seen it. Johnny accepts a great job, is preparing to move to the new location (or perhaps has even already moved there), and suddenly the company decides it no longer needs that role. Several things could happen in this case:

SECTION 1: LANDING 77

- ★ The company could simply rescind the offer, and let Johnny go.
- ★ It might consider Johnny for a different, existing role they believe would benefit from his experience/capability.
- ★ They might create a new role that is an awesome fit for Johnny and the company.

In any of these possibilities, issues relating to salary, relocation expenses, and similar monetary and other topics can become a very sticky wicket, full of unique circumstances and solutions.

The good news is that while business conditions definitely do change, having an unforeseen impact on your landing, extreme examples such as the aforementioned are rare, and most employers are empathetic enough to do their very best with you. Most are also savvy enough to know that word gets out about how they treat employees, and they don't want to do anything that will damage their reputation (employment value proposition) any more than is absolutely necessary.

If you find that things have changed when you land, stay objective. Remain professional. Learn all you can about the situation. Understand everything you can about how the change will impact the job you signed on for, and the opportunities it may reveal. Keep your cool, be reasonable, work with the employer, consider your options, and make level-headed decisions about your next move.

Detailed *Product/Service* Insights when LANDING

When landing, identifying your organization's product/services is key.

As the graphic above displays there are two general product/service areas for you to consider:

- ★ **Business** – These are the products/services the organization provides to customers/clients/consumers. They include

    legacy products/services that have been in their portfolio for some time, **current** products/services that are being delivered today, and products/services that are being considered for the **future**. Identifying the **risks** and **opportunities** for each, and which ones are "**cash cows**" or "**capital burns**," is not critical when landing. Simply identifying what the products/services are is sufficient in your initial days.
- ★ **You** – Recognizing yourself as a product that is providing a service to the employer can be a helpful mindset that enables you to think critically about your value-add, and how you might best be engaged to leverage your skills, capabilities, and experience. When landing, be mindful of your capabilities, wants/needs, value-add, performance, potential, aspirations, abilities, agility, availability, and actions, to continually assess your fit with the organization's needs, and how well the organization fits for you. Again, when landing, your focus should be on initial impressions. Keep your eyes/ears open for red flags and opportunities, but don't overthink every little thing.

Let's dig a bit deeper into YOU as a product/service...

When the employer extended an offer for you to join their team, they saw capability in you to do the work they need done and to fit well on their team. Congratulations! You did what you needed to do to convince them you were the best candidate for the job.

Now that you've landed, you need to pay attention to every possible data point that confirms your **capabilities** and that indicates opportunity for you to demonstrate them. After all, you want and need to show that you are worth the investment the employer is making. If you have capabilities beyond the current job, keep them in your toolbox, close at hand. You never know when the chance may arise for you to demonstrate these also!

We all have **wants and needs**. When landing it's wise to be mindful of yours; to vet how well this new gig aligns with them. We're not

SECTION 1: LANDING

suggesting acting like a self-centered, impetuous child, but failing to be mindful of your wants and needs can lead to some pretty negative downstream effects. Imagine you're in a new job, using your capabilities and making a difference. BUT…you're miserable. Perhaps you're working huge overtime or travelling extensively, throwing your work/life balance out of whack. Maybe you want advancement opportunities but are in a role that simply has zero upward potential in the near future (e.g., the boss is either a rockstar or the owner's offspring, and isn't going anywhere for several years). This disconnect between reality and your wants/needs will likely create some challenges over time.

Landing can be a challenging time. You're feeling the success of making it to this point in your transition journey, and you may be feeling a bit of excitement, anxiety, or stress about making a great first impression, getting a few wins out of the gate, proving your **value-add** and setting a strong foundation for the future. If you find yourself in this space, remember your past **performance**. You've had solid performance in the past, and there's no reason to doubt your ability to perform well in the present!

Certainly, when you are landing, your focus should be on today—identifying who's who and what's what. That said, it's wise to keep an ear open for future **potential** in this role, as well as within your company and industry. Do they align with your **aspirations**? Do you have the **ability** to do more/other at some future point? Does your **agility** align with the optempo, variabilities, and apparent trajectory of the situation? Will you be **available** when opportunities arise? Are you willing to take necessary **action** to bring your potential to life?

Finally, be attentive to your **fit** with the organization. Are you setting yourself up as a solid team member that adds value and fits well today? Are you reasonably comfortable with the situation? Are you receiving any initial feedback that indicates how others see your fit? What, if any, indicators are hitting your radar about where things are going in the future and how that may impact your fit tomorrow?

When landing, there's lots to do. Balance your focus and efforts. Don't obsess about yourself as a product/service, but occasionally make some time to consider it. If things are going well, drive on! If there are some concerns/red flags, build in time as you land to vet them, make decisions and take appropriate actions. You'll be glad you did.

Business Products/Services

Legacy products/services are those that have been around for a while; perhaps years or decades. Identifying what these are when you are landing gives you a peek into the company's history and may provide footprints from where the company started to where it is today. A great example of a legacy product is Harley-Davidson's Sportster. It has been in production since the 1950's!

Some products/services answer a **current** need. Think of those products/services that feed a fad. Fidget spinners are a good example. Several years ago, fidget spinners popped on the scene as the next cool toy for kids. They were simple little gadgets that allegedly helped kids reduce stress and focus better. They hit the shelves by storm, and just about as quickly they faded away. Identifying products/services in this category provides insights as to the lay of the land, especially in regard to potential product/service offering changes that may be on the horizon.

Some products/services are designed/developed/delivered with a **future** focus that aspires to answer an emerging need. Working with these types of products/services can be exciting, but it can also involve risk. Identifying what (if any) future focused products/services are in the company's portfolio, and how your role relates to them can be valuable information that helps you land well.

Every product/service offering a business may consider comes with **risks and opportunities.** Identifying the risks and opportunities of the products/services most closely related to your role can be time well spent when landing. Gaining insight into those products/services with high levels of risk may influence how you attack your role. Conversely, if you discover that you are working on a product/

service that has waning opportunities, you'll want to dig in deeper to consider the impact this may have on your future.

> ### DAVE STORY
>
> *"Risk of Doing vs. Not Doing."*
>
> *Risk is inherent in growth, but it is often far too easy to use that risk as an excuse to never even try in the first place. We say things like, "That acquisition or project is too risky, so let's scrap it." (Don't get me wrong, sometimes the risk is too high!) In the military, the risk is often high until risk mitigation measures are implemented. I spent several deployments as the senior enlisted advisor of a Special Operations Assault Force. Weather often introduced risk as it degraded our ability to see the target and could limit our ability to employ certain weapon systems.*
>
> *On one such deployment, weather had rolled in and was affecting our ability to see the targeted compound from certain altitudes. To fly lower would potentially alert the target and give the bad guys an advantage we didn't want them to have. During the planning process, I recommended that we roll the mission until conditions were more favorable. Not five minutes after I made that call, the Task Force Commander came to our planning room. "Dave, I get the risk of going, but what is the risk if we don't go?" See, this was a high-level guy who was directly responsible for American deaths and was very hard to locate. There were risk mitigation measures that we could take to lower the risk of going, it was much harder to mitigate the risk of not going. This mindset shift of looking at risk through both lenses is an exercise that I challenge everyone to try. Whether it is career planning or business decisions, what is the risk of not doing? Does it outweigh the risk of doing? Sometimes it won't...but sometimes it will.*

Some products/services are **cash cows**. They generate lots of revenue and lots of profit. Other products/services **burn capital** (money). They require a lot of money and other resources to become reality. Both can be important pieces of a business portfolio. Cash cows can provide relatively dependable sources of money that can be used for other purposes. Those that burn lots of capital can represent necessary investments in expanding current markets or establishing new ones. As they relate to landing, identifying which products/services are which, and how your role relates to them, can be valuable information that helps form your initial understanding of the business situation you're stepping into.

When landing it's not critical that you learn deeply and broadly about these, simply identifying what products/services exist and why is sufficient. Later, as you integrate, and thrive & survive, you can learn more deeply and broadly about them all, and leverage them for positive results.

LANDING SUMMARY

Landing is much more than getting your badge, access codes, and finding your desk. Getting the lay of the land goes far beyond the procedural tasks that encompass the first week or two on the job. Transitioning into a new role is seldom easy, and it can be overwhelming when it is so different than what you are used to. Dissecting your new role by the people, processes, and product/service will help you take a complex new environment and break it down into manageable and actionable components. A good landing is a catalyst to successfully integrate into the company and thriving & surviving in the long run. Whether this is your first job after the military or your tenth, answering the questions contained in this section will give you a good view of the landscape in the company, an initial glimpse into your firm's strategy, and an idea of where you should focus your priorities as you shift into the integration phase.

SECTION 2

INTEGRATING

CAREER AND LIFE JOURNEY ALIGNMENT – INTEGRATING

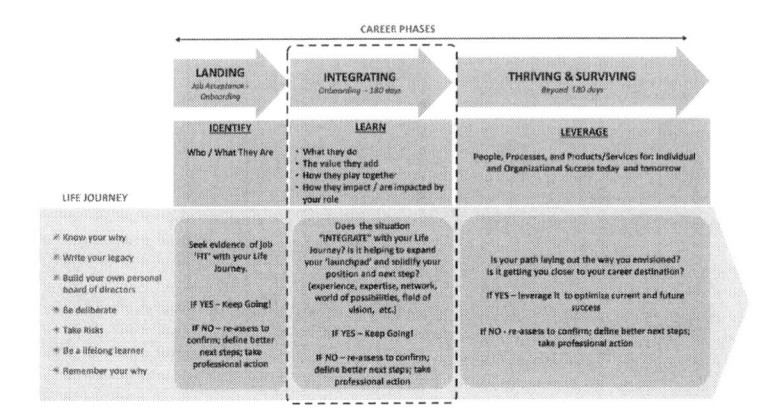

CAREER PHASES		
LANDING Job Acceptance – Onboarding	**INTEGRATING** Onboarding – 180 days	**THRIVING & SURVIVING** Beyond 180 days
IDENTIFY Who / What They Are	**LEARN** • What they do • The value they add • How they play together • How they impact / are impacted by your role	**LEVERAGE** People, Processes, and Products/Services for: Individual and Organizational Success today and tomorrow

LIFE JOURNEY

- Know your why
- Write your legacy
- Build your own personal board of directors
- Be deliberate
- Take Risks
- Be a lifelong learner
- Remember your why

Seek evidence of job "FIT" with your Life Journey. IF YES – Keep Going! IF NO – re-assess to confirm; define better next steps; take professional action	Does the situation "INTEGRATE" with your Life Journey? Is it helping to expand your launchpad and solidify your position and next step? (experience, expertise, network, world of possibilities, field of vision, etc.) IF YES – Keep Going! IF NO – re-assess to confirm; define better next steps; take professional action	Is your path laying out the way you envisioned? Is it getting you closer to your career destination? IF YES – leverage it to optimize current and future success IF NO – re-assess to confirm; define better next steps; take professional action

CAREER AND LIFE JOURNEY ALIGNMENT – INTEGRATING ACTION ITEMS

	LAND	INTEGRATE	THRIVE & SURVIVE
Know your why	Vet reality against your WHY to optimize happiness and success	Don't let new influences sway you unintentionally	Stay true to yourself; let WHY evolve if appropriate.
Write your legacy	First impressions matter	How you integrate with others impacts your legacy	Remember – your legacy is the result of what you do over time; don't get the cart before the horse.
Build your own personal board of directors	Identify potential PBOD candidates	Build relationships with PBOD candidates and listen to their counsel	Review PBOD members for relevance over time; change members as needed.
Be deliberate	Have a plan to land well; work the plan diligently	Work with others to understand how everything fits	Take intentional actions to optimize current success and future opportunities that align with your life plan.
Take Risks	Reasonable risks – don't stumble out of the starting blocks	Eagerly seek out others; introduce yourself; make connections; build relationships	Boldly seek and exploit opportunities to spread your wings, add more value, and expand your scope.
Be a lifelong learner	Identify the "Who's Who" and the What's What" of the new job	LEARN • What they do • The value they add • How they play together • How they impact / are impacted by your role	LEVERAGE People, Processes, and Products/Services for: Individual and Organizational Success today and tomorrow
Remember your why	To avoid being drawn off course in your new position	Share your unique value	To vet situations and evolving conditions for alignment with your overall life journey plan.

Introduction/General INTEGRATING Insights

Having made it successfully through the LANDING phase, your next task is integrating. As Bill mentions in his first book, employers hire people that have convinced them they are the best to do two things:

- ★ Successfully do the work they need done.
- ★ Fit well and add value to the team.

Once you've made your initial impressions, and landed with your feet under you, it's time to prove the employer right! It's time to start successfully doing the work that needs done and fit in with and add value to the team. This requires that you focus on several key areas:

- ★ Confirming your duties, responsibilities, and deliverables.
- ★ Learning the people, team dynamics, and organizational culture.
- ★ Understanding available resources and constraints.
- ★ Gaining awareness of headwinds and tailwinds that may help or hinder your success.

When you are integrating, you are moving past the formalities of the onboarding process, to learning how things really operate, and establishing your place in the organization. It is a formative time, full of opportunities, unknowns, and potential. It is a time to learn about the people, processes, and products/services that are core to your new organization and work environment.

As it relates to your life journey, the INTEGRATING phase of your career transition is all about situational awareness, ensuring that your situation aligns with your overall life plan. As such, key considerations for you at this point in your career journey should be:

- ★ Know Your Why—Don't let new influences sway you unintentionally.
- ★ Write Your Legacy—How you integrate with others impacts your legacy.
- ★ Build Your Own Personal Board of Directors—Build relationships with PBOD candidates and listen to their counsel.
- ★ Be Deliberate—Work with others to understand how everything fits.
- ★ Take Risks—Eagerly seek out others, introduce yourself, make connections, and build relationships.
- ★ Be a Lifelong Learner—Learn what your coworkers do, the value they add, how they play together, and how they impact/are impacted by your role. What they do, the value they add, how they play together, and how they impact/are impacted by your role.
- ★ Remember Your Why—Share your unique value.

"Capable" and "Credible" are two different things.

CAPABLE: (adjective) having the ability, fitness, or quality necessary to do or achieve a specified thing; able to achieve efficiently whatever one has to do; competent. Said simply – having the actual ability to do something successfully.

CREDIBLE: (adjective) able to be believed; convincing. Said simply – being capable of persuading people that something will happen or be successful.

Two important but very different terms.

You may be capable of many things.

You may have demonstrated capability in some very tough situations, throughout your time in the military and beyond.

However, and perhaps unfortunately, that does not make you automatically credible.

To be credible, you must cause others to believe; to be convinced that something will happen or be successful.

"Capable" is evidenced by past success.

"Credible" speaks to relevance and potential.

Integrating well is, in part, about becoming credible. It's about demonstrating to your employer that you can successfully do the work they need done, fit well, and add value to the team. It's also about creating positive, credible relationships with other people, internally and externally to your organization, so that you set a solid foundation for success. It's about communicating and demonstrating your capability in a relevant manner.

Understand the asks and the tasks. Coordinate efficiently and effectively with relevant others. Execute well. Follow up robustly. Seek feedback. Take action to reinforce what's working, and to shore up what isn't.

Once your capability becomes credible to the employer, you are on your way to integration success!

BILL STORY

"Capable, But Not Credible."

Imagine you are deployed, out there making good things happen in real-world, challenging environments. One day, a new guy arrives out of the blue. He says he's there to be your new platoon sergeant. You ask where he came from, what his background is and so forth. He shares that he had a long career in manufacturing serving in a variety of leadership roles responsible for revenue generation, profitability, operations, logistics, people, process, and more. He goes on to say that he's excited to be here and he is confident that his great leadership experience in manufacturing will be a great asset to the platoon's success. Sounds ridiculous, doesn't it? He may be capable in manufacturing, but there's no way in hell he's credible in your military environment. Well, guess what? When the tables are turned and you're asking an employer to

> *accept your military experience, it can sound just as ridiculous. Remember this once you've landed and are working on integrating well, then do your level best to make yourself credible.*

To integrate well, you need to add value — as the employer measures it.

Just as commanders are much more apt to approve a mission plan after a well-briefed concept of operations is delivered by people with credible experience and perspective, the ability to articulate your value, coupled with proven results, are what create credibility. Why? Because the more comfortable you are speaking your plan/value, the more likely it came from research and experience.

> ### *DAVE STORY*
>
> *"Understand How They're Counting."*
>
> *I got my job as Director, Firelands Forward, even though underqualified from a technical standpoint. I had a well thought out/researched plan and asked good, relevant questions that demonstrated I understood the employers' expectations and was able to put in place a plan to achieve them.*

As you integrate into your new role, get clear on expectations. Learn why they are important to the employer, and how they are measured. Understand how you fit and add value to each of them, and how the boss needs to hear about progress. Then, go forth and deliver to the very best of your ability.

Money drives business. You better have at least a cursory understanding.

Finance is the universal business language. Whether for profit, non-profit, publicly traded, privately held, large, small, startup, or mature, money is the commodity of every organization.

There is a language for everything. You didn't know the military language when you first joined, but you learned it. Get educated in whatever language the industry you want to join uses.

Likewise, employers that want to hire, retain, and maximize the value of veterans need to have a cursory understanding of the military language. This mutual, basic understanding of each other's lexicon will help both understand the different lenses by which each view problem sets.

For veterans, it doesn't matter what industry you are in; understanding how money is made, how expenses are managed, and how money matters are documented—as well as becoming literate in profit and loss statements, balance sheets, and so-forth—is relevant to everyone. While not every position requires the same depth and breadth of understanding, if you don't recognize the basics, you're behind the eight ball. Because of this, it's incredibly important to know how to read basic financial statements, and understand what decisions are being made (and why) based on the current strategy. Money is the universal language of business; if you want to integrate well across all pieces of your organization, you'd better understand the common language

DAVE STORY

"I Am in Waaay Over My Head...Not."

My first day of class at Ohio State University's Executive MBA program was the first time I had ever set foot in a college

> *classroom. During orientation, we introduced ourselves and gave a brief synopsis of our backgrounds. I knew that I was going to be going to school with talented people, but there I was, in a college classroom with a world-renowned brain surgeon, the chief of surgery for the cancer center, one of the top marketing professionals for Johnson and Johnson, and more. My first thought was, "I am in waaay over my head." I've been operating with high performing individuals for my entire professional career, but doing so in a profession and discipline that I knew. This was different. Learning accounting or business strategy with successful business leaders was incredibly intimidating. However, much to my surprise, I was able to not only keep up, but contribute to the overall learning experience of the class. It was incredibly empowering to succeed in another learning environment. It gave me confidence to know that I could speak the language of business, think critically using different problem-solving tools, and ultimately succeed in a different sector.*

You Can Do It

It is not uncommon for veterans to feel overwhelmed or intimidated by entering a whole new and unfamiliar world. Let's face it, many of us are in the civilian workspace for the first time. Most joined the military right out of high school or college. This is probably your first big boy/girl job. Totally normal. However, it's time to get over it.

You have a lot to learn; we've talked about that. But you also have a ton to bring to the table. Don't discount your prior experience, which is richer, broader and deeper than the vast majority of society. Be aware. Be confident. Connect your experience to the employers' needs, and then go make an impact!

As you start to get settled in your new position, this is often when the sense of being overwhelmed sets in. You have landed,

SECTION 2: INTEGRATING

have finished the onboarding process, and suddenly you find yourself face to face with real expectations, looking at you to deliver high level, real results. The technical/tangible stuff may not be totally familiar. But that's only part of the picture. There are multiple intangibles that make success happen – and veterans are highly skilled and experienced in this realm. Don't fall prey to the "oh shits." Be confident; you've done tough stuff before, and you can do this, too.

DAVE STORY

"Tangibles, Intangibles, 'Oh Shits' and Success."

Select members of the 75th Ranger Regiment hosted the Toronto Blue Jays for a week in 2019. We were asked by their coaching staff to discuss culture, and the way that we create a culture of accountability. One night, after a hard day of training, we were all standing around a campfire. Both Rangers and Major League Baseball players. Two groups of professionals in very different fields. There were two questions from their players that stood out to me, which I think bring some context into some of the intangible value that veterans bring to the workforce:

1. *How do you mentally prepare for a mission?*
   This one was pretty easy for me to articulate. I told the baseball player that I visualize everything that I'm going to do on the mission. Literally everything. Over and over again. I visualize what I am going to do in the helicopter at the one-minute mark, from as mundane of a task as unclipping the troop strap and handing it to the guy next to me. I visualize putting my hand on my safety lanyard so when the aircraft lands I can quickly unsnap. I build a mental map of how I am going to approach the target building, where

I am going to put the door charge, etc. I visualize contingencies. What happens if the door is open? So on, and so on. Even though I have practiced all of these things exhaustively already, visualization allows me to get more repetitions in. It allows me to think through the game plan if things go wrong, or if things don't look the way I thought they were going to look. This all allows me to perform when the game is on the line.

The nature of my military service may not reflect yours, but no matter what branch you served in or what your duties were, all veterans have been trained to perform complex tasks when the pressure is on. Veterans are also used to maximizing our training through visualization, and through preparation. The great news for us is that this is absolutely relevant in the corporate setting. Business leaders need to know that they can trust their managers in high-stake situations, whether that be in a boardroom or in a complex negotiation with a potential client. Now, this doesn't take away from the technical aspect of knowing the job, but what every employer hiring a veteran can count on is that after they know how to do their job, they will know how to prepare so that they can maximize the application of that knowledge base in complex and high stress environments.

2. *How did you make the decision to go into the room the night you got shot?*

   This question caught me off guard and I had to admit, I never really thought about it before. However, after a minute or so of pondering this seemingly strange question, the answer came to me. I told him, "I guess I made that decision fifteen years ago when I joined the Ranger Regiment." The reality is that I didn't think twice during the moment of truth because

SECTION 2: INTEGRATING

> *I had already mentally committed to my mission fifteen years prior when I volunteered to serve. You will likely not need to risk your life for your workplace teammates, nor should you expect the same from them; still, employers should know that when they hire a veteran, they are getting a team member who will be committed to the team, and that value is immeasurable.*

These, of course, are two small examples of the intangibles you can bring to the table. Be confident, and be aware of your surroundings. Bring your best, deliver it in a way that is well received, and know that your efforts are helping you integrate well.

Your new organization is what it is. It's not the one you came from.

DAVE STORY

"Great Intent. Great Message. Not So Much with the Delivery."

In 2016, Ranger Regiment reimplemented what they called "serving the charter," or "charter time." This meant that before you could assume a certain leadership role, you had to serve outside of the organization for at least twelve months. This was designed to serve two purposes: first, to broaden our experiences outside of the small bubble we knew; and second, to give back to the General-Purpose Force some of the skillsets we had gained in the Special Operations Community. It so happened that 2016 was the year that I was eligible for said leadership position, and so I was one of the first to execute this new policy and leave the organization for a short period of time.

For all the reasons you can probably imagine, my wife and I decided to go to Hawaii. We packed our stuff and headed 4,000 miles west on a new adventure. Shortly after we got there, I assumed responsibility for an infantry company and got to work. It's not that the company wasn't operating well, but there was a clear priority towards administrative excellence and little emphasis on tactical performance. I was full of vim and vigor, and had grand plans of changing that so that we could increase our lethality and proficiency on the battlefield, something that hadn't been as big of a priority previously. The team was getting better, and all the metrics that mattered to me were improving (marksmanship, medical proficiency, etc.). When my first 360 assessment came up, I thought I was going to crush it. I was confident that the team felt the same way I did, that we were on our way to where we wanted to go, and that there was a palpable culture shift because the team was getting to do what they signed up for.

Enter the most humbling experience of my military career. I couldn't have been more wrong about the pulse of the company. I had this preconceived view of what an infantry company should look like, and it didn't align with the most important stakeholders in the room...my employees. It turns out, they didn't want to be a Ranger company. It's not that they didn't want to evolve; they just wanted to drive that evolution. After all, many of them had served for years in the organization, while I had been there for mere months. Maybe one of the greatest leadership lessons of my career.

That wasn't to say my experience wasn't relevant, but the 25th Infantry Division wasn't Ranger Regiment, just like Ranger Regiment wasn't the 25th Infantry Division. I needed to learn my current organization, with our unique challenges and architecture, before I could influence real change.

So, what did we do about it? We all sat down and wrote

> our own collective Tactical Standard Operating Procedures Manual. We took a couple of months to capture how we, as an organization, wanted to operate. This was a collective process driven from within; not mandated from the outside. We captured how we wanted to standardize the way we set up our gun positions, what would be standard on our kits and what would be left up to the individual, how we would mark things, and more. While this started out as the most humbling leadership experience in my career, it also evolved into one of my proudest. Within the year, not only had our culture improved significantly (as demonstrated by the follow-up 360 assessment), but also had become, quantitatively, the most lethal and effective infantry company in the brigade. Bottom line: real and lasting change is generated from within the organization.
>
> Much like I was in 2016, you are coming into a new organization. You may feel the urge to start calling out things that you believe could improve the process or product. Resist until you fully understand the purpose behind the process, the context in which it exists, and the plan for it in the future. This doesn't mean don't ask questions; fire away! Again, the better you can build this understanding, the faster you will appreciate why it is the way it is (or the more effectively you will be able to recommend and implement needed changes). Only now, your solution will come with context and an understanding of how it fits within the larger business.

The military must build its talent, but in the civilian world, employers often buy talent.

As you integrate into your new role, it's wise to remember that you were brought into the organization via an interview and an offer.

The employer offered you a certain position, with certain pay and benefits, so that you could join the team and deliver certain results. Whether you came on board in an entry level or senior leadership position, you were hired for the role you were expected to fill.

This is a very different proposition than the military, where everyone starts as a "1." Whether E1 or O1, in the vast majority of cases, the military talent pipeline is filled from the bottom up. People are developed at every level for success at higher levels. This absolutely makes sense in the military – after all, you can't exactly go to other nations' military services to obtain a new Senior Chief Petty Officer, Lieutenant Colonel, or other.

As a normal matter of course, civilian businesses go outside their organization to obtain the best possible talent to fill their open roles at every level. Even the top-level executive roles are often filled by outsiders. This being the case, leadership and career development may not be nearly as robust as the military's. The logic here is, "I can pay good money to bring in someone that is ready to deliver–I don't have to spend time and money to train them up to get there." As you might expect, there are strong, valid arguments on both sides of this discussion. Dissecting these is beyond the scope of this book. Suffice it to say, as you integrate into your new organization, learn how they approach talent. If they're buying most of it, you need to understand what that means to your position and your future. If they're building it, make sure you are dialed in to how that works.

Leadership Expectations

Leadership means very different things in the civilian world. It rarely is as robustly understood as it is in the military. Investing in leadership development among the ranks of the civilian workforce is unfortunately rare, and where it does happen, the rigor, focus, and integrated nature of military leadership training is rarely replicated. While this may be a shock when you first join a new organization and begin to integrate, it is what it is. You'll be well advised to understand it, why things are the way they are, and the conditions that got the organization to where it is today, rather than blasting them for not having solid leadership development.

BILL STORY

"We're Training Them, Bill; It's What We Get Paid For."

My second job out of the military was with a $3B supply chain/ transportation company. I was brought in to lead the training function for a 1100-person air freight hub that processed ~three million pounds of freight a night. Part of this gig was leadership development for the facility's management team. At our first session (a multi-day off-site event), I was cofacilitating a session that could only be described as rudimentary. In the military context, we were covering topics that inexperienced E4s receive in their very first leadership courses. I was shocked. On a break, I pulled my colleague aside to express my concerns. She was an external consultant who had worked with the group previously. She was highly skilled and had spent her entire career in the civilian work world. I asked "How in the hell did this team ascend to their lofty positions of authority without understanding these entry level leadership concepts? What are we doing here?" My colleague chuckled and said, "Bill, we are training them. This isn't the Army. People land in leadership positions for different reasons—often because they were really good at some technical aspect of the work that needed attention. Sometimes because they were buddies with the boss. Sometimes they were simply the last person standing. Rarely are they fully ready for the leadership aspects of the job. The good news is the boss values leadership and wants his team to grow in that regard. That's our job. Break's over; let's go make leaders."

DAVE STORY

"Not All People in Positions of Authority Have Leadership Training."

I was working at the VA when the Afghanistan withdrawal happened. I knew that the way we left that country after twenty years of investment would create a substantial uptick in behavioral health issues for our veteran population. I was working in the C-suite office and wanted to check in with the Mental Health Services team to ensure that the administrators were supporting the surge of patients that would undoubtedly come. Nope. Not one administrator other than me, the new grad student intern, had talked to the department. Not one administrator understood the impact this would have on their patients. Nor would they until it reached crisis mode. Why? I can only make an educated guess, but I believe it was because there was not one veteran in the C-suite. They didn't understand their patients and as a healthcare organization serving a specific demographic, that's important. But the real problem is that they didn't really care to. Their priorities lied with meeting metrics set by their higher headquarters. In the VA, leaders seemingly could rise up the ranks as technical experts with zero leadership training. This resulted in a severe disconnect between practitioners and decision makers.

In the military, every leader has some sort of formalized leader training that is uniform and tailored to the specific needs of the organization at that time. From direct leadership training to organizational leadership to strategic leadership, at almost every level of increasing responsibility, that leader goes back to school and learns how to manage at the level in which he or she is assuming. All different and requiring a different set of skills. Not so much in the civilian world. Often, companies promote technical experts and put them

> *in management roles without equipping them with the right skillset to lead. Know this is a thing and while integrating into the company, try to identify and understand the different leader dynamics within your organization. It will pay dividends for you when trying to get things done.*

Innovation is a funny thing. It is a huge priority for some companies. For others, it is a necessary evil. The reality is, though, that innovation and change are constant. The world is ever evolving, and companies must evolve with it. As you integrate, learn how your company, division, department, function, team, and others see innovation. This knowledge can be very helpful to integration success. If you're an innovative person—always seeking ways to improve, grow, extend, or expand success—and the organization is innovation averse, you may be in for a tough row. If, on the other hand, you're a steady state solid performer, looking to do what you do with little change, and the organization is focused on innovation, the disconnect can also be challenging.

BILL STORY

"I Want New Ideas – But We Aren't Doing Anything I Haven't Already Done."

There was a company that was allegedly seeking a strategic talent partner to help it grow top line revenue 4x (from $100M to $400M annual revenue). A top-notch talent management professional joined the team as a member of the executive committee to help make that growth happen. At an early leadership team meeting, the boss commented that he was not happy with the current approach to strategic planning. He said the existing annual strategy planning process took too much work to produce, didn't convert into real action and results, and served little more purpose than to hold down shelves. He

> *asked for ideas. This new talent executive offered the 15-month rolling strategy concept (build your annual business strategy, monitor performance and build the 5th quarter strategy as you go). He'd seen it work well, especially in dynamic business conditions. The boss's response was nothing short of shocking. Paraphrasing his colorful retort, he basically said "I'm not doing anything I haven't already tried." WTF???If he had no intention of charting a new course or considering valuable feedback, then why did he even ask??? The new talent executive knew better than to press the issue, and had certainly learned a lesson. Innovation may be what they're asking for, but to integrate well, you need to understand what they really want.*

Learn when to lean on and leverage your military experience directly, and learn when to be more subtle. No doubt your military experience can add great value to most any organization. But as you integrate, you want to be sure how and when you dole out that experience. Much the way farmers' fields absolutely need rain, an unexpected driving downpour can do more harm than good, washing away the sprouting crops and the soil in which they are planted. To integrate well, remember you have two eyes, two ears, and one mouth for a reason. Observe, listen, think, and then professionally offer your insights and experience. Doing so will limit the risk of overwhelming others, will provide value, and might even create interest in what other great value you may be able to bring.

Pay attention to the culture, because it's the work world you're going to be living in. The near-universal support that surrounded you in the military is gone. Yes, you are part of an organization, and that organization may even offer some great benefits and an environment you love, but by comparison you're pretty much on your own. Need medical care? There's no troop medical clinic – you need to find your own doctors. Need groceries to feed the family?

There's no commissary. Looking for activities to enjoy? There's not much chance of an MWR (Morale, Welfare, and Recreation) agency to help with that.

Furthermore, as we've mentioned previously, no one cares more about your career than you do. Yes, you are part of a team, but if you don't prioritize 'Me,' you may not much be part of any 'We.' Be a solid team member, but remember that you have to look out for yourself and your career.

Integrating can take energy. There will be many new things to learn, new people to meet, new challenges to overcome, and new opportunities you'll have to figure out how to exploit. Be resilient. Keep a positive perspective. Be assertive without being aggressive. Press on, but know when to get off the gas and coast for a while to let the journey evolve.

It's probably good at this point to remind you that your former rank means nothing to most of the people around you. Some folks may know the difference between a private, a sergeant, a lieutenant, a major, and a general but most won't. Terms like "sergeant major" and "lieutenant general" may just make their heads spin. Further, there's often little correlation between military ranks and civilian job titles. Sure, there are some general, relative similarities, but even these get wonky from company to company, where employers can pretty much use whatever titles they want. Learn the company's structure. Understand what titles fit where. And for Pete's sake, leave your military rank at the door.

Your focus greatly impacts your success. Which way are you looking now that you've landed in that great new job?

When it comes to career transition, it is tempting to look backwards, holding tight to that which is familiar while avoiding that which is unknown. It may have happened to you when you were in job search. It may also happen to you once you have landed and are beginning to integrate into your new world.

ANYONE SEE A PROBLEM HERE?

TRANSITION <u>INTO</u> MILITARY

Then

TRANSITION <u>OUT</u> OF MILITARY

Looking Forward

Looking Backward

Consider this - when we joined the military, we transitioned INTO it. We joined a structured, organized, aligned environment where most everything around us existed to make us successful. Our focus was on the future. We were guided through our transition and our landing, and because of the common processes and experiences, and robust, focused resources, our integrating experience was often a non-issue.

Fast forward a few short years (or decades) and we transition OUT of the military. Even that simple phrasing indicates focus. Backwards. Toward the past, the familiar, and the known.

We get it. Most of us did it. But looking back is not what we need to be successful in transition.

Transitioning into the civilian workforce is not at all like your military experience. You are on your own (but for the network you build). The robust resources are gone. The community's focus on helping you succeed is nonexistent (but for the veteran-related resources with which you may decide to connect).

When you add a backward focus to the mix, you are making things harder for yourself!

So why bring this up now? After all, we're talking about integrating into a new role, not finding a new one! How does this impact

SECTION 2: INTEGRATING

integrating? Unfortunately, this is exactly the point at which this can become an issue.

Having gone through the challenges of the job search, there can be a sense of relief when you've landed (and that is a great, well-deserved thing). This can sometimes morph into a sense of security, wherein one begins to revert into their old behaviors, their prior mindset, their previous, familiar patterns. There can be a great temptation, to try to apply that which worked so well in your previous, military career, that you can forget that you are essentially the FNG (F*cking New Guy) who has yet to build up much credibility. Resist this temptation. Recognize your place at the table. Play chess, not checkers. Observe, assess, build relationships, make suggestions, and be part of the path to a better future, rather than just another FNG that can't get past his past. By the way – this challenge isn't unique to the military, few team members like it when any newbie comes in with a litany of "When I was at ___, we did it this way."

Yes, we need to remember our past, but we must focus forward - to the great unknowns, in a world that is very different than the military.

You will make your ability to integrate effectively far more successful by looking to the future, learning all you can about yourself and what lies ahead, and by leveraging all you have learned and experienced in the next legs of your life journey.

Integrating well requires a certain amount of vulnerability.

The term "vulnerability" gets a lot of play these days. Many alleged leadership gurus espouse it as the great key to leadership success. Their claims aren't without merit, but for vulnerability to be effective, it must be understood in context and in general.

Dictionaries define vulnerability as "the quality or state of being exposed to the possibility of being attacked or harmed, either physically or emotionally."

This is the antithesis of everything we learned and became in the military. Our purpose and entire professional development included great focus on eliminating the possibility of being attacked or harmed.

Further, regardless of military background, no person, group or business likes being exposed to attack. Great efforts and investments are expended on eliminating/mitigating risk of attack or harm.

So, how do we rectify the need for vulnerability as we integrate into our new roles and careers, without creating unacceptable levels of risk that might cause harm?

We suggest reframing the definition. Consider appropriate, helpful vulnerability as being open, honest, transparent, and exposed to others, to new ideas, to new processes, and to new products/services that are inherent in your new work world.

Yes, these can create some risks, but we liken these risks to parachuting and its inherent vulnerabilities. Jumping from a perfectly good aircraft while in flight is risky. You are inherently vulnerable to any number of unique threats that, but for jumping, would not exist. That said, with proper training, proper equipment, and proper awareness, your vulnerability is mitigated to acceptable levels with high degrees of success over innumerable instances.

As you traverse the integration period of your role, be open, be honest, be transparent, and be willing to expose yourself to others, new ideas, processes and products/services. You'll mitigate risk, and benefit greatly!

DAVE STORY

"The D1 Wrestler."

In Hawaii, I had a Division 1 (D1) collegiate wrestler in my Company. The guys thought that a combatives match between him and me would be the ultimate showdown. The old crusty Ranger and the young gun. However, here's the reality. I knew he was going to whoop me. I was never a wrestler, and although I could generally hold my own, there was no way I

SECTION 2: INTEGRATING

> *was going to even be a challenge to this guy. But nonetheless, I gathered the entire company around the quad and indulged the guys in what turned out to not be the ultimate showdown, as he submitted me in about two minutes. Even though I knew that he was going to beat me, I wanted to show the company a couple of things. 1. It's ok to fail, as long as you get better from it. 2. No one is above training.*
>
> *I have a buddy who leads a podcast called "Leading with Vulnerability," (Shout out to Yuma Barnett!) The premise behind his message is that leadership requires a sense of vulnerability. Why? Because leaders aren't infallible. Subordinates want to know that a leader understands what they may be going through, or the challenges they may be facing. Everyone fails at some point in their life. If you haven't, you likely aren't growing. Growing requires taking risks, and risk sometimes leads to failure. But we've all seen leaders who are unwilling to admit they have ever made a mistake, or ever failed. This is dangerous because it can create an environment where subordinates feel like they can't fail. Not only does this stunt growth, but it can create a culture where employees do not feel like they can have free and open dialogue with their leadership team. But, admitting to not knowing something or discussing failures can be uncomfortable and requires the courage to show vulnerability.*

Sometimes, vulnerability gets interpreted as humility. To a degree they are related. Lacking humility can certainly make it tough to be vulnerable. But they are two different things.

BILL STORY

"Too Much Humility Creates Unacceptable Vulnerability."

A couple of years ago, I was coaching a top-notch, high potential engineer. This young gentleman had amazing knowledge,

> *skills, and abilities. He could identify obstacles and opportunities, diagnose causes, and determine effective, efficient solutions for any product placed in front of him. He was clearly a great asset to his team and the company. The only problem? He was too humble. He rarely spoke up in meetings. When asked direct questions, his humility caused him to soft-pedal his responses. Over time, folks around him began to question his ability and/or willingness to be an active part of the team. He became vulnerable to their doubts. His progress in integrating well was stifled. I was brought in to coach him past this challenge. Over time, he began to realize that by over-focusing on humility, he was making himself vulnerable. He was so focused on being humble, that he presented an artificial weakness to the team. Further, he realized that he was robbing the team and the company of the great skills, knowledge, and abilities he carries, and by so doing, he was enabling bad vulnerability into the business. I'm honored to report that he successfully found a great balance, dialed down his humility to a more appropriate level, and became more open, honest, and transparent with everyone. His integration success soared, and he is on a very successful career track.*

Yes, be vulnerable. Yes, be humble. But remember, your employer hired you to deliver, and you are responsible for delivering your very best. As with all things, keep your vulnerability and humility in balance.

Integrating well also requires solid conflict resolution capabilities. Learning new things, building relationships with new people, and becoming a well-integrated member of a new team is rarely a clean, straight line. Bumps will appear in the road and inevitably, conflicts will arise. Maybe it's a difference in personalities, or maybe priorities conflict. Maybe, maybe, maybe. No matter the cause, to integrate successfully, you're likely going to have to practice some conflict resolution. The good news is that as military veterans, your leadership and other training and experience has provided you with a solid base of capability to successfully work through conflicts. When conflicts arise, leverage your experience. Understand the situation, apply appropriate interventions, and do your level best to find the outcome where everybody wins.

> ### *DAVE STORY*
>
> *"Conflict Resolution Styles & Levels."*
>
> *Just like you experienced in your military career, you will experience conflict and the need to resolve conflict in your new role. In one memorable instance, an organization that I had been trying to increase our ability to partner with publicly questioned one of our sources of funding at a board meeting. As a startup nonprofit which had not yet generated enough revenue to sustain itself, that was a big deal. I wanted to understand what was behind the question and the refusal to partner on several projects. In my military mind, I thought "Well, let me reach out to the CEO and resolve this as quickly as possible. I'm sure it's a misunderstanding and something we can quickly move past once we get in the same room together and work it out."*
>
> *Wrong. Bad move on my part. He refused to meet with me. As a director level and not a CEO level, I needed to bring in my boss. He wanted to work it out organization to organization on a formal level. I understood, but this outcome was not what I was used to or expecting. Legally, it probably protected both of us. But pragmatically, it took much longer to resolve, involved more people and organizations, and created additional conflict along the way. The point of this story is not to say which was the right or wrong way, but to highlight that conflict will happen, you will have to resolve it, and it may or may not be in a way that you are used to. At the end of the*

> *day, it doesn't really matter; what matters to your company is that it gets resolved and doesn't negatively affect operations.*

Experiences and Expectations: Differences may cause disconnects and make integration challenging.

We are all, at least in part, a product of our experiences.

Whether Army, Navy, Air Force, Marine Corps, Coast Guard, or Space Force; officer or enlisted; one term-and-out or full career; active or reserve, military veterans have unique experiences. GWOT (Global War on Terror) era vets have a different experience base than those who served in the Gulf War, Cold War, Vietnam era, and so forth. Special operators have a different experience than conventional forces. A Navy submarine officer has a different experience than an Air Force cook. The comparisons could go on at nauseum, but you get the point.

All this said, our diverse experiences as veterans are especially unique in the broader society where only ~seven percent of the population are military veterans, and only ~one percent of the population today volunteers to serve.

Integrating into your new work world will take some dedicated effort. Most of the population has never experienced anything remotely similar to what you experienced in the military. Even still, their experience is just as valid as yours. Their unique paths add great value and richness to the civilian workforce.

Given that you have entered their world when you landed in a non-military role, you are a bit of a foreign entity – some may find you unfamiliar; others may embrace you as a great new add to the team, full of new potential – or they may stand away from you, sizing you up to see just exactly who you are and what you're bringing to their work world.

Certainly, the more similar your new role and organization are

SECTION 2: INTEGRATING 109

to the military, the more similar folks' backgrounds and experiences are likely to be. Given the different experiences noted above, integrating can take real effort.

In the overall employment life cycle, development and retention are key to integrating.

Having landed and completed onboarding, you likely have your feet up under you. It's now time to focus on integrating.

There will be lots to do in many different areas.

As mentioned in the LANDING section, getting hired is just the start of your journey with an organization. Getting to your landing, you experienced how companies conduct talent attraction and recruitment. When you land you will experience their onboarding practices.

Integrating is the next step in your journey. Relative to the **typical employment life cycle**, the topics of development and retention come into focus.

ATTRACTION → RECRUITMENT → ONBOARDING → DEVELOPMENT → RETENTION → SEPARATION

Development and retention occur throughout the employee's time with the organization. There are many components to effective development and retention work, all focused on helping employees perform better in their current role; get prepared for potential future roles; remain positive, productive, engaged team members; and thrive & survive as the organization evolves.

TYPICAL EMPLOYMENT CYCLE RELATED TO INTEGRATING

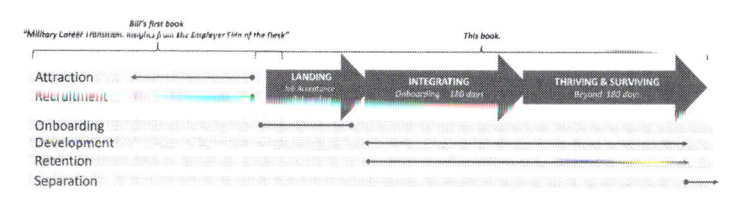

Development happens throughout your time with a company, and your career. Its focus is to help you perform well today and to prepare you for success tomorrow. There are many processes, practices, programs, and other activities in this stage. As a general rule, most employers' focus on development is far less robust than the well-evolved development and career management our military services employ.

Retention is also an ongoing concern, focused on keeping employees engaged, challenged, and continuing to serve as value-adding members of the organization for a long time. Employers dedicate significant attention and resources to retaining good talent. After all, losing good people who are trained, qualified, and experienced in their jobs is expensive. Lost production, disruption of the status quo, and recruiting new talent are all expensive. Whether it is engagement surveys, open door/open communications, benefit packages, quality of work-life initiatives, or any of a vast number of other approaches, employers know that retaining good people is good business. This is different than the military, where everyone is on a contract and specific assignments are for generally defined periods. Here, "employment at will" makes every employee's tenure with the company generally uncertain. Employers can release employees at any time, and employees can leave at any time. Understanding this difference can be enlightening as you progress in your integration efforts.

As with everything in life, your time with any organization will end. The separation stage recognizes this end, and the importance of handling it in a professional manner that is appropriate to the circumstance and respectful of both employer and employee needs.

Being aware of and attentive to this overall employment life cycle can be helpful to doing all this successfully.

Networking wasn't just for transition. To integrate well, you're going to need a solid network. Get out and meet people. Have a relevant, interesting elevator pitch. Learn what people and teams do, how they fit together, and how they add value to each other. Figure out who your go to peeps are. Build relationships broadly – you never know when an opportunity or need may arise that will benefit from your great network.

Be you. Will you need to adjust a bit to integrate well? Certainly. But you also have to be you. If you find yourself abandoning your core values, doing things you simply know are not right for you, or are otherwise disconnecting from yourself, STOP. Carefully consider what's really going on, what can be done to adjust things and correct course, and what you're willing to do. If the adjustments are reasonable and set well with you, drive on with them. If after careful consideration you know that adjustments in the current situation won't fix things, then make a plan for a professional exit to your next success.

INTEGRATING is time to start successfully doing the work that needs done and fitting in with and adding value to the team. This includes several key areas: confirming your duties, responsibilities, and deliverables; learning the people, team dynamics, and organizational culture; understanding available resources and constraints; gaining awareness of headwinds and tailwinds that may help or hinder your success and many others. You've integrated well into new situations before, be confident that you can and will do so again.

INTEGRATING is about LEARNING; Learning all you can about the People, Processes and Products/Services relevant to you and your role.

The Three P's - *People, Process, and Product/Service* **in INTEGRATING**

People

Introduction

During the landing process you identified who people were and where they fit in the organizational architecture. Now it's time to figure out how to all play nicely in the sand box together. Hopefully you took our advice and went a little deeper than simply gathering names during the LANDING phase; getting to know people on a more personal level and identifying some of their strengths, weaknesses and so on. Where do they fit in the process? Who is always late with their deliverables and who is always on time? How does the sales department interact with the marketing department? How do they impact and how are they impacted by your role?

This is like knowing the difference between your power running back and your speed back or knowing who can shoot the three under pressure and who can't. Remember that pie chart with people, process, and product, it's time to start adding some depth to it.

Integrating doesn't happen overnight; it can take weeks or months (or longer). You've got to perform well in your job and there's a lot to learn and understand, but paying attention to the internal and external people related to your role, learning about them, and continuing to grow your understanding of them is priceless work that can add real value to your current and long-term success.

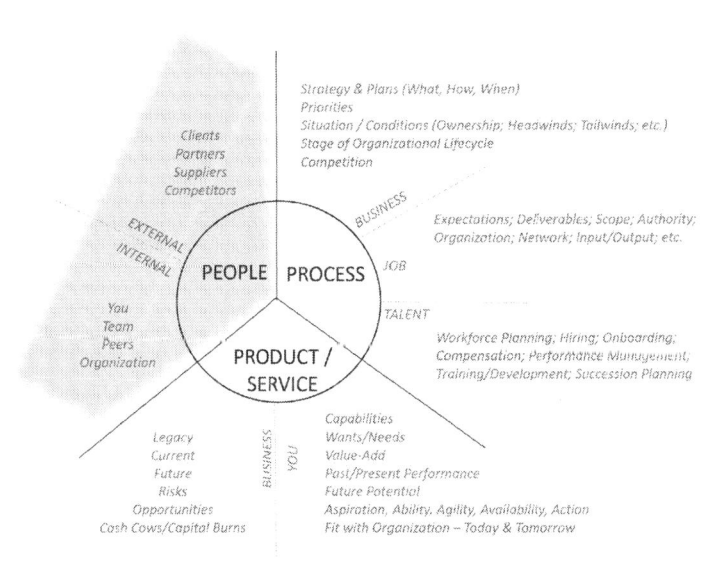

THE 3P MODEL – PEOPLE

Strategy & Plans (What, How, When)
Priorities
Situation / Conditions (Ownership; Headwinds; Tailwinds; etc.)
Stage of Organizational Lifecycle
Competition

Clients
Partners
Suppliers
Competitors

EXTERNAL
INTERNAL

PEOPLE | **PROCESS**

BUSINESS
JOB
TALENT

Expectations; Deliverables; Scope; Authority; Organization; Network; Input/Output; etc.

You
Team
Peers
Organization

PRODUCT / SERVICE

Workforce Planning; Hiring; Onboarding; Compensation; Performance Management; Training/Development; Succession Planning

Legacy
Current
Future
Risks
Opportunities
Cash Cows/Capital Burns

BUSINESS
YOU

Capabilities
Wants/Needs
Value-Add
Past/Present Performance
Future Potential
Aspiration, Ability, Agility, Availability, Action
Fit with Organization – Today & Tomorrow

General *People* Insights When INTEGRATING

Whether internal or external, the many people with whom you will interact all have unique interests, challenges, opportunities, expectations, timing, and so on. Learning as much as possible about all these helps you optimize your integration and helps you and the organization move ahead successfully.

Whether internal or external, people are your "stakeholders." "Stakeholders" are simply people you/your organization need/depend on to thrive & survive. While the term may sound new/different to you, the fact is as a military veteran, you've dealt with various stakeholders before throughout your military service. Perhaps they were sister units, international coalition forces, local governments, tribal leaders, or others, but you get the picture.

When downrange, you worked with and around many different stakeholders

Sister Units	International Coalition Forces
Joint US Forces	Local Governments
U.S. Government Agencies	Tribal Leaders
	Religious Leaders
Contractors	Relief Agencies & Volunteers

The same situation exists in business ... each stakeholder comes with their own value-add and expectations that influence the business

Employees	Owners
Benefactors	Investors
Government Agencies	Customers
	Unions
Volunteers	Communities
Creditors	Vendors/Suppliers

Learn everything you can about all the stakeholders. Learn their interests, timelines and expectations. Learn what they value, their challenges and opportunities. Use all your skill, diplomacy, and leadership to get familiar with them and build relationships.

Getting familiar with the various people, the stakeholders, in your world and building relationships with them are important components in your ability to integrate effectively.

Know what you know, acknowledge there's far more you don't know, and learn how you fit.

We all know what we know. Either by education, experience, dumb luck, or the school of hard knocks, we accumulate knowledge over time. That said, what we don't know will always far exceed what we do know. To integrate successfully, you need to keep this in mind and figure out how to handle those times when you aren't the smartest guy in the room. Be honest. Be humble. Let other stars shine and work with them to create success.

DAVE STORY

"Recon Ain't My Thing!"

After I got hurt, the command team decided to move me to the Reconnaissance Company. Their Senior Enlisted Advisor was moving on and the organization needed an external leader rather than someone from within (which by the way, is extremely common in the private sector). Here's the catch, I knew absolutely nothing about reconnaissance other than occasionally seeing their tired faces on the airfield. How was I supposed to lead an organization of senior (E8s, E7s, and E6s) technical experts in a field I knew very little about? I was intimidated, felt inadequate, and thought there was no way I was going to be able to lead this company to the caliber it deserved. Up to this point, in my last several prior assignments, I had been both the most experienced member and the technical expert. I could do almost any job in my previous organizations and had led at every level within them. To say this was going to be a professional challenge would be an understatement.

Here's what I learned shortly into my time at the company. It didn't need another technical expert. It didn't need any more reconnaissance expertise. There was already decades and decades of expertise and experience in that realm. They didn't need me to tell them how to conduct a night freefall infiltration into a tactical reconnaissance (which is a good thing). But, that's not what I was "hired" to do. What the organization needed was an organizational leader that could tie its members' technical expertise with the organization's operational priorities. It needed a leader who could set strategic priorities for the company that aligned with broader

> *organizational objectives. It needed a leader who could then turn this alignment into successful action. It just so happened that I did have experience with that.*
>
> *As you integrate, be clear about what you were hired to do. I needed to have a general understanding of reconnaissance, but I didn't need to be an expert in it. Just like you likely don't need to be an expert in every aspect of your industry. Having a deep understanding of what you were hired for and what value you are expected to contribute though will ensure you integrate into the company in the way you are needed.*

Detailed *People* Insights when INTEGRATING

As the graphic above displays (and as we saw in the LANDING section) there are two general populations for you to learn about:

- ★ **Internal** – This includes **you**, your **team**, **peers**, and **other organizational members** that may influence/impact you/your success.
- ★ **External** – This includes **clients** (the folks that are buying/consuming your product/services), **partners** (people/organizations outside your company that have established partnership agreements beneficial to them and your company), **suppliers** (those people/organizations from whom you/your company purchases goods/services that enable your business to operate), and **competitors** (people/organizations in the same market space with either a similar product/service, a replacement product/service, or a product/service that eliminates the need for your product/service. Said another way, competitors are others that want your customers.

Let's start with You and the other internal folks.

★ You – Understanding yourself, your capabilities, preferences, pet peeves, aspirations, and your "Why"/"How"/"What" are foundational to integrating well. Not every experience in your new role will be spectacular. Being self-aware will help you assess and respond to various situations in a way that stays true to you without over-reacting (or under-reacting).

How do you define yourself? While in the military, many of us define ourselves by our occupation.

DAVE STORY

"Dave the Ranger."

I know that my identity was completely wrapped up in my career. I saw myself as Dave the Ranger. While this may have been conducive to justifying my time away, whether training or deployed, it had an extreme negative effect during my transition into the civilian world.

After I got shot, I knew that I was going to deploy again. After spending so much time in Iraq and Afghanistan, I knew that I had to leave on my own two feet, or it would forever haunt me. While there, I went on a mission that on paper was like hundreds I had been on before. In fact, I had operated in that area plenty over the past fifteen/twenty years of war. But it was me that changed. During the mission, a round went through a wall right behind my back and it changed my life. I felt like I lost my identity in that moment because it affected me differently than any other gunfight I had ever been in. Why was I here, on the other side of the world from my family, fighting in the same place with the same people,

I had for the last almost two decades? I knew that my time in the community was coming to a close, but if I wasn't Dave the Ranger, then who was I?

I struggled with this throughout my transition into the civilian world, particularly in the workforce. In the Ranger Regiment, I was a technical expert and a trusted leader who spent the last eighteen years building my credibility. I had led 200-person organizations, had managed operations for an 800-person organization, and was trusted to make high stakes decisions. Now, I was the new guy, in a new field, with no credibility. I couldn't identify with being a benefits consultant or a hospital administrator. No one asked for my advice anymore. No one sought me out for my expertise. And while anecdotally I understood why, it was still incredibly difficult to accept.

Through this experience, I learned two major lessons that helped me overcome this identity crisis.

1. A feeling of insecurity at being knocked down a few pegs on the food chain provided a hunger to become an expert in my new field. Like everything, expertise takes work, and I certainly had some work to do. It also provided me the opportunity to work on myself. Oftentimes, we as leaders overlook our own development at the detriment to our organizations and this gave me the opportunity to work on myself, guilt free.
2. Hanging your identity on your occupation is dangerous. Although many will say that being in the military is more than a job (and I would agree to some extent), it is ultimately temporary and can change in an instant. It forced me to re-evaluate who I was and who I wanted to be. Instead of Dave the Ranger, could I be Dave the dad who loves his family and community

> *and prioritizes as such? The answer was yes, and I would argue that this shift allowed me to be more effective professionally.*

BILL STORY

"A Father, A Son and Their Titles."

My dad was a physician. Shortly after the Korean war he did two years as an Army medical officer, a year of which was as an advisor to the 3d ROK Army. After his Army service he and a colleague opened a successful family medicine practice. He was "Doctor Kieffer" his entire adult life. When he finally decided to retire, he was lost. While he would always be known as "Doc," he no longer was actively engaged in medicine. He had been so laser focused on his career that he had lost any identity beyond it. Rather than kicking back and enjoying his retirement, he forever bemoaned his loss of identity.

I loved my Army career. I loved being part of something bigger that impacted important things. It was my identity. No matter the rank or assignment, I embraced it all. When my life journey took an unexpected turn causing my career journey to depart from the Army path, I was lost. If I'm not "Captain Kieffer" then who the hell am I? It was a tough leg of my life and career journeys but in hindsight, I'm blessed to have faced the loss of identity when I did rather than later in life as my dad did. You see, I HAD to adjust. HAD to let go. HAD to be open to new possibilities. There were simply too many years ahead of me to not know who the hell I am. It took me longer than I'd have preferred, and it wasn't easy, but today I realize fully that my Army career, as important and impactful as it was, was only part of my career and life journeys.

It is natural to have these feelings while integrating into the workforce, especially if you have recently transitioned from the military. It's hard, and not acknowledging that could be a mistake. But figuring out why it's hard can lead you to next steps and solutions. Do you feel insecure because you're not an expert? Learn from your peers, put the work in and become an expert. Do you feel frustrated because you want to punch at your weight level and feel like you aren't doing that? Build your credibility by showcasing your ability to perform at a high level. Managing expectations and then building a plan to get to where you want to go will help overcome this sense of identity crisis.

Build your mentor bench. Because the military places such a heavy emphasis on building leaders, it is no surprise that most veterans have a handful of trusted mentors that they could call on throughout their military careers. It is also likely that these mentors have a diverse array of experiences and skillsets within the military. As military members transition between units and duty stations, this compilation of trusted advisors is a natural benefit.

Much like you learned during the job search phase of your transition, engaging mentors from outside the military is greatly valuable. As you integrate into a new job or new role, it will be important to start to expand this slate to include mentors in your new industry or new company. Knowing your strengths and weaknesses will help you identify those who possess the attributes that you want to grow in yourself, both professionally and personally. This doesn't mean discarding your mentors from your military career. Quite the opposite in fact. Growing your bench will help ensure that you have mentors, role models, and coaches who possess the skillsets and traits that will help you in both this phase of your career journey, and throughout your life journey.

SECTION 2: INTEGRATING

There is a lot to be done during the INTEGRATING phase and you are the star of your show. As you start to perform the actual work that you were hired to do, there is an opportunity to confirm your assumptions about how your skillsets pair with the work that needs to be done and self-evaluate what skills should be sharpened. It's a time to be confident in what you know and humble enough to ask for help. It's a time to learn what teammates you can rely on and which ones have ulterior motives, love to spread the office gossip, or who might otherwise impede your success.

As you learn all of this and begin to establish yourself as a value-adding entity, there are two things that are critical to remember. First, always be yourself. It will be hard to be truly fulfilled if you have to put on a mask to work every day. Second, know that your leadership style and way you interact with your teammates might need to change slightly. These aren't mutually exclusive concepts and don't have to be in conflict with each other.

★ **Your Team** - In the military, it's a universal truth that "no one fights alone." From our very first days in uniform, we are taught to think and act as a team. The civilian world has a stronger focus on individual performance than the military (the "Me versus We" phenomenon) but being a good team player is still important. Integrating well with your direct teammates makes a real difference in your overall success. So how do you integrate well with teammates? Leverage your great teambuilding experience to integrate well:

- ✯ Build Relationships.
- ✯ Demonstrate flexibility and adaptability.
- ✯ Cooperate with other team members.
- ✯ Have a willingness to help others.
- ✯ Respect others.

Sound familiar? They should, because they are straight out of every military branch's leadership and team building publications.

An important part of integrating well (especially if you're in a "people leadership" role) is to understand your team, and their professional interests/aspirations. Some want to be leaders. Others want to focus on the technical work. Take the intelligence community for example. This is an important, complex, far-reaching community that requires extensive technical expertise to fully achieve its mission. While there are certainly many great members of this community that are interested in, and highly qualified for, leadership roles, there is also a large portion of the population that seeks to stay focused on the technical work. They're great at the intelligence stuff, and they love doing it! The military's "up or out" mentality and its focus on leading at every level can be both a great asset (lots of leaders enables agile, decentralized capability in fluid environments) and a challenge (trained, experienced, technically proficient people are often pulled away from the work they love, to take on leadership roles they're not especially fond of). By and large, it works for the military.

The civilian work world is a bit different. It doesn't understand leadership in the same way as the military, and there may well be multiple opportunities to stay in a technical path doing the work you love to do.

Yes, you still need to be technically and tactically proficient in your role, but assignments may change less frequently and the push into leadership roles may not be as forceful.

As you learned in the military, to integrate effectively, you need to learn your team.

Regardless of whether you are in a "people leadership" position or not, understand their aspirations, interact with them well, and be aware of how the environment aligns with them. Build relationships that go beyond the deliverables, do all you can to help them achieve the future they seek; support others' life journeys as you travel yours.

BILL STORY

"Dual Career Ladders."

One of the major corporations for which I led global talent management had a large, diverse engineering function. There were hundreds of highly capable engineers doing great work across every business and product line. Some of these great engineers sought "people leadership" positions, focusing less on the technical aspects of engineering and more on the broader people, process, and product aspects of the business. This was awesome for many reasons, not the least of which being the credibility these technical experts brought to the table with internal and external stakeholders. On the other hand, there were many engineers who wanted nothing to do with managing anything. They were skilled in the technical aspects of their career field and wanted to continue in the technical realm.

Progression in the management lane was pretty clear: start as an Associate Engineer, then become an Engineer, Manager, Senior Manager, Director, Senior Director, Vice-President, and ultimately Chief Technical Officer.

There was no similar progression on the technical side. Once you became an engineer, you were an engineer. As you might expect, this was a pretty dissatisfying situation for our technically focused team members. You see, while they didn't want to be managers, they (like everyone) were very interested in progression; some pathway forward that recognized their technical contributions and gave them a larger opportunity to contribute even more. We tackled this issue by creating a "dual ladder" career path. An Associate Engineer's next step was Engineer. Engineer's next step was Senior Engineer, and so on all the way to the very top of the technical ladder until reaching the level of Senior Technical Fellow (which was a peer to a Vice President on the engineering manager path). This worked very well, addressed key talent concerns, and provided a unique set of opportunities for our great technical talent.

* **Peers** – Peers are those folks with relatively similar roles at relatively similar levels in the company, with whom you may/not have regular interaction, and who are working in different departments, divisions, units, or functions of the organization. Let's say for example that you are an engineering project manager responsible for operationalizing a newly engineered product. Depending on the size of the company, you're likely to have peer managers in operations, supply chain, HR, IT, finance and other areas with whom you'll need to effectively interact to accomplish your mission. Making this happen effectively and efficiently is significantly impacted by how well you've integrated with them. Take a lesson from your transition – NETWORK! Once you've landed, continue to meet people, ask what they do, how they fit in the organization, how your respective positions interact (and for what). As you integrate, continue the discussions, learn their capabilities, priorities, challenges, opportunities, aspirations etc. When it comes time for you to work with these peers, you'll be glad you did!

BILL STORY

"Peers & Performance."

When I was head of global talent management for a $3B+ supply chain/transportation company, I was tasked to implement a global succession planning strategy and process. (These focus on identifying successors to top leadership positions

> *across the enterprise, and when well done, provide a means to understand talent needs, identify pipelines of top-talent, and emplace approaches to develop this top talent for ever-larger roles. Ultimately, the purpose is to ensure there are qualified candidates, ready to assume top leadership roles, with little to no dip in organizational performance.)*
>
> *As you might imagine, there are many different perspectives about what good actually looks like for this type of global process (most frequently driven by whatever fires are burning hottest for the various stakeholders). I engaged the top-level leaders from around the globe, gained their input and perspectives, learned their priorities, and got some idea of what good looked like for them. I analyzed the commonalities, the conflicts, and the gaps. I realized that this was no small task. I then engaged with my peers – the HR leads from each of the global regions (who like me, were also direct reports to the global Chief Human Resources Officer). Since they had direct support relationships with the top global leaders, they were able to provide deeper, highly valuable insights that clarified some information and cleared the deck of some apparent conflicts and gaps.*
>
> *My previous efforts to get to know these folks and to build professional relationships paid off. Frankly, we were not all best friends, but we had mutual respect and regard, and were able to work together and successfully bring this complex initiative to fruition.*

★ Organization – There will always be people in the broader organization that have seemingly zero relevance to your job. Certainly, there will be people with whom you'll never interact for role-specific tasks. That said, to integrate well it's still worth your time and effort to keep your eyes/ears open to who these folks are, how they fit, what value they bring, and so on. You never know when an unexpected opportunity may arise that changes your assignment and puts you in direct contact with these good folks.

The beauty of the military is that it is designed and organized for interoperability. Whether it's one unit or one branch working with another, there is a commonality in organizational architecture, roles, and rank that is hard to replicate in the private sector. For example, a company commander in the Army or Marine Corps has a very similar scope and authority as a squadron commander in the Air Force. A battalion in the 82nd Airborne looks very similar to a battalion in the 4th Infantry Division, etc. This means that when a public affairs officer (or any other position) moves from one organization to another, he or she knows with relative certainty what the org chart will look like, what roles will do what, and the general chain of command structure. In the private sector, this is not necessarily the case. A CFO (Chief Financial Officer) can have vastly different roles from one company to another. Likewise, a project manager in one department could have a completely different scope than in a different department in the same company. Therefore, it is so important to learn the details of the organizational hierarchy and understand who influences what, who can make what decisions, and how/if that changes when conditions shift.

Next, let's consider external people relevant to your role.

No job or business exists in a vacuum. There are many other people outside the company that impact and are impacted by you and your business. They too have specific perspectives, interests, challenges, opportunities, expectations, timing, and so forth. Four common types of external people with whom you should integrate well are **Clients**, **Partners**, **Suppliers**, and **Competitors**. (Note – there are others e.g., government officials that may have an impact, but those vary broadly by company, industry, market, etc.). Begin by integrating well with these four populations and learn who the relevant others are in your specific role.

- ★ **Clients** – These are the individuals and organizations that are buying/consuming your products/services. They are your source of revenue (in a for-profit company) and the community you serve (in a nonprofit company). Without their demand for your products/services, the organization (and your job) go away. Once you've landed and are integrating, be sure to gain a good understanding of who the clients are, why they are buying/consuming your product/service, what their priorities are, challenges, opportunities, constraints, future plans, and so on. Even if you are not in a customer facing role, having a solid understanding of the clients makes you a more valuable employee.

BILL STORY

"Getting out of the Ivory Tower."

One of the most genius leadership moves I've experienced was when the CEO of our global $3B+ supply chain/transportation company decided that every member of the executive team would be assigned as the executive lead for a major client company. They would be the top-level point of contact for the client company's top leader to connect with. For example, the Chief HR Officer was the primary executive lead for a key global client that happened to be a name-brand, multi-billion-dollar global computer manufacturer. Certainly, sales teams and others continued to manage the dailies, but this top-level, executive relationship was a unique approach that

> *added value in so many ways. The client was more confident in their value to us, and our executive team members became more deeply invested in the customer facing aspect of the business—ultimately adding great value to the business and how we operated.*

- ★ **Partners** - Partners are people/organizations outside your company that have established partnership agreements beneficial to them and your company. For example, years ago, when Bill was working with a major tier-one automotive supplier, that company partnered with another large tier-one supplier for the development and commercialization of various drivetrain and power transmission products. You see, each company had expertise and experience in certain aspects of these products that the other didn't. By partnering, they were able to design and produce products the market needed that neither could produce alone. Learning and understanding who your business' partners are, how they operate, and their unique areas of excellence can provide invaluable insight as you integrate, and add to your individual value proposition.
- ★ **Suppliers** – Those people/organizations from whom you/your company purchases goods/services that enable your business to operate. Whether they provide mission critical materials, administrative supplies, transportation services, telecommunication capabilities or others, suppliers are critical to any organization's success. Learning and understanding them, their goals, business models, constraints, etc., are important to your ability to negotiate service agreements that are a win-win for you and them.
- ★ **Competitors** – Other organizations that are competing with your firm for market share. Much like the military, it is important to know your competitor. What is their value

proposition? Their strategy? What does their supply chain look like? Their pricing models? And so much more. One substantial difference from your military experience, however, is the proximity and frequency in which you will interact with your competitors. It is very probable that you will be in the same boardrooms, conferences, or job sites, competing for the business of the same people and organizations. To integrate well, you need to learn all you can about your competitors. Build smart relationships with them. Understanding what information you should and shouldn't share while building a working relationship can pay dividends if and when the market landscape shifts.

DAVE STORY

"Competition; Unlike Anything I'd Seen Before."

One thing that I loved about the military is that no matter what branch you were in, regardless if we disagreed on the how, we were all at least rowing in the same direction. At the end of the day, the overall goal was the same...we all wanted each other to succeed. There was a sense of cross-agency sharing of information, collaboration between organizations, and a sense of trust between external partners. The first time I encountered an organization that was deliberately hindering our success, I kind of went into shock. I felt like it was a personal attack and could not understand why their organization wanted to see us fail. Had we done something to them? Did they not like me as a person? Maybe and maybe not, but most likely they viewed us as a competitor. They thought we were going after a share of the market that they had dominated for a long time. If we took business away from them, that means lost revenue and lost revenue is not good in any business.

Process

Introduction

Simply identifying the processes that you will be utilizing or that affect the ability to do your job is fine during the LANDING phase, but during the INTEGRATION phase, it is important to learn and understand them. Why do certain processes exist? Why do they work the way they do? What are the performance metrics? Why do they matter? What results do the processes enable? Where are they efficient and where are there potential bottlenecks? Understanding processes will help you become proficient at your role, better able to add value, and better position you for success in the long term.

THE 3P MODEL – PROCESS

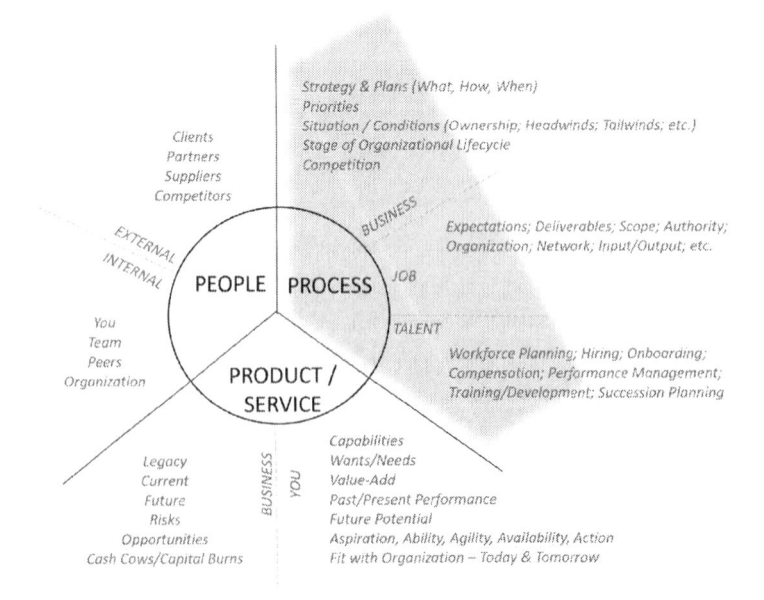

Strategy & Plans (What, How, When)
Priorities
Situation / Conditions (Ownership; Headwinds; Tailwinds; etc.)
Stage of Organizational Lifecycle
Competition

Clients
Partners
Suppliers
Competitors

BUSINESS

Expectations; Deliverables; Scope; Authority;
Organization; Network; Input/Output; etc.

EXTERNAL
INTERNAL
PEOPLE | PROCESS | JOB

TALENT

You
Team
Peers
Organization

PRODUCT / SERVICE

Workforce Planning; Hiring; Onboarding;
Compensation; Performance Management;
Training/Development; Succession Planning

Legacy
Current
Future
Risks
Opportunities
Cash Cows/Capital Burns

BUSINESS | YOU

Capabilities
Wants/Needs
Value-Add
Past/Present Performance
Future Potential
Aspiration, Ability, Agility, Availability, Action
Fit with Organization – Today & Tomorrow

General *Process* Insights when INTEGRATING

As we noted earlier, when integrating, learning and understanding the processes relevant to your role and your career is key.

Processes, Procedures, and Practices

As military veterans, we're accustomed to having a process for everything. It seems there's some manner of document that outlines the what/when/how for every aspect of our role.

This condition may exist in the organizations you join in the civilian world; or it may not. Larger, more established firms are more likely to have more formalized processes than newer start-up firms. No matter the age of the organization, nor how well documented things are, or what terms are used to describe them, there are norms for how things get done. These exist for a reason: maybe they've been well considered and proven best, maybe they're just how things have always been done, or maybe exigent circumstances caused them to arise out of an emergency. No matter the case, they are what they are. As you integrate, learn them, explore their genesis, their effectiveness, their constraints, and opportunities to either extend their success or enhance them.

BILL STORY

"No Procedure? No Problem. What's your Practice?"

Process and procedure matter. Sometimes especially when audits, investigations, or other similar inquiry-type actions are in play. On more than one occasion, I've experienced outside agencies inquiring (properly, legally, and appropriately) about the company's process for particular activities. The general intent of these queries is to see if you've "said what you do and do what you say." Often, if there's no documented process,

> *the next question is, "Okay, what are your practices? How does this stuff typically happen?" So why make this point? Because in the civilian work world, even if there is no process map, procedural manual, or similar, common practices are recognized as valid. As you integrate, don't just look for the manual; watch how people behave, and see what they do, how they communicate, and what impact it has. Then you will be gaining insight into what the real processes are.*

Success for most organizations depends on repeatable, high-quality solutions at the lowest possible price. They need to know they are making the best bang for the buck. Their customers (internal and external) need to know they can count on the product/service they're investing in delivering as promised.

Having clear, understood, effective, and evolving processes is key to making all this happen. Solid processes help set standards, establish understanding, and drive behaviors, all of which enable cost-effectiveness, quality and repeatability.

Ink on paper won't do it. You need to know and understand what the processes are and how they work. When you landed, simply identifying what processes exist was sufficient. Now that you are integrating, it's time to LEARN all you can about the processes relevant to you and your role. Seek them out. Read them. Discuss them with others to find out how they really work.

No process is forever. As you learn about existing processes, be mindful that they all exist in fluid environments and must evolve over time to ensure relevance, repeatability, quality, and cost effectiveness that optimizes business results. Learn the processes. Learn the context in which they exist, the variables impacting that context, and willingness of the organization to update them.

Better is the enemy of good…know the opportunity cost of process improvement. If you are a veteran, you have likely practiced process improvement throughout your military career. It is something that is built into our DNA. The old saying, "Always improve your foxhole," perfectly encapsulates this position. We are not suggesting that process improvement does not have its place in the private sector, nor are we saying that you shouldn't personally try and be better every day. However, it is wise to remember that there is an opportunity cost for everything. If you are putting your effort into one task, you are not putting that effort into another. There are some processes that are good enough. It is easy to get so wrapped up fixing something that didn't need fixing in the first place, that you could overlook the business priorities that help maximize revenue, foster growth, and improve your company's position in the market. Know when it is a priority and when it isn't. Know what processes need to be improved and what are already working well enough.

Detailed *Process* Insights when INTEGRATING

As the graphic above displays there are three general process areas for you to consider:

* **Business** – Processes related to strategy, plans, priorities, situation/conditions, stage of organization's life cycle, competition, and other topics impacting the enterprise.
* **Job-specific**—Processes related to your job, expectations, deliverables, scope, authority, organization, network, input/output etc.
* **Talent-related** – Processes relating to the way in which the organization's talent is planned and managed, workforce planning, hiring, onboarding, compensation, performance management, training/development, succession planning, etc.

Why are these three process areas important? Because they encompass the broad areas in which you will exist and by which your career will be impacted. There are innumerable additional details inside each of these areas, but the topics we note herein are the ones that are broadly applicable.

Business Processes

- ★ **Strategy, Plans & Priorities** – Learning and understanding your organization's process for developing and executing strategy, developing plans, and identifying priorities can be important to your integration. Think about it – if you know what the strategy is and how it was developed (what the plans are and why, what the top priorities are, and what/how products/services fit strategy), you are in a strong position to integrate broadly and deeply, and to quickly add real value to the organization. For example, Ritz Carlton's business strategy is more than providing luxury amenities to their guests; it's about providing their guests with a luxury experience. This strategy guides many of their business decisions, including empowering their employees to make decisions regarding customer experience, investing in training facilities, and creating an integrated eco-system of information sharing to ensure it captures guest preferences across their enterprise. We discussed identifying your company's strategy in the LANDING phase. However, learning and understanding how your role fits within this strategy is a little more complex, and it is critical to integrating well. If you were hired as a general manager of a Ritz Carlton, the difference between providing a luxury facility and providing a luxury experience may sound nuanced but it has some big differences, that should play a heavy role in your decision-making process. For example, do you give your check-in attendants the autonomy to make room upgrades within a certain threshold to compensate for unmet needs? How do you train your staff to ensure that every interaction makes the customer experience luxurious?

    Organizations where employees at all levels know,

understand, and embody the company's strategy are almost always more successful. There is a reason that Ritz Carlton is one of the world's most successful hotel brands ever. That said, where do you find the strategy if you are not part of the executive team? Depending on the company, it may be a common internal discussion. Your leadership team should know your company's strategy and lastly, you may be able to find it in the company's annual report (if they have one). If this is not a common part of internal discussions, seek out mentors, peers and others that work in this arena that can help enlighten you. Connect with them. Build solid relationships. Pick their brains. Learn all you can from them.

★ **Situation/Conditions** - In the LANDING section we discussed identifying indicators of your situation/conditions. As you integrate, it's time to build these into your routine, to learn and understand trends, and to know what to look for as your situation/conditions continually change. If you may recall, earlier we talked about the ball bearing market and its relation to commodity steel prices. In 2021, the United States imported more steel from Russia than any other country. Because commodity prices are largely based on supply and demand, an interruption to Russia's steel exports could have a significant impact on the price of steel. A ball bearing manufacturer likely will be paying attention to and integrating this information into his/her calculus about how much raw material to keep on hand, production rates, supply chain variability, and many other relevant topics. As you integrate into the company, learning what indicators to pay attention to is only half the battle. Using that information to make smart business decisions is the ultimate goal.

As you integrate into the company, you will start to see the correlation between external indicators and internal figures and metrics. You will see which ones have a direct correlation and which ones are more indirect. Paying attention to changing conditions will allow you to make informed decisions in an ever-changing environment.

- ★ **Stage of organization's life cycle** - As we noted in the LANDING section above, businesses tend to follow a life cycle from Launch/Startup to Growth/Expansion, then Shakeout/Stability, Maturity, and Decline. Each of these phases has unique priorities and their evolution from one phase to the next will likely impact your role. Dramatic evolution from phase to phase may/not happen during your integration period but learning all you can about where the organization is in its life cycle, the speed at which it is evolving, the priorities, influences, challenges, opportunities and several other variables will certainly help you integrate well. Partner with others who can share information and insights. Talk with front line folks, mid-level leaders, senior staff and executive leaders to get as broad, deep, and robust a perspective as possible.
- ★ **Competition** – Understanding where your competitors are positioned and where they are trying to position their product or service in the market and what that means for your product or service should be part of the calculus when determining strategy. Some competition can improve brand awareness. During the height of the Coke /Pepsi face off, both brands benefited greatly from each other's advertising. In 1975, the cola war between Pepsi and Coke heated up when Pepsi launched their Pepsi Challenge campaign. From 1975 through the 1980's, both companies gained an incredible amount of market share from the increased publicity. More recently, the introduction of the iPhone effectively erased Blackberry from the smartphone market for more than a decade. Depending on your role in the company, this may be integral to your day-to-day job, or it may be something that requires only general awareness. Because competition is such an integral piece of strategy development, whether

it is existing competition, threat of a substitute product or service, or entry of a new company into the market, it needs to be part of your thought process when making business decisions.

Competition is ever present. It isn't always a bad thing, and it isn't always a good thing. But it is always a thing. Knowing who your competitors are and what their strategy is will help you identify pathways to creating your competitive advantage. Gaining knowledge about competitors can come from many sources, but the marketing department can be a good place to start when learning about your competitors. They may have everything from a detailed competitive analysis (an in-depth examination of strengths, weaknesses, differentiators of competitors) to more general market research. As you integrate into your role, understanding your competition is critical to developing a holistic picture of your company and how this ever-present factor effects strategy.

Job Specific Processes

★ **Expectations** – When you landed, you likely had the opportunity to get clear on the expectations for your role: what you need to deliver, cultural norms, and so on. As you integrate, it's time to bring these expectations to life and to learn as much as possible about what it takes to perform at the highest possible levels. Stay situationally aware to understand the headwinds and tailwinds impacting these expectations. If challenges arise, assess them, do some root cause analysis, problem solve, and bring potential solutions to the proper people so they can be overcome. Where opportunities exist, take a similar approach so they can be positively exploited. Be sure to keep the right people involved! Changing expectations in a vacuum is rarely a pathway to success.

- **Deliverables** – As you integrate, pay attention to your deliverables. Are you delivering the quantity and quality you need to? Are you delivering on time? Are you working with all relevant others positively to make all this happen? If the answer to any of these is anything less than a resounding "YES," then you need to go into After Action Review (AAR) Mode. Use that great military AAR experience you carry to dive into the situation, deconstruct it, identify where things are off track, and prepare new go-forward plans for improvement.
- **Scope & Authority** – If all went well when you landed, your scope and authority are well-defined. Understanding your left and right limits, decision trees, information flow, lead times, etc. not only benefits you, it also benefits your team members, peers, and other internal and external folks. When integrating, be mindful that business circumstances are never static. They are constantly evolving. This evolution impacts every bit of your role. Sometimes the impact is barely perceptible and requires no change. Other times the changes rock your whole work world and require significant adjustments. Keep your eyes and ears open to ensure you're adjusting appropriately.
- **Organization** – When you landed, the organization was structured in a certain way. Likely this was done intentionally to best serve business needs. As you integrate, the probability of a massive, unexpected restructuring is low. If things are relatively static, learn all you can about how the organization is structured, why it is structured that way, how the various divisions, departments, functions, and groups interact. Note where things are rocking and where they are rocky. Be attentive for opportunities to help smooth out the rocky spots, and to extend the success of those areas that are humming along well. If there is a restructuring on the horizon, learn everything you can about it. Understand that reorganizations might bring new opportunities for you, they may have zero

SECTION 2: INTEGRATING

impact on you, or they may cause new, difficult challenges. Depending on your position, you may or may not be able to glean much information (re-organizations are often held quite confidential). You may or may not be able to influence the change much. But learning as much as possible puts you in the best possible position to understand the landscape and prepare to integrate effectively.

★ **Network** – Far too often, people stop networking when they land in a great new gig. Big mistake. Networking is a critical activity to effectively integrate in your new role and company. There are new people in and around you that have varying degrees of relevance and impact on your ability to perform well. Learn who they are, how they fit, what makes them tick, how you can help them succeed, and how they can help you succeed. Further, building and nurturing a broader network (beyond the people related to your role) can help you integrate faster and more effectively. You never know when someone is the unexpected key to the kingdom. You probably networked your butt off to get introduced to the opportunity that resulted in your hire. That's great, and building that network is important, not only for getting the job but also for doing the job. Don't stop networking just because you got hired or landed. Who in the company do you need to know? What external stakeholders will influence your ability to be effective in your role? Continue to network throughout your career; it was important to your transition; it is important to landing well, and it will be important to integrating, thriving & surviving as long as you are in the workforce.

★ **Input/Output** – Identifying the inputs to and outputs from your role and the processes by which they flow are important. This knowledge provides you with valuable intelligence about where reliable, dependable, repeatable processes may be replicated, where weak points might be improved, and a general sense of the direction of your workflows.

Talent-Related Processes

* **Workforce Planning** – Previously, we encouraged you to identify what you can about how the company manages its workforce planning, as it is a good indicator of its overall talent strategy. While integrating, you have the opportunity to learn more about how this actually plays out and how effective it is bringing the business strategy to life. If you are a "people manager," are your requests for hiring, organizing and shaping your workforce being heard and are appropriate actions being taken to enable your team's success? If you are an individual contributor, are you seeing people being hired in the right places to help move the business forward? Or are you seeing the workforce shrink, and individual roles being loaded up with new tasks and requirements? Keeping your eyes/ears open and learning about the workforce planning process and its impact on people, teams and business can be helpful as you navigate your integration journey.
* **Hiring** – Learning the ins and outs of the hiring process as you integrate can provide valuable insight into business conditions and priorities. Is the process substantially stable and similar to what you experienced when you came on board? Has it become more streamlined? Have hiring restrictions been imposed? Are there new, draconian requirements in play (e.g., the business president has to personally approve EVERY new hire?) Or has the hiring process dropped certain expectations due to challenges bringing in new talent? (e.g., eliminating/changing pre-hire drug screens) All of these are indicators that the situation has changed – maybe for the good or maybe not.
* **Onboarding** – You experienced the onboarding process firsthand when you Landed. Whether it was a great experience or a bust, it provided a glimpse of how the company approaches their overall talent processes. Remember what

SECTION 2: INTEGRATING 141

you experienced. If it was positive, learn if/how it sets the stage for other talent-related processes, so you can participate in/contribute to extending the positive impact. If your onboarding experience was not so good, consider how you might work with relevant others to share your insights and be part of improving the experience for others coming in behind you. Since you are still fairly new to the organization, be mindful that you may not know all the context that caused onboarding to be as it is. You want to be a helpful part of the solution, not a nagging pain in the ass.

- ⋏ **Compensation** – Having identified the compensation process upon landing, when you're integrating its time to learn how that process really works, and to do the right work that enables you to earn your keep (and maximize your bonus if there is one). Pay attention to payroll and how accurate/timely it is. Ensure your benefits enrollments are complete and current, and all deductions/allowances are accurate. Most employers are dedicated and diligent in keeping compensation processes on track, but in the end, you need to pay attention and take action as necessary.

- ★ **Performance Management** – No matter how robust the company's performance management process is (or isn't), you need to perform to the very best of your ability. Understand the overall goals and expectations, seek out feedback (in a manner that fits with the company's norms) and go make good things happen. If you are a "people manager," do the right things for your people. If you're an individual contributor, go do great things. In either case, remember that delivering top results and fitting well with the team are both critically important to integrating well. No one wants a jerk who only delivers results, nor a nice guy who just can't produce. Also, if you find the performance management process lacking, assess whether or not you are in a position to help improve it. No one wants the FNG to call their baby ugly, but on the other hand, your perspective, experience, and expertise may be just the thing to help make valuable improvements.

> ## DAVE STORY
>
> *"Needs Improvement."*
>
> *My first civilian annual performance evaluation from my board really threw me for a loop. I was used to being "top blocked" on my NCOERs. From a young NCO to a senior NCO, I was used to outperforming my peers (throughout the Army), and my evaluations showed it. I kind of expected my annual performance review to go somewhat similarly, which is why it was such a shock to see a block checked "Needs Improvement" next to public speaking on my evaluation. I wasn't happy, and even felt betrayed until I took a step back and realized the difference between this evaluation and my NCOERs in the Army.*
>
> *NCOERs are available for leadership teams to see throughout your career in the Army, are used for promotions, and most importantly are a comparative tool to evaluate performance amongst peers. You are being evaluated compared to your peers, not your personal potential. Like anyone else, we want to continuously improve and want honest feedback on how we can do so. Your performance evaluations may be comparisons between your performance and your potential, which while very different can be a great approach! The board wasn't telling me that amongst all the directors that they'd seen, my public speaking was in the bottom 20%. They were saying that they knew I could improve that aspect of my performance and they expected me to do so. Completely different. To be clear, this is not how every civilian performance management process works. It is how it worked in this case. Understanding this has been a great help to integrating well.*

SECTION 2: INTEGRATING

- ★ **Training/Development** – When you were landing, figuring out what deficiencies exist in either your foundation of knowledge or skillset and what opportunities exist both internally and externally to address these deficiencies was sufficient. Now, as you integrate, it's time to really learn how the company addresses training and development. Is it a priority? Do they view it as a cost, or as an investment? Are processes in place to assess training needs, develop interventions to address those needs, and evaluate their results? Is training handled internally by company experts or externally by paid vendors? Is the focus on training people to perform well in their current job, or is it to develop them for future assignments? It's quite likely that the training and development processes will look very different than what you experienced in the military. Most are not nearly as rigorous, well developed, or as thoroughly integrated as what you're used to. It is what it is. Learn all you can about how it works in your new company. Take actions to get yourself as much training and development as you want/need. If you're a "people manager," do the same for your team. Partner with the appropriate company leaders to help improve training and development processes where you can.

- ★ **Succession Planning** – Now that you have your feet on the ground and are beginning to integrate into your new role, team, organization, and environment, you'll want to start learning about how succession planning works. It likely won't be as robust as the military (where the progression from 1 to 2 to 3 and so on is so very well established) but there will definitely be some process. It may have some focus, structure, set of activities, guidelines, expectations, optempo, and so forth, or it may be little more than "the boss promotes who he wants when he wants." No matter what, knowing what it is helps you better understand the succession environment, helps you set expectations, and can be informative about what steps to take as you continue to integrate.

Product/Service

Introduction

When integrating, it is time for you to start bringing your experience and abilities to bear, and to start making an impact. You will likely find that some of your experience will be easy and enjoyable. Some of it may be challenging. Some of it just "is." This is all totally normal.

You've likely had similar experiences before, taking on a new assignment or moving to a new unit. That said, this is a whole new world. The difference is especially impactful for your first couple gigs after the military. Over time, as you get a few more job changes/transitions under your belt, you will get to be a pro at this.

During the INTEGRATING phase, it is necessary to not only understand what your products/services' value proposition to consumers is, but the strategy behind it. Let's take Southwest Airlines for example. Southwest has long been considered one of the most successful airlines in the history of commercial aviation. In fact, Southwest is one of the few airline companies that has been consistently profitable over time. Their product is low-cost air travel, but this alone is not enough to account for their success. There have been other low-cost airline companies that haven't been nearly as successful. Achieving low cost while maintaining high quality service is what sets them apart. While not perfect, Southwest has been deliberate and consistent in achieving efficiency to drive down operating costs. For example, they only purchase one kind of airplane in order to systemize their training pipeline and minimize the variety of parts, equipment, etc. They are also deliberate in their hiring process, diligently assessing customer expectations and then attracting, recruiting, and selecting team members best qualified to meet or exceed them. They understand that their customer experience depends on far more than the technical aspects of their

SECTION 2: INTEGRATING 145

employees' roles. Thus, they seek candidates that contribute to a more pleasant customer experience.

Once you know the products or services that the company offers and the strategy behind it all, the key to integrating well is to figure out how you can add value to it. You were hired for a reason and whether that was as VP of operations or as the person who puts the product in the box, you can (and must) add value. Figure out what the competitive advantage is and how your role affects it. Is speed of delivery the competitive advantage that your company's product offers? How do you make it faster, or more cost effective?

THE 3P MODEL – PRODUCT/SERVICE

Strategy & Plans (What, How, When)
Priorities
Situation / Conditions (Ownership; Headwinds; Tailwinds, etc.)
Stage of Organizational Lifecycle
Competition

Clients
Partners
Suppliers
Competitors

BUSINESS

Expectations; Deliverables; Scope; Authority;
Organization; Network; Input/Output; etc.

EXTERNAL
INTERNAL
PEOPLE | PROCESS   JOB

You
Team
Peers
Organization

TALENT

Workforce Planning; Hiring; Onboarding;
Compensation; Performance Management;
Training/Development; Succession Planning

PRODUCT /
SERVICE

BUSINESS | YOU

Legacy
Current
Future
Risks
Opportunities
Cash Cows/Capital Burns

Capabilities
Wants/Needs
Value-Add
Past/Present Performance
Future Potential
Aspiration, Ability, Agility, Availability, Action
Fit with Organization – Today & Tomorrow

General *Product/Service* Insights when INTEGRATING

When integrating, understanding your organization's products/services and the strategies behind them is key.

Organizations produce/provide certain products/services for a reason.

Perhaps they arose because of a particular passion the founder(s) had. Maybe they meet a need in society. Perhaps they think they have "a better mousetrap" or have developed a way to offer the product/service at lower cost, higher profitability, or better quality. No matter the reason, to help you integrate well, it's a good idea to dig below the surface and really understand the what, why, who, how, and when behind the products/services. The deeper/broader knowledge will make you a more valuable asset when future-focused discussions and decisions arise. It can also help you see around corners to if/how your role may be impacted (good or bad) by product/service-related decisions.

Few products/services exist forever without change.

Changing consumer wants/needs, increasing competition, technological advancements, new/unexpected opportunities, risk diversification, increasing company & brand reputation, utilizing excess capacity and various other reasons can impact the products/services your company provides. These changes can impact you, your role, your career and ultimately your life journey. Years ago, Coca-Cola decided to change its spectacularly successful recipe for Coke. They branded it "New Coke." It was an epic failure. Many good people were tied to the efforts to create New Coke, and unfortunately, when it flopped, some number of these good folks' jobs were impacted. Likely some lost their jobs, others were reassigned to other positions, and some kept their jobs but were refocused on new projects. Regardless of the details, the point is that a product change caused real impact on people, their career and life journeys. Be mindful of where the winds of change are flowing. Consider their impact on the products/services you support. Leverage opportunities. Build contingency plans for potential challenges/obstacles.

Integrating well depends on always being mindful that YOU are a product providing a service to your employer.

Don't ever lose track of your responsibility to lead and manage your career journey. Keep track of your capabilities, expertise and experience as they grow over time. Consider any gaps you may have and take action to close them. Be diligent in assessing and understanding your value as a product to the employment market for today and for tomorrow.

Detailed *Product/Service* Insights when INTEGRATING

The two general product/service areas that we discussed in LANDING still apply to INTEGRATING:

* **Business** – When landing, it was enough to simply identify the products and services your organization offers. As you integrate, it's time to learn all you can about these – why they exist, how they came to be, what customer needs they answer, how they are produced, their profitability, and so forth. You won't learn all this overnight, but with dedicated attention, you'll get smart on all of it – and that knowledge and awareness will help you be and become known as a value adding member of the team.
* **You** – We advised that when landing, you should be mindful of your capabilities, wants/needs, value-add, performance, potential, aspirations, abilities, agility, availability, and actions, to continually assess your fit with the organization's needs, and how well the organization fits for you. As you integrate, this remains important, but with this external focus also comes the risk of becoming totally focused on everything but "YOU." Be careful not to fall into that trap. Yes, you have a lot to learn. Yes, you need to integrate well and thoroughly, but you must

also stay attentive to how YOU are doing and how well the new environment aligns with your definition of success. As some often say, "If I'm not having fun, I'm outta here." Check in with yourself occasionally. Check your inner fun meter. If it's all good, bravo! Drive on! If it's trending the wrong way, objectively assess the situation, and consider potential paths forward.

Business Products/Services

When it comes to the INTEGRATING phase, learning about legacy products/services (those that have been around for a while, for years or even decades) and understanding their history can be very helpful. It provides context about where the product/service and the company overall came from and how they got to where they are today (good or bad). It can provide useful information about customer wants, needs, and expectations. Further, learning all you can about legacy products/services can be informative about the relevance of your position today and tomorrow.

As we noted in the previous section, some products/services answer a **current** need. During the INTEGRATION phase, learning about these often-short lived products/services can provide valuable perspective on the viability of your role. For example, if your role is totally focused on a fad (short-lived) product/service, you may need to start contingency planning for other options when it eventually sputters to an end.

Learning about **future** focused products/services as you integrate into your new role can reveal some exciting opportunities (it may also present some high-risk dead ends). If your role is tied to future focused products/services, be aware as you integrate of the ones with the highest potential for success and the highest probability of coming to life. Make decisions and take actions that position you for success (however you define it).

Learn and understand the **risks/opportunities** associated with the products/services most closely related to your role. Consider how those risks/opportunities might impact your potential for success in the near and long term. Develop countermeasures to mitigate the risks and to exploit the opportunities, so that your career can proceed in a manner that best fits your overall life journey.

As they relate to integrating, learning as much as possible about the **cash cows** and **capital burners**, (and how your role relates to them) is a good investment of your time and effort. Learning how to best support either and understanding how their existence helps (or hinders) the overall business strategy can position you as a strong contributor to the success of the products/services, and the business overall.

When integrating, learning as broadly and deeply as possible about the company's various products/services should be a priority for you. Knowing their various strengths, vulnerabilities, risks and opportunities can help you not only provide the highest-level performance possible, but it can also be helpful as you manage YOU as a product that provides a service to your employer.

You as a Product/Service

YOU are product, providing a service to your employer. Sounds pretty odd to say that, but this perspective can be an important one to remember as you integrate. You have capabilities, wants and needs; you bring a level of performance and potential; you have aspirations, abilities, agility, certain amounts of availability, and are able to take actions—all of which can provide real value to your employer. Keeping all this in mind as you integrate helps you keep perspective and balance between giving your all to the employer and losing yourself along the way.

As with LANDING, the INTEGRATION phase provides opportunity and data points to confirm and demonstrate your **capabilities**, showing your employer that you are worth their investment in you.

Deploy your capabilities relevant to the job. Have your additional capabilities nearby in your toolbox, ready to use them when the opportunities arise.

As you integrate, it's wise to assess how the situation and environment align with your **wants and needs**. Are they being met today? If not immediately, is there a reasonable possibility that they might be in the future? Or do indicators show that there is a notable disconnect that leaves your wants and needs out of the picture? No one would suggest making any rash judgements or taking impulsive action, but being attentive to how well your wants and needs are being met is prudent so you can address disconnects thoughtfully and proactively to bring things into alignment, (or consider alternatives that are more acceptable).

Integrating can feel like a pretty long haul. Getting the lay of the land, learning "Who's who and what's what" and how it all fits together doesn't always come easy. Performance can be the great equalizer. Remembering your strong **past performance** and recognizing wins in your **present performance** are both helpful throughout your INTEGRATION phase. One of the most valuable lessons from most change management gurus is to "recognize the small wins and celebrate successes." Do this as you integrate. It will reinforce the good days and bolster you when challenges rear up.

As it is often said by pilots, "Always keep your eye on the dials and on the horizon." While integrating, you'll be wise to keep a dual focus also – on today and on tomorrow. Focus on what's currently on your plate and deliver top-notch results—but also have the foresight to consider your **future potential**. Does the business situation seem likely to provide potential that is attractive to you? Do circumstances seem to support your **aspirations** and **abilities**? Does the playing field offer room to demonstrate your **agility** and **availability** to take meaningful **action**? If there are apparent disconnects, do yourself a favor and explore them while you integrate. Finding yourself in a position where future potential does not align for you is never a good thing in the long run.

DAVE STORY

"Pilots Keep Their Eyes on the Dials and the Horizon."

Don't Get so Focused on Tomorrow that you Lose Sight of Today" - Remember when I talked about my running journey? Rediscovering my love for running is not where it ends. The work wasn't done. I decided that a love for running and racing didn't have to be mutually exclusive and I ached for the race environment again. The support for everyone that crosses the finish line, the respect for people's inner competition with themselves, and a general feeling of we do hard stuff. I decided to sign up for Ironman Ohio 70.3 and got to work.

After months of training, race day came and went. I finished, but it wasn't pretty. My time was about an hour and a half slower than my PR. I walked most of the run and pretty much limped across the finish line. Nevertheless, I learned two important lessons that day, and I think they are relevant to long term success in the workforce and in life.

> 1. *Celebrate the wins. When I crossed the finish line, I was almost in tears. I was so frustrated that I had to walk...that I was so slow. I mean, what the heck was all that training for? I was sulking away to the holding area where I saw my wife (she beat me by more than an hour, by the way). She had tears in her eyes too—but her tears were happy tears. She was so damn proud of me. See, Libby remembered the journey, when it was a struggle for me to walk around the block. While I was looking at where I wanted to go, she was in the moment, and this moment was a win. It's great to have a strategic plan on where you ultimately want to go, but don't forget to celebrate the wins along the way. That promotion might not*

have been the one you wanted, but it took work to get there. Celebrate it.
2. *You have to put in the work. Because of the training volume and general convenience, I did most of my training on the treadmill. But (and this is a big but), because I was still having a hard time lifting my leg over long distances, I did all my treadmill training at a negative one incline. I mean all of it. I was getting faster; I was making progress (or so I thought) and was generally feeling optimistic...until one week before the race, when I ran outside for the first time. Talk about an "oh shit" moment. I could barely finish five miles, and not because I was out of shape but because I was literally hitting muscle failure in my hips. Although I knew I would finish the race, even if I had to walk (and I did, a lot), I also knew it was going to be so much more painful than it could have been, because at the end of the day, I hadn't trained the right way. The lesson here is that there are no short cuts to systemic success. You have to put in the work. Even if you find a work around that makes life easy for a while, it's going to catch up to you and likely at the worst moment. The good news is there's a sure way to overcome it, and even though it won't be easy, putting in the work will ultimately always win over the shortcut.*

And finally, be attentive to your **fit** with the organization. Business conditions are always fluid. Position yourself as a value-adding team member **today** and attend to evolving conditions that may impact your fit for **tomorrow**.

INTEGRATING SUMMARY

Integrating is a critical step in one's career and life journey. A successful integration can and will pave the way for you to thrive & survive in your new role. As you can see, integrating is much more than identifying people, processes and products/services, that play an important role in your new position. It is learning and understanding how you fit and interact with these 3Ps. This is a time where you really learn how these different aspects interact with each other in order to create a business output that creates revenue or value for your customers.

One more word of advice and caution. Be careful of beginning the INTEGRATION stage too early. Fully invest in your landing first. Trying to understand different processes without identifying all of the necessary components of the business or your role can lead to unnecessary heartache. The more you start to understand the bigger picture, the closer you will be to being able to leverage your talents to increase people, process, and product value—the theme of our next section, THRIVING & SURVIVING.

SECTION 3

THRIVING & SURVIVING

CAREER AND LIFE JOURNEY ALIGNMENT – THRIVING & SURVIVING

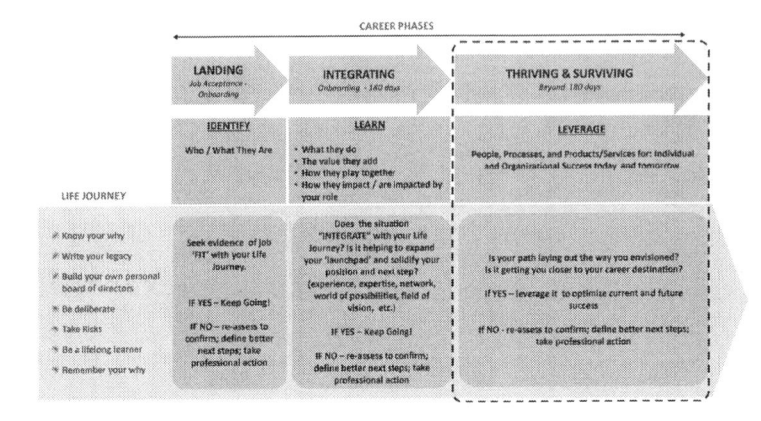

CAREER PHASES

	LANDING Job Acceptance – Onboarding	INTEGRATING Onboarding – 180 days	THRIVING & SURVIVING Beyond 180 days
	IDENTIFY Who / What They Are	**LEARN** • What they do • The value they add • How they play together • How they impact / are impacted by your role	**LEVERAGE** People, Processes, and Products/Services for: Individual and Organizational Success today and tomorrow

LIFE JOURNEY

- Know your why
- Write your legacy
- Build your own personal board of directors
- Be deliberate
- Take Risks
- Be a lifelong learner
- Remember your why

| Seek evidence of job "FIT" with your Life Journey.

IF YES – Keep Going!

IF NO – re-assess to confirm; define better next steps; take professional action | Does the situation "INTEGRATE" with your Life Journey? Is is helping to expand your "launchpad" and solidify your position and next step? (experience, expertise, network, world of possibilities, field of vision, etc.)

IF YES – Keep Going!

IF NO – re-assess to confirm; define better next steps; take professional action | Is your path laying out the way you envisioned? Is it getting you closer to your career destination?

IF YES – leverage it to optimize current and future success

IF NO – re-assess to confirm; define better next steps; take professional action |

CAREER AND LIFE JOURNEY ALIGNMENT – THRIVING & SURVIVING ACTION ITEMS

	LAND	INTEGRATE	THRIVE & SURVIVE
Know your why	Vet reality against your WHY to optimize happiness and success	Don't let new influences sway you unintentionally	Stay true to yourself; let WHY evolve if appropriate.
Write your legacy	First impressions matter	How you integrate with others impacts your legacy	Remember – your legacy is the result of what you do over time; don't get the cart before the horse.
Build your own personal board of directors	Identify potential PBOD candidates	Build relationships with PBOD candidates and listen to their counsel	Review PBOD members for relevance over time; change members as s needed.
Be deliberate	Have a plan to land well; work the plan diligently	Work with others to understand how everything fits	Take intentional actions to optimize current success and future opportunities that align with your life plan.
Take Risks	Reasonable risks – don't stumble out of the starting blocks	Eagerly seek out others; introduce yourself; make connections; build relationships	Boldly seek and exploit opportunities to spread your wings, add more value, and expand your scope.
Be a lifelong learner	Identify the "Who's Who" and the What's What" of the new job	LEARN • What they do • The value they add • How they play together • How they impact / are impacted by your role	LEVERAGE People, Processes, and Products/Services for: Individual and Organizational Success today and tomorrow
Remember your why	To avoid being drawn off course in your new position	Share your unique value	To vet situations and evolving conditions for alignment with your overall life journey plan.

Introduction/General THRIVING & SURVIVING Insights

BILL STORY

"Thriving & Surviving – The Long Haul."

I've been thriving & surviving in the civilian work world for well over two decades. Some days have been easy; others, not so much. Some legs of my career and life journeys meshed well. Some clashed in ways obvious and subtle. There were times when things got me down, and there were times when I was buoyed by the rising tides of great positive things.

My career journey has included multiple transitions—from the military to my first civilian job in a small pseudo-governmental office; from there to an HR/talent management career in the transportation/logistics industry; then on to the heavy manufacturing industry, followed by the consumer goods manufacturing industry, all the way to today as an entrepreneur.

Along the way, my life journey evolved, as well. Marriage, divorce, births, deaths, significant health events, new opportunities to serve my community, new ways to enjoy life, and new challenges and obstacles all arose for me, as they do for everyone.

Over time, I began to realize and appreciate that to thrive & survive in the long run, I needed to:

- ★ *Be keenly aware of my surroundings.*
- ★ *Stay well informed and knowledgeable as broadly and deeply as possible.*

> ★ *Always keep a dual focus on today and tomorrow.*
> ★ *Seek balance in all things.*
>
> *Perhaps most importantly, I learned that success is what you define it to be. No matter the headwinds, tailwinds, challenges, or opportunities, to thrive & survive for the long haul, YOU have to define your success. That may mean riding a great job and career path to the top. It may mean facing tough family, social, or work conditions and making difficult decisions to change your situation and path. But in the end, there's really no getting around it - success is what YOU decide it is.*
>
> *My hope is that by sharing my experiences and insights, you are able to define your success and navigate the long haul to thrive & survive well.*

Having landed well and integrated solidly, the next leg of your successful career journey is to thrive & survive. Just like the battlefield, the civilian work world is fluid. Various influences, internal and external, controllable and uncontrollable, exist that continually shape the landscape. Customer demands evolve. Markets grow and shrink. Supply chains face differing challenges and opportunities that impact suppliers' ability to meet your needs and budgets. Financial markets ebb and flow. Ownership changes. Companies merge, acquire, and divest. These and so many more variables impact your work world. Some positively, some negatively, some are just different.

As these changes arise (and they surely will), you'll be faced with challenges and opportunities, and may have to make decisions about whether to stay, go, or attempt to adjust your employment situation.

In this section, we offer insights to the longer-term future of your career, so that you have "Intelligence Preparation of the Career Battlefield" for the long term, that will help inform your decisions.

Thriving & surviving is all about leveraging your capabilities,

SECTION 3: THRIVING & SURVIVING 159

skills, experiences, and your understanding of and relationships with the people, processes, and products/services that surround you.

To be clear, leveraging in this context means working positively with and through all these to overcome challenges, optimize opportunities, and achieve individual and organizational success today and tomorrow. It DOES NOT mean "taking advantage" or using them for negative or self-serving purposes.

As it relates to your life journey, the THRIVING & SURVIVING phase of your career transition is all about situational awareness, ensuring your situation aligns with your overall life plan. Are you getting closer to your career destination? If YES – leverage it to optimize current and future success. If NO - re-assess to confirm; define better next steps; take professional action.

Action steps to thrive & survive in a manner that is well-aligned to your life journey:

- ★ Know Your Why - Stay true to yourself; let your WHY evolve if appropriate.
- ★ Write Your Legacy – Remember, your legacy is the result of what you do over time; don't put the cart before the horse.
- ★ Build Your Own Personal Board of Directors - Review PBOD members for relevance over time; change members as needed.
- ★ Be Deliberate - Take intentional actions to optimize current success and future opportunities that align with your life plan.
- ★ Take Risks - Boldly seek and exploit opportunities to spread your wings, add more value, and expand your scope.
- ★ Be a Lifelong Learner – Leverage people, processes, and products/services for individual and organizational success today and tomorrow.
- ★ Remember Your Why - To vet situations and evolving conditions for alignment with your overall life journey plan.

BILL STORY

"Thriving & surviving in any organization is a bit like planting grass."

I recently re-landscaped part of my yard.
Planted a large patch of grass.
Selected and prepped the soil.
Researched and obtained just the right grass seed.
Spread the seed intentionally.
Watered regularly.
I waited and watched for nature to do its thing.
As I waited, I noticed birds and rabbits eating some of the seeds.
Days later, I saw the first inkling of green pop through the surface.
Small at first. More as time went on.
Some patches grew robustly. Some not so much. Some not at all.
I got more seed, planted the bare spots again.
I'm seeing new growth there too now.

How does grass apply to your career?
To build a successful career, you:

★ *Must have some manner of goal (to have a beautiful lawn). Without a goal, you may land individual jobs but you are less likely to land positions that are seedlings of a great career. (This said, there may be times where the practical realities of your situation dictate that you take a job in order to meet current needs, rather than turn away from them, holding out for that ideal career move.)*

SECTION 3: THRIVING & SURVIVING

- *Need to do the prep work. Build your base and do your research. Grass grows best in soil that has been prepared. Same for your career. Prepare yourself for the future. Learn what you need to learn. Build a network that helps you perform well today and connects you to future opportunities.*
- *Must do the work. Plant the seeds. Water them. Nurture the relationships. Enable opportunities to evolve.*
- *Must be patient. Few things in life are overnight successes. The obvious big wins are most often the result of many years hard work that is unnoticed by the masses.*
- *Need to remember that your career search and growth does not happen in a vacuum. Other people and forces are omni-present. Some of these are supportive and well-intended. Some are neutral and just happen to occupy the same space. Others are out to get whatever they can with no regard for your intent, desire, effort or investment. There will always be birds, rabbits, and other vermin that will "eat your seeds."*
- *Recognize the successes, small wins and windows of opportunity. Just like the small buds of grass, great career opportunities often first appear almost imperceptibly. Maybe it was a chance meeting with a powerbroker. Maybe your contribution to a small project yielded great results. Maybe your new idea sparked interest in someone who had, or knew of, a need you can now suddenly solve. Keep your eyes/ears open for these seemingly small occurrences; they can open doors you never knew existed and can help create a career you never imagined.*
- *Must be resilient. Stay at it. Keep planting the seeds. Continue to nurture them. Be resilient in the face of adversity. Find a way through, around, over, or under roadblocks and challenges.*

Keep You and Your Career a Priority.

It's been said that no one cares more about your career than you. With rare exception, this is very true.

Similarly, one of the greatest challenges military veterans face in the new civilian work world is the shift in focus from "WE" to "ME." From day one of all military training, the focus is on the team: being a strong team, being a valuable team player, thinking and acting with the team always top-of-mind, and subordinating yourself for the good of the team. This team-focus is critical in the military, and it is highly valuable in the civilian work world.

Still, in order to thrive & survive over the long term, you need to look out for yourself, to do what's right for you, your current success and your future. There's nothing dishonorable about this – unless you're being a jerk about it, or hurting others along the way. When operating in the civilian work world, you must strike and maintain a very careful balance between being a team player and being your own "Chief Marketing Officer."

> ### *BILL STORY*
>
> *"When Focus on WE Puts a Hurting on ME."*
>
> *During one of my jobs, I got so focused on the "WE" that I let my contributions and efforts go unrecognized. I truly lived the "WE" ethos: gave all the credit, absorbed any criticism, and minimized recognition of my contribution to the cause. Good stuff in my mind! That's what leaders do, right? Yes, of course, but what I didn't properly consider is that not everyone holds this same ethos. Some folks eagerly seek out and exploit opportunities to puff themselves up, marketing team successes as their personal wins, and are not above submarining others*

> *to move themselves ahead. In this case, a peer team member took every opportunity (valid or not) to leverage wins and losses to his advantage. His contribution to the team was minimal, but his self-promotion was astounding. I faced a dilemma wherein I could challenge his self-promotion and appear rather small/petty, or I could focus my efforts on the good of the order and let the chips fall where they may. I chose the latter. This gentleman was a master at self-promotion, a smooth talker, and effectively bull shitted a key decision-maker to his own advantage. (The success added to his annual cash bonus and to his list of project wins.) I knew I made a material, positive impact on the success of this initiative, and I was pleased with that, but by not paying attention to the fact that others were spinning a yarn about their contribution, I was not properly recognized for the results I generated. Lesson learned. I ALWAYS put mission first and ALWAYS recognized the team, but from that point forward I made damn sure I kept track of, and told the story of, my contribution. It felt selfish at first, but over time I realized that if I don't tell my own story, no one else will, and that can hinder my ability to thrive & survive successfully.*

Balance Technical and Soft Skills; Leverage Your Intangible Skills to Achieve Tangible Results.

Thriving & surviving in any organization is about being capable enough, broadly enough to achieve planned results and be a great member of the team. This requires a balance of both technical and soft skills that are sufficiently developed and appropriately deployed to make a difference today, and to demonstrate success potential for tomorrow.

We know how difficult job hunting and career transition can be, especially when your technical capabilities may not be so obviously well-aligned with job opportunities - as is the case for many military veterans.

Most veterans come to the job market with experience and capabilities that are great value-adds for many jobs. These capabilities are often viewed as soft skills (which we all know are some of the hardest things to do well). They are also sometimes referred to as "intangible" skills. Now, there is no doubt that these intangible skills are important to individual and organizational success, but as you continue your career journey and endeavor to thrive & survive professionally, you'll do well to remember that businesses need tangible results. For-profit companies need to produce products/services that consistently meet/exceed customer and market expectations, and they need to do so profitably. Nonprofit organizations need to achieve their mission successfully, so they fulfill their purpose, serve their benefactors' needs, and remain attractive recipients of donor funds. Be sure your intangible skills are accordingly applied in a value-adding way that helps achieve tangible results.

As Bill notes in his first book, employers hire people that have convinced them of two core things:

- ★ They are able to successfully do the work that needs done (technical/tangible skills).
- ★ They will fit well and add value to the team (soft/intangible skills).

Employers (and their hiring teams) often bring this truth to life by first exploring and considering the candidates' technical/tangible capabilities, then assessing their soft/intangible skills.

In transition and job search, the relevance and impact is fairly clear; the candidate that is most convincing on most fronts gets selected.

But is this relevant to thriving & surviving in the long run? Absolutely!

Discussion and decisions regarding pay, bonuses, opportunities and assignments inevitably include consideration of your technical/tangible capabilities AND your soft/intangible skills. These discussions may address how well aligned your capabilities/skills are for your current role, how they may impact your readiness for broader assignments at the same level, whether or not you're ready for a promotion, etc.

> ### BILL STORY
>
> *"Tangible/Intangible Balance."*
>
> *A long tenured finance professional was being considered for promotion to a more senior finance role (direct report to the CFO). He was well known for his technical/tangible capabilities. Even though he was a rockstar technical finance expert, as his promotion was being discussed, several folks questioned his soft/intangible skills. They had heard that this good gentleman was a bit rough around the edges, very direct, and sometimes not as easy to get along with as might be desired. After much conversation, the decision was made to promote him – and provide him with some feedback and training to help shore up the soft/intangible spots. He took the assignment, worked very hard at both the deliverables and his development. It was rocky at the start. He was producing outstanding results, but his learning curve on the soft/intangible skills was a bit steeper and longer than anyone hoped. In addition, the perception his team held of him (based on prior experiences) was challenging to change. In the long run, the decision was made to adjust his role to more of a senior individual contributor, with less interaction with others. He*

> *worked hard to do all the right stuff, but the optemo was quicker than the speed at which he could rebalance.*

Lesson learned here? When considering promotions/new assignment opportunities, be sure to:

★ Know and balance your technical/tangible capabilities and your soft/intangible skills.
★ Learn and understand the job's deliverables, core responsibilities, technical/tangible capabilities and soft/intangible skills.
★ Vet how well your technical/tangible capabilities and soft/intangible skills align with the job.
★ Recognize that people's perceptions (positive and negative) can impact your ability to thrive & survive.
★ Realize that business optemo and the time it takes you to achieve balance may not always sync.

BALANCE YOUR CAPABILITES WITH EMPLOYER NEEDS

Technical/Tangible		Soft/Intangible
Your Capability = Employer Needs	*SUCCESS*	Your Capability = Employer Needs

Thriving & Surviving is About Performance, Potential, Growth, and Rebirth.

No matter how "big" you are, how much you enjoy your current gig, or what you think is next in your career plan, sometimes things happen. Uncontrollable forces invade your reality and create changes that are unexpected. These may be great, positive surprises, or they may be the last thing on earth you'd ever want.

No matter the nature of the change, nor how traumatic or positive it is, you CAN start again and grow into something amazing!

There are two primary attributes that anchor individual and organizational ability to succeed: balance and agility.

This mindset is rooted in military experience, as every servicemember past and present could relate to the familiar saying, "Plans only last until first contact." Agility is the inherent key to success.

Certainly, having a career plan is important, but having the ability to adjust well when things change (and they will) is the real secret sauce. Leverage your military experience. Build a plan. Have a PACE plan. Understand the battle space and employ your great agility skills to create success!

Credibility is critical to successfully thriving & surviving.

When you landed the gig and successfully integrated, you earned some level of credibility in your new organization. This is great, but credibility is ephemeral and can vanish quickly.

As your time in the role and with the organization goes on, you'll need to ensure you are willing and able to grow both your capability (ability to do new things) and your credibility (the degree to which you convince others to believe in and trust that you are the right person to do the work that needs to be done, and to be the best fit for the team). This means more than simply getting smart on a new topic. It's about others' perception of and belief in your ability to perform in all aspects of the job.

As a military veteran who has successfully landed and integrated into your new job/company/career, there's little doubt you can get smart on damn near any topic that may arise. It's no BS. You are among the most agile, adaptable, development-focused people on earth! You are highly capable and have seemingly endless desire and ability to grow your capabilities and add value to something meaningful.

As your time with an organization grows, so does your capability. But just like your job search, networking, and interviewing experience early in career transition, capability alone is not enough.

To keep the great role you have, and/or to grow your career over time, you must also continually expand your credibility.

In short, making yourself credible is a capability you need to get smart on.

So, how do you grow your credibility?

SECTION 3: THRIVING & SURVIVING 169

First, be mindful that credibility is temporal – it can evaporate over time, and you'll likely need to prove yourself over and again. This is not some personal attack or indictment of you as a person. Business conditions change, leadership position incumbents change, peers change, team members change, needs change, and each of us needs to be able to demonstrate that we have the chops to do what needs to be done. It can be hard. (The phrase "What have you done for me lately" comes to mind.)

This need to continually prove yourself can take a toll. It can wear you out. BUT ONLY IF YOU LET IT! Do the best work you can do. Be the best team player you can be. Learn all you can learn. Build the best network possible. Then let the chips fall where they may. Sometimes the grass looks greener (and it might really be) – but remember, you'll need to make yourself credible in that new green field also.

Think about your military career. Each new assignment, each change of station, each new school. As the FNG, you entered these new situations relatively unknown. Perhaps the folks there heard something about you. Maybe they saw your profile or heard about you through their network. This may have provided some level of awareness, but it didn't give you credibility. You had to establish that once you arrived on station. It is a very similar situation in the civilian work world, with a couple notable exceptions:

1. 93% of the population never served in uniform. They don't have a common network, base of experience, perspective, etc. with you.
2. In the civilian world, you don't wear your resume on your chest; there is no rank insignia that gives you positional authority.

Your credibility curve will be steeper and longer than any PCS, and you'll have to be far more situationally aware and agile than ever before.

Business conditions change. Leadership teams change. The

winners in the thrive & survive game are those who adjust to both, and that build credibility no matter the headwinds/tailwinds.

> ## *DAVE STORY*
>
> *"Just Because You Met the Standards Once, Doesn't Mean You Meet the Standards Now."*
>
> *One of the things I love about the Ranger Regiment is the systematic need to "re-blue" yourself throughout your career. Rangers don't go through selection just once. Senior leaders could go through a selection process up to four times throughout their career in order to stay in the organization. This wasn't always the case. Around 2010, the Ranger Regiment changed its policy, which made it mandatory for Non-Commissioned Officers to go through the Ranger Assessment and Selection Program before they assumed responsibility of a platoon and again before they assumed responsibility for a company. As you can imagine, not everyone was thrilled with this change. The Regiment lost some good NCOs during this transition. Some because they opted out and some because they did not pass. But just because they were good NCOs did not mean they were the right fit at the right time. Could they adapt to a changing operating environment and therefore a shift in the needs of the organization? Were they willing to?*
>
> *I went through selection three times to stay in the Ranger Regiment. Once to get into the organization, and again before I both assumed responsibility of a platoon and a company. I also taught the course for two years. Each time was different because the Regiment was different. As needs changed, the organization changed with it and therefore we had to grow as leaders to be the best leader for the organization in the current and future environment; not the past.*

DAVE STORY

"Forcing Myself to Get Better; Deciding to Go Somewhere New and Create Credibility with a Whole New Crew."

Around the 2011 timeframe, I taught Ranger Regiment's Assessment and Selection program for senior NCOs and officers. It was a great experience, but after two years or so, it was time for me to move on and get back to the assault teams. I had spent almost a decade in 3rd Ranger Battalion in Ft. Benning, GA. I had established a pretty good reputation while I was there. I could have gone back when my time teaching was complete. There was a job for me. I could have relied on my previous reputation. I knew almost everyone, and they knew me. However, I wanted a change. I wanted to go somewhere, where I had to prove myself all over again. I wanted to challenge myself because I knew that this challenge would make me better. And so, I took a job at 1st Ranger Battalion in Savannah, GA instead.

It was not easy. No one knew who I was. I made mistakes, and while in 3/75 those mistakes likely would have been overlooked because of my reputation, they were not in Savannah, and so I had to work my ass off to regain my credibility. I grew more in that first year as a leader than throughout the entirety of my career up to that point. I had an amazing team and with that team, we became one of the most proficient in all of Ranger Regiment at that time. I am convinced that my growth was almost entirely due to putting myself in a position where I could not rely on past performance to drive current performance. That reputation will eventually deteriorate if you do not continuously grow and improve. The move forced me to do so, and, to this date, it is probably one of the best professional decisions I have made. Sometimes you need to *force yourself out of your comfort zone, whether by changing positions, teams, locations, organization, etc. to catalyze both your career and professional growth.*

BILL STORY

"The New Boss."

During one of my assignments as a senior level HR/talent management executive, we had extensive change in the C-suite. While the folks entering these top-level positions were highly qualified, each change created a new set of expectations that impacted the overall organization, my function, my team, my job, and (potentially) my future. New incumbents came with their own perspectives, preferences, priorities, expectations, and ways of doing business. One of these was particularly impactful. When my direct boss changed, I wanted to make a great first impression. I did my research, learned as much as possible, and prepared a robust, thorough introduction/overview of our priorities, strategies, structure, ongoing projects, current metrics, future plans, and connecting points with key players. It was some really good work, befitting of any staff introduction to a senior miliary leader. At my introductory meeting with the new boss, I provided a copy of this great work (in hard copy and electronic format) and offered to discuss it at whatever day/time was most convenient. Little did I know that the function I led (global talent management) was not a top priority for his early days. Maybe it was because I had it all squared away, and there were no burning issues; maybe he just didn't really value it. Maybe, maybe, maybe. Given my military background, I employed the "last standing order remains" mentality, and kept driving on. Eventually, the boss met with me, considered the overview, gave it a positive nod, and noted that we'd be making some changes to the process. As much as I recognized his authority to do so, this was my baby; I had built it, deployed it, and operated it with great success. He was the new guy, and he was changing things! This felt like a threat to my success, my position, and my future.

I did my level best to adjust. Some of the changes really did make sense; some not so much. Many of my top-tier internal clients (my boss' peers) preferred my way. What could have been a simple matter of adjusting process, however, became a notable "people" issue. That shift materially changed the work environment and my on-the-job enjoyment. It also meant I had to establish credibility with my new boss, both technically and behaviorally, in that I had to show that I could be supportive of him even while his peers favored my approach and processes. It was a delicate place to be. Establishing my technical credibility was relatively easy. Creating credibility with him on the behavioral side, however, was a bit bigger challenge. He didn't like that his peers had high regard for me; it seemed to threaten him. We managed to work together for over a year, but in the end, we just didn't gel, and we came to mutually agreeable terms to part ways. This was not a change I had planned for, but it was one that I had to deal with all the same. In hindsight, it forced me into some much-needed reflection and consideration about what I was doing, how I was doing it, and what I really wanted for my career and life. It opened my eyes and ears to new paths that I hadn't really considered before.

BILL STORY

"New Ownership."

I joined a Fortune 500 company after it had emerged from bankruptcy. I was brought in to design and deploy a global talent management strategy. It was a rare opportunity to actually create something meaningful from a clean sheet on a global scale. Having emerged from bankruptcy, the company was under new ownership. Private equity (PE) owners now called the shots, and as you might expect, they had tough financial covenants we had to hit. This new ownership created notable change across the company and at every level. Structures changed. Expectations changed. Priorities, timelines, and behaviors all changed. These changes disrupted the status quo. Simply "maintaining" was not good enough anymore; each and every team member had to make a real, positive impact in order to keep their seat at the table. I liken our process during this critical period to "saving a crashing aircraft." We had to get laser focused on the urgent, critical tasks that would stop the descent. Long-term, future-focused efforts were put on a back burner unless part of the plan was able to make a positive, near-term impact on our ability to achieve our financial covenants. As my mission was to design and deploy a global talent management strategy, I had to be very wary that every step in the plan, every action item, was able to produce near-term return while simultaneously building a solid foundation for future success. Fortunately, I understood the situation and was able to adjust my approach, plans, and actions to provide credible near-term impact that built a solid foundation for the future.

BILL STORY

"We Got Bought."

Several years into my tenure with BAX Global (a multi-billion-dollar global air freight and supply chain company), the gigantic German rail and transportation company Deutsche Bahn (DB) bought us. They found our operations attractive and accretive to their current business and longer-term strategy. As you can imagine, bringing together two multi-billion-dollar, global companies is no small feat. The complexities and intricacies are nearly unimaginable. The potential impact (positive or negative) is huge. Every bit of the respective organizations' people, process, and product/service components were checked, vetted, and assessed to define what they were, how they worked, how they fit amongst themselves, and how they were likely to fit and interact across the newly merged companies.

As this process evolved, it was clear that tough decisions were going to have to be made. Redundant people, processes, and products/ services would have to be either optimized so they complement each other in ways that make good business sense, or eliminated to reduce costs and complexity. As the head of global talent management, I found myself in a potentially precarious spot. Did DB have another similar incumbent? Was talent management even a priority? If so, were the processes aligned? So many questions. I knew I had to make myself credible in this new environment and with the new leadership team at the top. I worked hard to learn everything I could about their priorities and perspectives. I developed relationships with as many as possible. I packaged all my deliverables to the best of my ability to meet/exceed their expectations. Apparently, it worked. Not only did I survive the inevitable headcount reductions, but I was also invited by DB's Chief HR Officer to address the top 200 HR leaders across all of their then-240,000-member workforce. I built the credibility I needed in a very complex, challenging time of change.

> ### BILL STORY
>
> *"Market Crashes/Budget Slashes."*
>
> *Around 2008-2009 the US and global economy tanked. Financial markets crashed, revenue opportunities evaporated, costs skyrocketed, supply chains became strained, and so forth. As the recently hired head of global talent management for a $7B automotive supplier, I knew that I had to ensure and bolster the credibility of my function, my position, and my ability to remain as the incumbent. To do so, I had to lead the function as a true business partner, cognizant of the economic conditions and proactive in my actions. The business focus was laser tight on cost savings, margin preservation, and adjusting business structure, strategy and practices to ensure we could achieve our financial covenants and remain a high-quality provider of automotive components, and an attractive investment opportunity for the investment community. In short, this meant that for me to remain credible, I had to find creative ways to ensure all talent management, training, learning, succession planning, performance management and related areas were delivered with clear line of sight to critical business objectives. There was no room for "nice-to-haves," and abandoning the "must-haves" was not an option. We had to cut heads. We had to defer programs. We had to find no/low-cost solutions to complex problems. It wasn't easy, but I was able to make positive progress that answered real business issues and was thus able to enhance my credibility with the top leaders and others throughout the company.*

Let's revisit the typical employment life cycle, to see how it relates to thriving & surviving.

TYPICAL EMPLOYMENT CYCLE RELATED TO THRIVING & SURVIVING

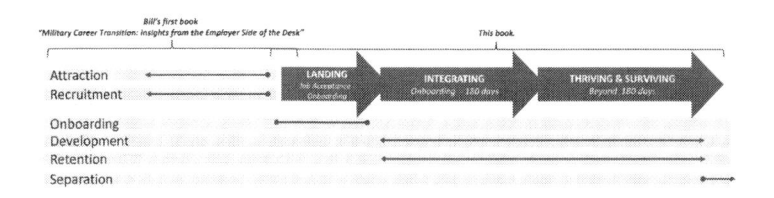

As we discussed earlier, the development and retention phases of this cycle are highly relevant to thriving & surviving over time. You will likely want to develop as you go, learning new things and gaining new experiences. Assuming you are a value-adding member of the team, your employer will likely be focused on retaining you. Attending to both of these streams is time well spent and can notably influence your career and life journeys.

Development is an extended part of your time with the company. Its focus is to help you perform well today and to prepare you for success tomorrow. There are multiple processes, practices, programs, and other activities in this stage. As a general rule, most employers' focus on development is far less robust than the well-evolved development and career management our military services employ.

All this said, you need to explore every avenue to continue to develop. Perhaps it is via company provided/sponsored programs. Perhaps it is via new assignments that afford you the opportunity to learn and do new things. Or perhaps you will have to create and implement your own development plan. In some cases, where things just aren't lining up, you may have to move on to another company to bring your development plan to life.

No matter the situation, remember that you are the captain of your career and life journey, and you have the opportunity and responsibility to chart the course that works best for you.

Retention is also an ongoing concern throughout the typical

employment life cycle. Employers have invested in you and, as long as you are performing well and adding value, it is in their best interest to keep you engaged, challenged, and continuing to serve as a value-adding member of the organization for a long time. Employers dedicate significant attention and resources to retaining good talent. After all, losing good people who are trained, qualified, and experienced in their jobs is expensive. Lost production, disruption of the status quo, and recruiting new talent are all expensive. Whether it is engagement surveys, open door/open communications, benefit packages, quality of work-life initiatives, or any of a vast number of other approaches, employers know that retaining good people is good business.

To truly thrive & survive in the long run, you as an employee also need to attend to retention. Is this a place you really want to be? Are you able to deploy your capabilities here? Do you understand how you fit and how you are adding value? Are your wants, needs and aspirations being met? Are you having any fun? Is your life in balance, or are your days consumed with work? Do you have the time and energy to dedicate to your family, your friends, yourself, or anything other than work? These and other questions are worth asking yourself occasionally to validate if you're in the right place for you. If you're mostly answering "yes," bravo! Drive on! If not, carefully consider the gaps, their causes, and potential solutions. Vet your relationship with your boss and/or other people in positions of authority. Decide if/how you might bring your concerns up, and what the likely outcomes of these discussions might be. Engage trusted mentors to check you, to offer insights, and help you achieve a balanced perspective. When the time is right, take action. If conversations are reasonably likely to help, have them. If after thoughtful consideration you know that leaving is your best option, do it wisely. Start your job search so you have a landing spot before you leave. When you do leave, do so professionally. The civilian work world is smaller than you might think, and you don't want to burn bridges you might need to use in the future.

Organizations have a life cycle. They are where they are. It impacts how they operate – and how well you might thrive & survive.

TYPICAL ORGANIZATIONAL LIFECYCLE

Launch / Start up	Growth / Expansion	Shakeout / Stability	Maturity	Decline
High Risk/Reward	Proof of Concept	Formalizing	Established Products	Stagnant/Declining Sales
Disruptive	Revenue Growth Focus	More Structured	Steady Customers	Shrinking Margins
Passion	Operationalizing	Becoming Specialized	Incremental Growth	Asset Divestitures
New Idea(s)	Some Specialization	Gaining Market Share	Cost Effectiveness Focus	Rising Debt
All Hands	Setting Metrics	Operational Improvements	Efficiency Focus	Stagnant Management
Fast Pace; Change	Seizing Opportunities	Talent Focus	Operational Excellence	Save/Sell?
Few SOPs	Some SOPs	Etc.	Bureaucratic	Etc.
Etc.	Etc.		Etc.	

We mentioned this earlier, but it is especially important to understand where your organization is in its life cycle in order for you to thrive & survive in the long run. Because it is so important, we'll dive into the details here, looking at each phase and the focus, culture and priorities typically associated with them:

★ **Launch/Startup** – As the name implies, this is the start of it all. The bringing to life of someone's dream/idea/vision. Not all launches/start-ups are created equal. Some are well planned, thoroughly resourced, and highly organized. Some, on the other hand, are more like energetic, enthusiastic puppy dogs who go headlong into whatever's in their path. Both can be successful, but both can just as easily be abject failures. Startups may be new idea(s) in existing markets, or they may be totally new, disruptive ideas, approaches, and organizations that bring something completely innovative to the world. Characteristics of businesses in this life cycle phase typically include a lot of passion for the business/product/idea, a fast pace with much change, many new and evolving ideas about what to do and how to do it, few SOPs (standard operating procedures), an "all hands on deck" mentality, and the expectation everyone will do whatever it takes (whether it's in your job description or not) to drive success. This phase tends to have an environment of high risk, with potentially high reward.

★ **Growth/Expansion** - Having launched, the next phase is growth/expansion. Given the innumerable variables impacting every new organization, there's no set norm from a timing standpoint as to when this shift occurs. Regardless of when it happens, moving from launch/startup to growth/expansion shifts focus and expectations. In this phase, organizations typically begin focusing on proof of concept (proving that their product/service really does what they say it will do) and revenue growth (demonstrating that the product/service can and does generate revenue). These are both foundational topics that businesses must focus on. They need to deliver on their product/service's promise, and they must make money to cover the costs of bringing the product/service to market and producing/providing those products/services. The business will also start focusing on operationalizing the work, specializing where it makes sense, creating some SOPs, and establishing metrics. It will also be highly attentive to seizing opportunities to get their product/service into more markets and customers, and to evolve/refine existing products/services or introduce new products/services that answer new customer/market needs.

★ **Shakeout/Stability** - At this point in the organization's life cycle, things are becoming more routine, predictable, and stable. The business processes are likely to become more formalized. More structure is likely to be emplaced. Specialization may become more prevalent. Focus typically shifts to gaining market share and improving operations. Talent is often a higher priority at this point in the organization's life cycle—defining the talent needs, acquiring top-tier talent at the lowest possible cost, implementing robust performance management practices, training and developing people, planning for a bench strength of successors, and so on. Organizations at this phase are well-advised to keep their eyes on the prize: delivering on their promise to their customers and markets, and not become so enamored with process that they become overly-bureaucratic and cumbersome.

- ★ **Maturity** – At some point, the organization will be pretty well "grown up." It will have established products/services, a steady stream of customers, and its processes will be well-proven. Businesses in the maturity phase tend to focus on incremental growth, cost effectiveness, efficiency, and operational excellence. Businesses in this stage of development run the risk of becoming overly bureaucratic, more inwardly focused, dependent on proven products/services (rather than on discovering/developing new, innovative ones), and becoming less relevant to their customers' needs and the evolving demands of their markets. Think of the classic buggy whip story–wherein the market for buggy whips (which were used to drive horses that pulled wagons and carriages) evaporated with when their product became obsolete at the introduction of the automobile.

- ★ **Decline** - At some point, companies face decline. The reasons are myriad, but regardless of the reasons, sales become stagnant/begin to fall, and profit margins begin to shrink. At this stage of the game, divestment of assets will become part of the conversation, debt levels may rise in order to shore up the financials, the management team and their practices may become stagnant, and discussions about whether to save or sell the business may arise.

So, why is this relevant to thriving & surviving?

There are great opportunities and challenges in every phase of this life cycle. Each phase has the potential to be a great job, or even career experience. As the organization evolves through the phases the expectations, culture, and work expectations evolve also. In order to thrive & survive over time, you need to be aware of where the winds are blowing and how that is impacting your role, and the people, processes, and products/services around you.

For example, let's assume you join a brand-new startup. At first things are great! It's a high risk/high reward situation, fast-paced, and full of passion and new ideas. You've got your hands in every pot and have relatively free rein to make an impact. Things are going well for you *and* the company. Sales are growing. Market share is growing. New clients are clamoring for more. The demand for consistent, high-quality goods at a competitive price begins to grow.

To achieve these needs, focus shifts from the new, "disruptive" stuff you love, to building SOPs, documenting processes, emplacing quality and other controls, and so forth. All of these are necessary and good things to help the company evolve.

The only problem? This isn't what you want to be doing, and you find your enthusiasm waning for the job you once found stimulating. Now what? Well, you must take a hard look at the situation and yourself. Can you do what needs to be done? Do you even want to? Does the organization see you as a fit for these new needs, or does it only see you as a successful, value-adding contributor in the prior situation?

If answers to these questions are positive, great! Keep doing what you're doing, adjusting to the evolving circumstance, building new capabilities and relationships, and going with the flow!

If not, however, you're going to have to do some soul searching to define your next steps. Are you willing and able to adjust your preferences and develop your capabilities? Can the organization's perception of you expand to see you in a new light—one that causes them to want and need you on the team in the future? What are your alternatives to this job? Do you have a network to leverage for new opportunities? What are the pragmatic realities of your situation? Do you need to suck it up for a while to keep the income or benefits for you and your family? If so, how long? What is your plan to begin the

SECTION 3: THRIVING & SURVIVING

transition process to a new gig? There are many questions that you'll need to ask and understand. There are many things to consider. If you find yourself in this position, remember–thriving & surviving in the long run doesn't mean just sticking it out in a bad situation. It means making tough decisions and taking actions that put you in the best possible position to achieve success, as YOU define it!

BILL STORY

"Evolution, Revolution, Thriving & Surviving."

My last corporate gig was leading global talent management for a $3B+ consumer goods manufacturing company. It was mature. The customer base was solid. Products were established. SOPs were in place. Growth was generally incremental and there was great focus on operational excellence and cost effectiveness. We were evolving the global talent management strategy and practices. Everything was going along as one might expect. Then a new idea arose, a potentially game-changing approach to the manufacturing process that could potentially change the industry. In terms of the organizational life cycle, we had a startup right in our midst! To thrive & survive in my role, I had to flex in multiple directions. I had to support the core, mature business in the way it needed, and at the same time I had to adopt startup practices in support of this new and exciting business potential. I considered the situation, reflecting on how I prefer to work, my capabilities, and the practical realities of the situation. I knew the load was too large to handle alone. I knew I had a small but capable team that had some bandwidth. I decided that I would approach this by delegating more of the existing work for the mature portions of the business where I could, and I would focus more of my time and attention to partnering with

> *this "internal startup." It worked! The legacy business all got completed on time and to standard, and the internal startup received appropriate support to move forward.*

Beyond the typical organizational life cycle, there are many influences and events that shape structure and culture – and each of these can impact your ability to thrive & survive.

Business, like life, is never static. It is always changing. Sometimes, the change is gradual and nearly imperceptible (like water eroding rock). Other times, it is immediate and obvious (like a hurricane destroying petroleum refineries on the eastern seaboard). Sometimes it can be anticipated (your competition will ALWAYS seek ways to grow their business). Other times, it comes seemingly out of the blue (unexpected political shifts strangle supply chains).

Some of these influencers and events include:

- ★ *Market force changes* – Changing customer needs, new market complexities, mergers/acquisitions (with you and/or your competitors), supply chain changes etc.
- ★ *Technology Advancements* – Innovations in technology that help optimize your processes, products/services, or that make your product/service obsolete, etc.
- ★ *Ideological, Psychological, Social, Moral, Ethical changes* – Greater focus on environment, sustainability, social causes, different social norms in different cultures/nations, etc.
- ★ *Political Change* – Impact of new elections or political upheaval/conflict in various parts of the world where business is conducted, etc.
- ★ *Legislative/Regulatory Change* – Changes due to newly adopted (or recently rescinded) laws and regulations that impact (positively or negatively) your business

★ *Weather / Natural Events* – Hurricanes, tornadoes, floods, volcanos, pandemics, etc.

These events and others can have a material impact on business. Thriving & surviving in the face of these takes agility, ability, and a real spirit of teamwork to work with others to overcome the challenges and come out as positively as possible on the other side.

> ## *BILL STORY*
>
> ### *"Hurricanes and Refineries."*
>
> *During my tenure as head of global talent management for a major global consumer goods manufacturer, the US mid-Atlantic coast was struck by a hurricane. Its impact destroyed or disabled numerous petroleum refineries and related facilities, creating a huge gap in the supply of the raw materials required to make our products (mostly plastic bottles).*
>
> *Everyone in the supply chain had certain levels of contingency plans in place, but no one could have anticipated (nor afforded) the magnitude of damage this hurricane unleashed. We found ourselves in a tight spot, unable to obtain what we needed to make the products we committed to our customers. This was an uncontrollable event that had a material impact on our business, and on all businesses that depended on the supply of petroleum products. Our procurement team went into overdrive, developing creative solutions that mitigated the impact as much as humanly possible. A large part of their success was due to the positive personal relationships built with people across companies, industries and markets over time. For sure, the business suffered, but the yeoman's work by dedicated people reduced the impact as much as possible.*

BILL STORY

"Plastic Bottles."

Pollution has long been a concern across the globe. Recycling plastics has been one of the key focus concerns for years. The interest and focus in this regard have continued to grow. I saw firsthand how this concern changed one company. The major global consumer goods manufacturer I worked for was a leading producer of plastic bottles and containers globally. It always had a focus on recyclability of their products, but over the years, that focus grew to become a central part of the business, including the creation of a sustainability team that looked at several related aspects. From collection of used bottles, to recycling practices, to exploring how to maximize use of recycled materials, this group attended to important topics that without public interest, might not have otherwise received such diligent focus.

BILL STORY

"No Matter Your Title or Tenure, Shit Happens."

One of my clients was a retired US Army O6 with a stellar military career and fantastic record of success in the civilian world. A senior leader with a for-profit, privately held company providing a variety of services across a broad portfolio of industries, he was responsible for the profit and loss of three different service lines. The challenge he faced was that he reported to the business president (who had a reputation as a sub-par leader). That president reported to the CEO and the board of directors.

My client shared a story that is, unfortunately, all too

common for both military veterans and civilians alike. While preparing their annual strategic plan, revenue and profit targets became a contentious point of discussion. The president demanded targets that were unrealistic. They weren't stretch goals meant to incent better performance; they were simply not achievable. My client proposed somewhat smaller (but infinitely more realistic) targets and provided logical, well-considered reasons for them. To be clear, these goals were not easy – but they were at least in the realm of reason. His peers agreed. The president ignored the recommendation and required the higher targets. The CEO and the board, while skeptical, wanted to support their president and approved his unrealistic targets.

Throughout the year, business results consistently fell short of those unrealistic goals, landing roughly where my client had advised. At all recurring business reviews, my client again proposed revising the targets, but despite all evidence, the president stuck with his unachievable goals, and the CEO continued to agree.

As the year came to a close, it was clear that the targets were not going to be met. The CEO called in the senior team. At this meeting the CEO took a different tact. He asked what the hell needed to change. He emphatically implored all participants (including my client) to take off the gloves and be totally honest and transparent about what went wrong and how to fix it. Now, this kind of situation can be tricky. If the reality is that the president is not good, everyone needed to be very careful in how that "honest and transparent" dialogue unfolded if they intended to keep their jobs. A couple folks dipped their toes in that pool, and their comments were reasonably well received. My client joined the fray, professionally and clearly addressing the elephant in the room – this problem happened because the president was not good. Addressing the real issue directly changed the entire course of events.

> *The meeting closed soon after. My client was called to the CEO's office, where they shared further detailed conversation. The CEO acknowledged that the president was not exactly stellar, but out of the blue he also commented that my client was "too military." My client was stunned. "Too military? WTF? He was asked to be "honest and transparent" - and he had been. (To be clear, he is an exceptionally articulate, professional, poised leader who at this point had nearly a decade of success as a civilian executive.) They discussed a variety of go-forward options. When the meeting ended, the CEO told my client he appreciated his candor, that he had to consider next steps, and that they'd reconnect in a couple weeks.*
>
> *A couple weeks later, the CEO invited my client back to his office. He announced that he had considered his options and decided to reorganize the company, eliminating my client's position. (This is a tactic that often happens when companies are trying to oust someone—I've seen it too many times to count.)*
>
> *So, what's the point of this long story? How does it relate to thriving & surviving?*
>
> *Shit happens. No matter your capability, your experience, your style, your leadership, your professionalism, your dedication, or anything else, there are times when uncontrollable, nonsensical factors carry the day. You'll never be able to perfectly read the tea leaves, but be aware of your surroundings. Be mindful that you don't know what you don't know. Don't live in fear of the negative potential, but always have a PACE plan in case the unexpected arises.*

Complexity is the norm.

But for a very few uniformed services, (police, fire, emergency services) the civilian operating environment is very different than the

SECTION 3: THRIVING & SURVIVING

military. Some of the differences are obvious—combat is not part of work life. Most jobs do not require life or death decision-making, nor do they involve confronting armed enemies.

There is no "deployed" life versus "garrison" life.

All that said, be wary not to underestimate the complexity and rigor of the civilian workplace. There are many plates spinning all the time, each requiring attention to ensure that they keep spinning atop their spindly poles.

One of the more subtle but impactful differences is that in the civilian workplace, businesses are *always* on production. As we noted in the LANDING section, the common military cycle of "train, deploy, refit, and repeat" doesn't exist in the civilian world. To effectively thrive & survive in the long run, you need to recognize this difference, as well as its impact. It can be a grind. Maybe not the same grind as the gig pit at jump school, or the same grind as a tough training evolution, but a never ending, all-consuming grind that comes from unrelenting expectations for results day in, day out, week after week, month after month, and year after year. If you're not cognizant of how the grind is impacting you and your ability to perform well today and prepare well for your future, you are harming your ability to thrive & survive. Recognize the difference. Leverage your experience in a way that is relevant to the situation. Adapt, improvise, and overcome.

BILL STORY

"Yesterday's Solution to Today's Reality."

Years ago, we had an opening for a shift supervisor at a manufacturing plant. This plant was in a rural, sparsely populated area where finding great talent was a notable challenge. To our surprise, we had a young USMC veteran apply. He had just moved to the area to be closer to his wife's family. The plant manager interviewed and was impressed with this young USMC veteran candidate. He asked me to chat with the young man and get back with him. I was impressed. This was a capable, appropriately educated, mature-beyond-his-years candidate. I was also a bit concerned that the line team members and the broader plant team were not ready for his well-developed small team leadership skills. You see, this was not exactly a high-performing plant, and many of the supervisors had been there for decades. The plant manager was trying diligently to improve things, and he thought this USMC veteran might just be a great add to make good things happen. I advised the plant manager of my positive and negative impressions, cautioning him that if he hired this young veteran, he needed to prepare his immediate boss (the operations manager), his peer supervisors, and the team. The plant manager agreed. A change was needed, and the small team leadership this veteran brought might just be the ticket.

The plant manager hired this veteran; coordinated the onboarding with his direct boss – the operations manager to set clear goals, prepared a robust introduction to the line team, and worked hard to set the stage for success. Indeed, the new supervisor hit the ground running. He had a solid "get to know each other" session with his new team. He shared his goals. He listened to his team's goals, aspirations, ideas, and concerns. Things started off well. When production misses or quality issues arose, he led AARs, asked for ideas, and implemented the ones with merit. Production and quality metrics were on the rise. Team attendance improved. Discord and noise amongst teammates quieted. The operations manager took note. He was impressed, and so he began providing this new supervisor opportunity to share his winning ideas with his peer supervisors. While some peers loved it, others emphatically did not. The new guy was showing them up. He was doing it better and faster than they were. In short order, the air got tense. These peer supervisors went to the operations manager to complain. The operations manager was now faced with a dilemma. On the one hand, he had several long tenured, average/below average performing supervisors that were pissed. On the other, he had a high performing newbie, who was doing everything that needed to be done, and very well at that! All this against the backdrop of an employment market that made finding high quality new employees and supervisors a very tough task. The manager decided to advise the new supervisor to "dial it back a bit." He noted that most folks here "strive for mediocrity;" to be just good enough not to get in trouble, but not to work any harder than necessary. He advised the new supervisor of the difficulties obtaining new talent, reminding him that he had been brought onboard to help drive change.

As you might imagine, the young USMC veteran supervisor was shocked. "Strive for mediocrity?" Really? How in the hell is that a strategy for success? In a relatively short period of time, and after multiple conversations, he decided that this was simply not the place for him. He left. We could argue all day about the various alternative solutions that the players might have chosen to achieve a better outcome, but the fact of the matter is that for this young, capable USMC veteran, thriving & surviving meant picking your battles and deploying your talents in places that fit for you. Moral of the story? There are complexities in every organization. Some may be apparent. Some may be obscure. If you find yourself in a similar situation, understand how you define success and assess your situation thoroughly. Decide if the situation aligns. If so, keep going. Give it your all and make a positive impact! If not, get into transition mode and begin a smart journey to your next success.

Risks are very different, but risk management is the name of the game, no matter your industry, function or job.

Identifying, managing, and mitigating risk is a large part of effective leadership and management in the military. Afterall, precious lives, expensive equipment and potentially even national security interests hang in the balance. Most civilian companies don't share these same risks, but rest assured identifying, managing, and mitigating risk is an inherent part of their business. Some may have robust risk management processes, while others may approach the topic in a less sophisticated way.

Understanding risk, its impact, and how it is handled in your new industry, company, job can be a huge benefit to your ability to thrive & survive. As military veterans, your experience and perspective may be a great asset that, if applied well, can positively influence your thriving & surviving success.

So, what does "applied well" exactly mean in this context? It means being aware of your situation: the gaps, challenges, opportunities, and nuances. It means understanding the players and their interests, priorities, risk tolerance, and agendas. It means leveraging your experience to assess all this and create solutions that mitigate risk to reasonable, tolerable levels, and then taking action within the scope of your role (or maybe a bit further) to bring those solutions to life. Doing this work well can be a strong, positive contributor to thriving & surviving today and tomorrow.

> ### *BILL STORY*
>
> *"Risk Management."*
>
> *The topic of training and developing current employees came up during a budget discussion. The purpose of the proposed training was to shore up employee skills so that production,*

> *productivity, and quality problems were reduced or eliminated. The CFO (Chief Financial Officer), doing his diligence to ensure costs are always reduced as low as possible, said "This is going to cost a ton of money! What happens when we train people and they leave? Not only have we lost the money, but we'll also have to spend more money to replace the people that left, and spend even more money to train the new people!" His boss, the CEO (Chief Executive Officer) responded, "What if we don't train them and they stay? The costs of production, productivity and quality problems will never improve!"*

Never underestimate what you don't know.

Thriving & surviving is somewhat more art than science. No matter your experience, education, network, relationships, or anything else, there's simply no way for you to know everything that's going on or understand what all the factors are that are influencing things behind the scenes.

Do your level best to know and experience as much as possible as deeply and broadly as you can. Diligently build and nurture a robust network of people who are relevant to your current situation and potentially value-adding to your future.

But also get comfortable knowing that you'll never know everything, and that those unknowns can have real impact.

As a military veteran, you likely have experience in fluid, fast paced environments chock full of unknowns. Of course, you didn't do this in a vacuum. The military's rigorous training and robust SOPs can't cover every possibility or contingency, but they provide a great framework from which you can adjust when the unknowns rear up.

The civilian work world generally is not as structured as the military, however. Your organization likely won't have robust, integrated training that comes anywhere close to the military's. Do yourself a favor: take whatever steps make sense to you to get good at "seeing around corners" and use this skillset to help you deal with a world of gray, filled with unknowns.

THRIVING & SURVIVING is about LEVERAGING People, Processes and Products/Services relevant to you and your job, for Individual and Organizational Success today and tomorrow.

The Three Ps - *People, Process, and Product/Service* in **THRIVING & SURVIVING**

The "People, Process, Product/Service" model we've used throughout this book has great relevance here. The added dynamic is the shifting sands of time. As we've defined them, LANDING focuses on your first 30 days or so. INTEGRATING is generally your first 180 days. THRIVING & SURVIVING, however, is evergreen. It encompasses the rest of your time in a job, with an organization, and in the workforce overall. Many variables and innumerable change possibilities will impact you, your role, and your overall situation in ways positive and negative, large and small. Sometimes subtly. Sometimes dramatically.

THE 3P MODEL APPLIES AS YOU PROGRESS OVER TIME

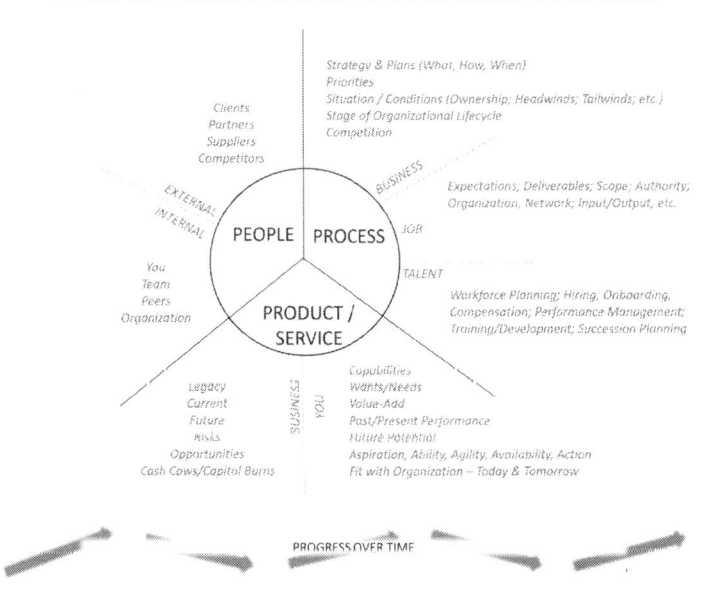

Strategy & Plans (What, How, When)
Priorities
Situation / Conditions (Ownership; Headwinds; Tailwinds; etc.)
Stage of Organizational Lifecycle
Competition

Clients
Partners
Suppliers
Competitors

EXTERNAL / INTERNAL

BUSINESS

PEOPLE | PROCESS

JOB

Expectations; Deliverables; Scope; Authority;
Organization; Network; Input/Output; etc.

You
Team
Peers
Organization

PRODUCT / SERVICE

TALENT

Workforce Planning; Hiring; Onboarding;
Compensation; Performance Management;
Training/Development; Succession Planning

BUSINESS / YOU

Legacy
Current
Future
Risks
Opportunities
Cash Cows/Capital Burns

Capabilities
Wants/Needs
Value-Add
Past/Present Performance
Future Potential
Aspiration, Ability, Agility, Availability, Action
Fit with Organization – Today & Tomorrow

PROGRESS OVER TIME

We will dive deep into each area providing insights that help you gain awareness of common considerations to:

- ★ Successfully thrive & survive in the ever-changing work world.
- ★ Be a value-adding member of the organization.
- ★ Ensure you are taking care of yourself and your career.

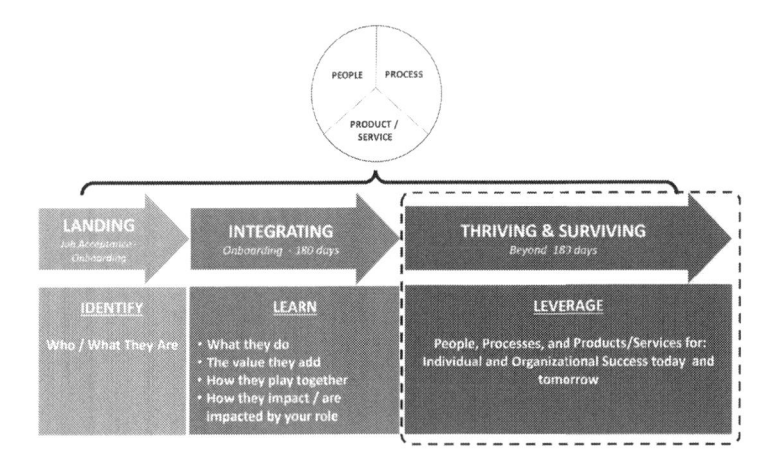

LANDING
Job Acceptance
Onboarding

INTEGRATING
Onboarding - 180 days

THRIVING & SURVIVING
Beyond 180 days

IDENTIFY
Who / What They Are

LEARN
- What they do
- The value they add
- How they play together
- How they impact / are impacted by your role

LEVERAGE
People, Processes, and Products/Services for:
Individual and Organizational Success today and tomorrow

People

Introduction

People really are the heart of it all. Whether internal or external, without people there is nothing. No customers. No teammates. No partners. No colleagues. No suppliers. And so on.

When you landed, you learned who some of the various people in your new world are.

As you integrated, you gained some initial understanding of some of these folks and met even more people.

To thrive & survive, you need to continue to broaden and deepen your understanding not only of the people, but also how you build and leverage relationships that help you, them, and the organization succeed.

SECTION 3: THRIVING & SURVIVING 197

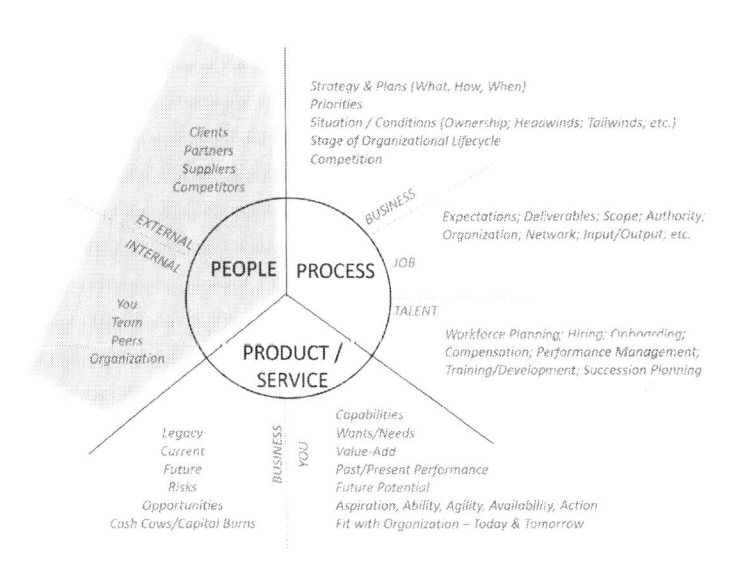

THE 3P MODEL – PEOPLE

Strategy & Plans (What, How, When)
Priorities
Situation / Conditions (Ownership; Headwinds; Tailwinds, etc.)
Stage of Organizational Lifecycle
Competition

Clients
Partners
Suppliers
Competitors

BUSINESS

Expectations; Deliverables; Scope; Authority;
Organization; Network; Input/Output; etc.

EXTERNAL
INTERNAL
PEOPLE | PROCESS

JOB

TALENT

You
Team
Peers
Organization

PRODUCT / SERVICE

Workforce Planning; Hiring; Onboarding;
Compensation; Performance Management;
Training/Development; Succession Planning

Capabilities
Wants/Needs
Value-Add
Past/Present Performance
Future Potential
Aspiration, Ability, Agility, Availability, Action
Fit with Organization – Today & Tomorrow

Legacy
Current
Future
Risks
Opportunities
Cash Cows/Capital Burns

BUSINESS | YOU

General *People* Insights When THRIVING & SURVIVING

"Stakeholders" will always be part of your journey to thrive & survive.

As we mentioned in the LANDING and INTEGRATING sections, stakeholders are the people you/your organization need and depend on. Identifying who they are and learning as much as possible about their interests, timelines, and expectations, as well as the challenges they face and the value and opportunities they bring, sets an important foundation.

Leveraging all this information over time, building solid relationships, staying abreast of changing conditions, and welcoming new stakeholders as they appear is all important to thriving & surviving in the long run.

So, how do we go about making this happen? By balancing skill, diplomacy, and leadership!

- ★ Leverage the networking lessons you learned when in career transition/job search

    - ☆ Know who you are and what you bring to the party.
    - ☆ Have a purpose.
    - ☆ Have an interesting pitch that compels the other parties to want to hear more.
    - ☆ Ask your ask.
    - ☆ Offer to help them – recognize their wants/needs, and help as best you're able.
    - ☆ Thank them!
    - ☆ Follow up. Stay in contact, and fulfill your commitments.

- ★ W.A.I.T. – Great, value-adding relationships exist where people converse effectively. Oftentimes that means listening more than talking, which can be hard, especially in fast-paced, pressure filled work environments. After all, we want to ensure others hear what we have to say, and be sure they clearly understand us. So, we sometimes talk more than we listen. This may not be your best bet when attempting to build and maintain value-adding relationships with stakeholders who have real potential impact on your ability to thrive & survive. To help successfully do so, check yourself. Ask yourself, **W**hy **A**m **I T**alking (W.A.I.T.)? If you're babbling on just to hear yourself speak, or restating yourself for added effect, maybe it's time to quiet down a bit and try engaging your ears rather than your mouth. Let the other party speak, share their perspective, or offer their thoughts. You'll be glad you did.
- ★ Be respectful of their position, acknowledge their perspective, and build bridges between their needs and yours.

- ★ Involve common connections that can help each of you. Everyone loves a "win-win" outcome!
- ★ Think beyond the moment. Keep the future in mind, consider how today's actions will impact tomorrow, and take actions that will positively impact both.

Pay attention to who the "Silverback Gorillas" and "Ambitious Chimps" are.

Everyone you'll encounter in the civilian work world will have different levels of power, influence, sway, impact, motivation etc.

Some will truly be the heavy hitters, the true alpha "Silverback Gorillas." Either by position, personality, charisma, technical expertise, broad/deep network connections, formal or informal influence or credibility, or other, these are the folks who can legitimately make things happen. They are the ones with whom you want to build and maintain your best relationships, because they are the ones that are most likely to influence your ability to thrive & survive.

Be mindful of the "Ambitious Chimps," however. These are folks with grand aspirations who have yet to grow into truly impactful positions. They are not necessarily bad people, nor are they useless. In fact, their drive for something more can be of great value to your efforts to thrive & survive. On the other hand, their ambition could be so strong/focused as to cause them to try to leverage you towards their success, without regard for you or your career. As you build and develop relationships with your stakeholders, keep your eyes open and your thoughts clear.

Detailed *People* Insights When THRIVING & SURVIVING

Consistent with our LANDING and INTEGRATING sections, we address the same populations of people here, focusing on thoughts to help you LEVERAGE each in a positive manner that helps you thrive & survive in the long run.

- ★ **Internal** – This includes **you**, **your team**, **peers**, and **other organizational members** that may influence or impact you on your path to success.
- ★ **External** – This includes **clients**, **partners**, **suppliers**, and **competitors**.

Let's start internally.

- ★ **You** - While self-understanding was important to landing and integrating well, it becomes even more important as you attempt to thrive & survive over time. As we've mentioned earlier, no one cares more about your career than you do, and continuing as your own Chief Marketing Officer will always be value-adding to your career and life journeys.

  To do this successfully, you need to have a solid handle on who you are, what you bring to the party, and how you define success.

  You need to be aware of your **capabilities** and your **wants** versus **needs**, assessing both your **past and present performance** as well as your future **potential and value-add**. You need to assess your **aspirations** for the future, how your **abilities** line up with future opportunities, and how **agile** you can be in your ability to change with ever-evolving business conditions. Consider your **availability** to take on something new, your bias towards **action** (or the absence of it), and think—above all—about how well you **fit** with the organization – both **today and tomorrow**.

  This understanding will evolve over time as you gain experience and expertise, but it won't magically appear. You must make a dedicated decision and take definitive action to making self-awareness and understanding an everyday part of life.

Without this awareness and understanding, you may find yourself existing in a role that isn't quite a fit. You may find yourself constantly overtaxed with work that in no way fits your abilities or preferences. You may be thoroughly unsatisfied, unhappy, and unproductive, with little idea why. You may find yourself constantly chomping at the bit, eagerly awaiting the opportunity to really run and bring all your skills, capabilities, and experience to bear and make a great impact! Alternatively, you might also find yourself thoroughly satisfied in the role and happy with your daily duties, but not sure why! Without some level of self-awareness, the chance of understanding why it is working so well is pretty low. Further, your ability to replicate this success in the future becomes quite random.

Knowing yourself is a powerful advantage to understanding where you are professionally. It is a great launchpad for your ability to thrive & survive in the long run of your career and life journeys.

So, how does this happen? How do you gain understanding and self-awareness?

On one hand, you could depend on the company to help you. If your employer offers training, learning, assessments, or other leadership/professional development resources, they may be helpful. Unfortunately, not every company makes such wise investments.

In the end, depending solely on the company for your self-awareness / understanding is a fool's game. Understanding yourself ultimately depends on you, and the responsibility to make this happen falls upon your shoulders.

KNOWING "YOU" TO THRIVE & SURVIVE

Make time to reflect on....

> What's really important to your life and career journeys.
>
> How your current situation aligns with what's important.
>
> Where you want to be in the long run (life and career).
>
> How your current situation is helping you get there.
>
> What your plan is to better align with what's important and to get you from where you are today to where you want to be.

Talk with trusted colleagues, family, or friends to help you. Consider engaging with a coach/advisor who has relevant expertise to help guide you to self-discovery and greater self-awareness. Leverage these folks to help you thrive & survive.

You are always in a much more powerful position to thrive & survive if you know who you are, what you bring to the party, how you define success, where you are, where you're going, and how you plan to get there. Purpose and direction rule the day, rather than wondering about it all and hoping the winds of change might randomly blow you towards some great place.

BILL STORY

"Know Thyself."

I was in the early stages of a coaching engagement with a senior executive in a Fortune 500 company. On one occasion we were sitting in a bar in San Francisco, having a drink and catching up on things. I could tell something was up.

This gentleman had a solid career and a track record of success. He was technically competent, had strong, positive relationships with his teams, peers, clients, and vendors. He had a great family life. By all accounts, he was a success!

But something was missing. He had a persistent sense that there was something else he should be doing; something with a higher purpose. As our conversation continued, he shared with me that one of his family members had special needs. She was well cared for, loved by her family, and thriving to the extent of her abilities.

Over the years, while my client had grown professionally, he had also grown personally. His experience with this special family member planted a seed of desire to help others in the special-needs community. At first, he simply ignored the nudge. He focused on helping his special family member and on extending his professional career. But the feeling wouldn't go away; in fact, it only grew over time. He wasn't sure what to do with it. The satisfaction he gained from his job began to decline, despite the fact that he knew he was doing good work, making an impact, and reaping great financial rewards.

I asked him what he would do if he wasn't doing his current job. He said, "I'd be helping folks with special needs live their best lives." I asked, "What's keeping you from doing that?" He studied his martini and finally said, "Nothing, I guess. Financially, I'm set. My family is supportive. I guess I'm just not sure where to start, and leaving the security of a successful career is a bit scary."

This started a series of discussions and actions to help him clarify what he might best do to fulfill the need. Eventually, he parted ways with his corporate career and began working in a fulfilling capacity helping special needs folks live their best life. This was the best thing he could have possibly

> *done for himself, as it engaged both his passion and sense of purpose, and breathed new life into his career.*

If you find yourself in a job, role, or career feeling the yearn for something different, pay attention. Don't be rash, but think it through, consider your situation, discover your options, then make decisions that will help you thrive, survive, and live your best life – whatever that means to you.

★ **Your Team** – Thriving & surviving in the long term is rarely a solo endeavor. While some of us may be a bit more introverted, and some jobs may be more individual contributor than people leader, we all are part of some type of team. In the LANDING section, we used the sports example of wrestling, where competitors are on the mat alone, but their points go to the team. In the INTEGRATING section, we noted that no one fights alone - reinforcing that military truth that no matter your job, the organization, or the mission, we are all part of a team.

The sense of team in the civilian work world often looks quite different than it does in the military. Yes, teams exist in the civilian world, and they are important, but things are different. Out here, you are much more on your own. "Me" overtakes "We." Your success is yours to make. That said, success rarely comes to those who don't know, understand, respect, regard, and play well with team members.

As with sports, there are different positions team players may fill in the civilian workplace. These positions vary by organization, just as they do by sport. Their duties vary. The qualifications for success vary. For example: on an American football team, tackles have critical roles. They are key cogs in both offensive and defensive strategy and plays. These teammates tend to be big - physically large, exceptionally strong, and able to provide explosive strength as they perform their duties. They hardly ever touch the ball. Only in rare circumstances do they score any points; their job is to shape the playing field and enable others. Kickers are also critical members of the team, and sports history is replete with examples of tight games that were won by a last-minute, well-executed kick. A kicker's focused ability, precision, consistency under pressure, high visibility, and performance under exacting conditions are unique. Clearly, tackles and kickers are both important parts of the team. Just as clearly, though, they provide unique value, and are rarely interchangeable.

In business you will find team members playing a variety of roles. Some are defined by the job: the operator, the supervisor, the accountant, the IT specialist, your HR partner, and so on. Beyond the technical deliverables of each team member's position, people bring other, less tangible qualities to the team that are just as important. Understanding these less tangible team member roles, and who's offering what can be an important asset as you attempt to thrive & survive. Some of these roles include:

TEAM MEMBER ROLES

Role	Value
Sounding Boards	A set of ears with whom you can share your thoughts.
Blind Faithful	Offer a mirror/echo chamber of your every thought.
Naysayers/Devil's Advocates	Provide critical insight and perspective that may help you sharpen your focus or bring pragmatism to your passion.
Technical Experts	Provide knowledge in areas with which you may not be so familiar.
Sage Purveyors of Wisdom	Provide broader, deeper insights based on relevant experience.
Fresh Eyes	New players with bright, eager outlooks and insight.

Sounding Boards – These are the people with whom you can share thoughts and bounce ideas. They add value by letting you bring your thoughts to life, and can provide solid, respectful perspective that may reinforce, refine, or refute your ideas.

Blind Faithful – These folks are the mirrors and echo-chambers for others' ideas. While simply mirroring others can lead to the risk of group-think, these folks can also be great, positive teammates during times of uncertainty and stress, when the last thing you need is one more person pointing out just how wrong you are.

Naysayers/Devil's Advocates – These teammates provide critical insight and perspective that can help sharpen your focus and improve things for you and the team. On the other hand, these folks can be a real pain in the ass. If their intent and behavior shift from being helpful to simply being a thorn in your side for the sake of being a thorn in your side, then you'll need to be mindful of how you engage with them and how you manage the relationship. Listen to the Naysayers' point of view, but don't let them shape your definition of what is in the realm of possible.

Technical Experts – These folks know the technical bits of their jobs in and out. Their abilities in areas next to but different than yours can make all the difference in the team's success. They provide value as ideas emerge, when plans are being developed, as business is being conducted, and after the fact. Their technical insights can provide immense help that precludes failure, overcomes challenges, and/or opens doors to otherwise unseen opportunities.

Sage Purveyors of Wisdom – These team members are the ones who have "been there, done that." They provide broader, deeper insights based on relevant experience. They

SECTION 3: THRIVING & SURVIVING 207

may have been in the company or industry for some period of time, or they may have come from entirely different backgrounds. Either way, do yourself a favor and listen to them. Consider their input and perspective. They quite likely have faced what you're facing and can be great assets in your journey to thrive & survive. However, just because they have great insight doesn't mean that you should let them stand in the way of innovation just because "this is the way it's always been done."

Fresh New Players – These are the teammates who are newer to the field or industry in which the team is operating. They bring bright eyes, eager outlooks, and fresh insight that can add immensely to the team. Welcome them. Listen to them. Consider their perspective. You just might find you, your team, and your future better off for having done so!

To thrive & survive in the long run, you need to identify, learn, and leverage your team members to bring out the best in them, and to benefit from the value they bring!

★ **Peers** - Peers can make or break your thriving & surviving success. As described previously, peers are other folks in roles at a similar level/scope to you. They may come from any of the typical functional areas (operations, finance, engineering, sales, IT, HR, legal, etc.). They may be folks with your same role in a different division/department of the same organization (think plant managers of the widget and wahtzit divisions).

All of your peers will have their own priorities, motivators, agendas, relationships, egos, and abilities. Some will be great colleagues, offering you support, encouragement, insights, information, resources, and other valuable assets that help you succeed. Others will simply coexist in your orbit; they will neither help nor hinder you. Others still will be thorns in your side. For whatever reasons, they will create drama, build obstacles, and otherwise intentionally get in between you and success.

As you travel your career journey, thriving & surviving to the best of your ability, take note of your peer group.

★ Some of your peers may be little more than part of the landscape, your paths never crossing and opportunities to work together nonexistent. Be open to chance encounters with them; they may just be the connection you never knew you needed!
★ Recognize that some peers will be thorns in your side. Understand what they are doing. Do your job well. Don't let their shenanigans distract you. Don't let them win.
★ Rest assured that the vast majority of your peers are great people who want to win and are more than willing to help you win also! Engage with them. Help them succeed. Let them help you thrive & survive!
★ Bear in mind that as time goes by and people and positions evolve, today's peers may be your future boss, or you may be their boss.
★ Note that your peers are part of your network. Develop the best relationships possible. Beyond your current work connection, you may both benefit from a positive relationship in the long run.

BILL STORY

"Peers."

On the upside, I've been blessed with many great, positive, supportive peers who understand that it is better to be a "go-giver" than a "go-getter." They've been there for me in times good and bad, and given me valuable, honest feedback in the true spirit of improvement. They partnered easily and helped create innumerable successes. Their primary assignments may have been focused on different specific deliverables, but they understood that no one succeeds alone and that being a great partner benefits everyone involved.

On the downside, though, I've also experienced a few peers who simply made things hell.

One was long-time personal friends with the boss, and while being technically capable, he depended on the relationship with the boss for seemingly everything. As my career grew, my wins accumulated, and my relationship with the boss developed, this gentleman became quite jealous and insecure. This led to him making several overt and covert attempts to undermine me. From simple smack-talk at the water cooler to working with other team members to contravene my plans, this gent was a master at passive-aggressive resistance. It got so bad that at one large business meeting, where our boss made some congratulatory remarks about my work to his C-suite counterparts, my nemesis said "Well, I guess I'm not the favorite anymore." What an unfortunately immature commentary from a person in a notable position of authority.

Another was so focused on moving up the corporate ladder that he would do anything necessary to clear out anyone who even appeared to be competition. This person was reasonably competent in his area of expertise, but he was more-so highly skilled in the art of self-promotion – the classic brown-noser. His focus on advancement far outpaced his focus on doing the right thing. He was exceptionally adept at sniffing out opportunities to submarine colleagues, ingratiating himself with senior leaders and doing whatever was necessary to make himself look good – no matter the collateral damage to peers or anyone else. Did he ascend to reasonably senior positions? Yes, he did. Did he have ardent followers? Yes, he had a handful of followers that were more than happy to ride his coat tails, no matter what that might have meant to the good of the order (or their personal integrity). BUT...people at the very top saw through him and his antics. There was no way he'd ever be selected for the top job – which was the object of his desire.

Another had been promoted far above her capability and was too proud to admit she was in over her head or receive well-intended assistance. She was insecure, acidic, and argumentative with damn near everyone. When she was tasked with new, challenging deliverables, rather than reaching out to her peers who had experience and expertise in these areas, she went off on her own, googled a few things, and came up with her own way forward. There was no doubt she worked hard or that she was trying her best to deliver, but she made life for herself and her peers far more difficult than it needed to be. As an example, at one point the company was updating our succession planning process. I was the global lead responsible for designing and emplacing an integrated strategy and practices across all divisions, functions, and countries. My peers were all on board to work together and make this a great success—all except one. She attended meetings and either failed to engage, or put up every roadblock possible to hinder progress and success. Meanwhile, she was burning the midnight oil coming up with her own approach. We all knew what she was doing, and I advised the appropriate leaders. The rest of us moved ahead together. When show time came and each division, function, and country leader had to present their succession plans, they all looked the same—except one. Needless to say, that didn't go well, and my peer was invited to assume a very different role not too long after.

★ **Organization** – As we described in the LANDING and INTEGRATING sections, there will always be some number of other folks in the organization with whom you need to interact to make progress, knock down doors, etc. Some of these you may only have infrequent contact with. Some may have seemingly zero relevance to you, your job, or career.

When you were in job search/career transition, it was important to build and nurture a broad, deep network. When you landed and were integrating, building and nurturing remained a value-adding activity. As you focus on thriving & surviving in the long run of your career and life journeys, growing and developing a robust network is even more important. Remember, thriving & surviving is about executing well today and preparing for your future. Knowing people across the organization (and more broadly, your industry and/or career field), building a strong network, and leveraging it for long term success is a powerful resource for both current and future success.

Knowing who to call is one thing. Actually knowing that person and having a positive relationship with them makes all the difference, though. It can help with a current time-sensitive project. It can help open doors to new opportunities. It can provide insight to options and solutions to challenging situations that you alone did not consider. And who knows? You may just get promoted, assigned to an entirely new role, division, or function someday. Wouldn't it be great to have some connections before you land?

BILL STORY

"You Build Bridges Before You Need Them."

On one occasion, I was tasked with designing and deploying a global performance management process. Given the size *and scope of the company (~$4B revenue; ~4000 employees in 126 countries) this was no simple task. Harmonizing the business planning process, team and individual goal setting approach, performance feedback cycle, performance feedback models, data security/privacy, integration with compensation practices, and so many other factors made this a notably complex initiative. Success was only going to be achieved with and through people in every business unit, function, country and location. They all knew things that I had no way of knowing. They all brought insight and perspective I'd never be able to gain on my own. They all had relationships that were critical to gaining initial buy-in, enabling effective deployment, and ensuring value-adding execution of the process in their areas.*

For example, the IT lead for Europe had great insight re: European Union employee data privacy requirements. Prior to this project, I had only seen this person's name on an organization chart. We had never met, spoken, or even traded emails. Fortunately, I had the presence of mind to reach out to him in the early project planning phase. His partnership, experience, and professionalism were invaluable to the successful design, launch, and execution of our new performance management process in the EU. Similarly, I connected with our Asia-Pacific HR leader to gain his insight on the cultural implications of a new performance management process. He shared similarly invaluable perspective about how performance management is received in the various Asia-Pacific nations, which helped us design country-specific solutions that were also well-aligned with the overall, global process. Without these great members of the larger organization, my task would have been far more difficult, and the levels of success would have likely been diminished.

SECTION 3: THRIVING & SURVIVING 213

People really are the key to success. Know yourself. Understand your team and your peers. Build and nurture a quality network throughout the organization. Leverage the positive relationships and improve the challenging ones where you can. These efforts will be time well-spent and will always pay long-term dividends.

And now for the external people.

★ **Clients** - Without clients, the people who buy or consume your organization's products and services, you don't have a business. In the LANDING section, we advised simply identifying them. In the INTEGRATING section, we recommended learning about them. When thriving & surviving, leveraging your knowledge about them and building relationships with them are critical to current and long-term business success. Think about it: if you are building and selling a product that no one wants or can't use, you won't be in business long. Client preferences, demands, wants, and needs change over time. Knowing which way the winds of change are blowing is mission critical. You learn this information by building strong relationships and communicating openly.

BILL STORY

"If You Build It, They Will Come – NOT."

Our company designed and produced a new, cutting-edge driveshaft for heavy vehicles. It won awards for the new product, its design, its creative new manufacturing process, and

> *other things. It was lighter, stronger, and possessed everything our customers said they wanted and needed. On paper, it was the ideal solution, but in reality, it flopped. Why? Because this great new driveshaft couldn't be installed in new trucks without a multi-million-dollar redesign of the customers' production line—which, as you might expect, was not going to happen. If we'd had a more robust relationship with our customer and a deeper, broader understanding of their overall situation, we could have made different decisions that were more beneficial to us and our client.*

★ **Partners** - Partners are those people and organizations outside your company with capabilities that you and your company do not have. No individual or organization can possibly possess every conceivable capability that may arise over time. Finding and engaging with partners who cover your blind spots, bring the needed expertise you lack, or otherwise help you move forward to success, is smart. They can be great assets on your career and life journeys to thrive & survive.

Successfully discovering and engaging with great partners starts by first having a clear idea of your goals, capabilities, and gaps. Having these, the next step is to explore relationships with partners who can cover your gaps, add to your capabilities, or bring a mutually beneficial something to the equation. This works best when you've built a strong network of great relationships *before* you are in need. Leveraging partner capabilities and relationships provides great, positive impact on your ability to thrive & survive in the long run.

SECTION 3: THRIVING & SURVIVING

> ### BILL STORY
>
> *"Competitors Here; Partners There."*
>
> *A large manufacturing firm I worked for provided parts to various segments of the automotive industry. Most of these parts were related to power transmission and management. As you might imagine, we had a number of well-established, large, successful competitors (and a number of smaller, newer ones too). On one occasion, a great new opportunity arose in one of our customer markets. We had expertise in a key area of this opportunity, but not in another. One of our large competitors had the expertise we lacked, but did not have the expertise we had. Because a relationship of respect existed between the two companies, a partnership was created to join forces, leveraging our respective strengths to cover our individual shortcomings, and to create an attractive solution to the customer's new need. All the right legal steps were taken to protect our individual interests, and structure the partnership in a way that properly answered all legal requirements. With this partnership, we were able to seize an opportunity, leveraging a strong relationship and creating a win that otherwise likely would not have occurred.*

★ **Suppliers** – No journey has ever been successful without supplies. Whether food, water, fuel, ammunition, repair parts or other, every veteran knows that supplies are critical to their mission. The same applies to thriving & surviving in the civilian work world. As we've noted earlier, suppliers are individuals or companies that provide a product or service, for a fee, that you need to successfully complete your mission. No matter the nature of your job, or your organization, you'll engage with suppliers.

Somewhat like engaging with partners, successfully engaging with suppliers starts by knowing your goals, capabilities, and gaps. The next step is to identify what supplies you need to close the gap and achieve your goals. What do you need? When? How many? What specifications? What are your price requirements? These are some of the relevant questions that you need to be asking.

Understanding all this, it's time to search and find suitable suppliers. Start by looking at what "is." Your organization may have great existing suppliers. They may have supplier relationships that are good but can be improved. Or maybe there is no current supplier for what you need. No matter the case, explore folks/organizations that can cover your needs and bring something mutually beneficial to the table.

To thrive & survive relative to suppliers, think beyond the transactional. Seek to build business relationships that are win-wins. Always ensure your needs are filled, but do your best to help your supplier meet their needs, as well. Business conditions will change over time; sometimes it's all positive gumballs, rainbows, and lollipops. Other times, headwinds and challenges make for a very rough ride. Having strong supplier relationships helps you thrive & survive no matter what conditions exist.

BILL STORY

"Payment Terms."

A while ago, I heard of a company that was facing some difficult headwinds. They were being impacted by a general economic downturn and several industry and market specific challenges that reduced sales, causing their customers to delay payment on their accounts. (Said another way, their

SECTION 3: THRIVING & SURVIVING 217

> *customers were delaying their accounts payable, which delayed the company's accounts receivables—thus disrupting their own cash flow and negatively impacting their ability to pay their own payables on time). In this case, the company was pretty squared away and had specified payment terms for all customers (they had pre-agreed terms that required customers to make payment in full within 30 days of the sale, charging interest for the remaining balance on late or absent payments). Suing customers for non-payment was certainly an option, but that can be costly in terms of money, time and relationship equity...and it doesn't necessarily help get the cash flowing quickly. In order to ameliorate the situation, the company went to their challenging customers and worked out reasonable, agreeable terms that made the best of a tough situation. The company also contacted their suppliers (to whom they owed money for products and services provided) and requested that their payment terms be extended. The suppliers with whom they had a great relationship agreed. Some others did not. Moral of the story? In order to thrive & survive, you need to have strong, positive, mutually beneficial relationships with your suppliers.*

★ **Competitors** - As you've likely figured out by now, competitors are, at their core, other people and organizations that want your customers and their business. To thrive & survive, you need to leverage all the information you've identified and learned about them, to maximize your competitive advantage and minimize their attractiveness to your current and future customers. Focus on what makes you and your business more beneficial and valuable for current and future customers. Don't slip into the negative world of slamming your competitors; beat them fair and square by being better than they are. Tell your story better than they do. Build relationships better than they do. Provide better products/services than they do. Perform better than they do. Outperform your competitors in helping your customers to make money, save money, save time, and reduce risk. Then, you'll truly be on your way to thriving & surviving.

People really are at the heart of everything. Learning as much as possible about them, building great relationships, and positively leveraging that knowledge and those relationships are critical components to successfully thriving & surviving.

Process

Introduction

Like it or not, processes are part of life. They may be robust and long-established, or they may be in their infancy, serving as little more than recurring practices that meet evolving needs.

Regardless of the nature of the process, your ability to identify them, operate within them, contribute to their evolution, and successfully employ them to deliver expected results are critical to your success over time and the level to which you thrive & survive.

Three key process areas we will focus on are:

- ★ **Business**
- ★ **Job**
- ★ **Talent**

THE 3P MODEL – PROCESS

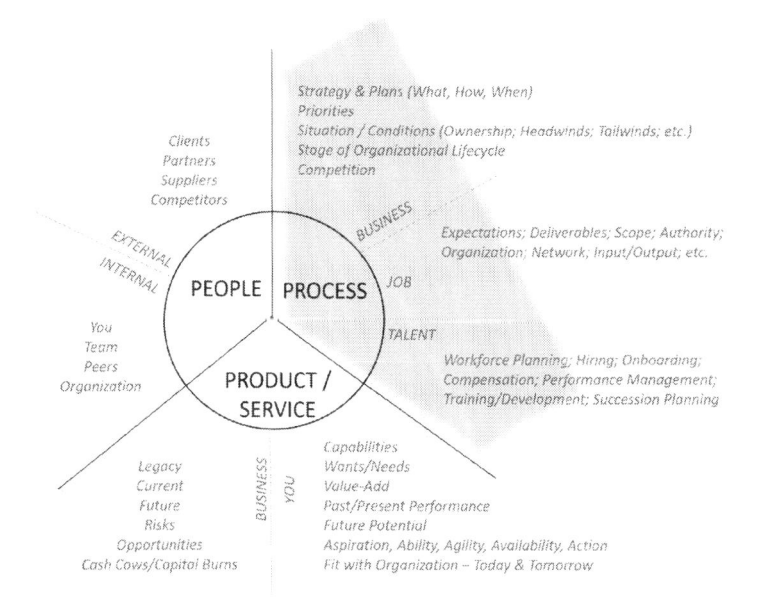

Strategy & Plans (What, How, When)
Priorities
Situation / Conditions (Ownership; Headwinds; Tailwinds; etc.)
Stage of Organizational Lifecycle
Competition

Clients
Partners
Suppliers
Competitors

EXTERNAL
INTERNAL

PEOPLE | PROCESS

BUSINESS | JOB

Expectations; Deliverables; Scope; Authority;
Organization; Network; Input/Output; etc.

You
Team
Peers
Organization

PRODUCT / SERVICE

TALENT

Workforce Planning; Hiring; Onboarding;
Compensation; Performance Management;
Training/Development; Succession Planning

BUSINESS | YOU

Legacy
Current
Future
Risks
Opportunities
Cash Cows/Capital Burns

Capabilities
Wants/Needs
Value-Add
Past/Present Performance
Future Potential
Aspiration, Ability, Agility, Availability, Action
Fit with Organization – Today & Tomorrow

General *Process* Insights When THRIVING & SURVIVING

Processes Evolve. Every process, no matter how effective, efficient, or familiar, must evolve over time. The world and all its various pieces and parts are always changing, and these changes inevitably will impact processes. To thrive & survive in the long run, you'll need to not only know, understand, and be able to use existing processes; you'll also need to be situationally aware, noticing the tides of change and the impact those changes are having on the processes that are part of your world.

Look for opportunities to improve processes. No matter how good a process may/not appear to be, having a continuous improvement mind set will always be beneficial to your long-term success. As noted above, the world is always changing and impacting processes in new ways. The changes may be a slow evolution, where the impact is barely perceptible (like the story of the boiling frog who is placed in a cool pot of water, that is placed over a low fire, gradually heating up the water so slowly that the frog doesn't notice it until the heat becomes life threatening). Opportunities to improve processes may also come from sudden, major changes that arise out of nowhere. In either case, realize that you may have the opportunity to make a meaningful, positive impact by suggesting/making process improvements that lead to improved business results.

Don't get stuck in the "we've always done it this way" mindset. We've all seen this happen. People getting so stuck in the past—in what's comfortable and familiar to them—that they have no desire to change. Now, we're not suggesting random change for the simple sake of change. That is reckless, and generally not good for business or your career. On the other hand, as a military veteran, you bring a great capability to assess situations, adapt to fluid environments and adjust as needed to achieve success. As you travel your career and life journeys, doing your best to thrive & survive in the long run, leverage your great abilities to overcome the "we've always done it this way" demon when it arises.

DAVE STORY

"Having the Right Equipment for One Situation, Doesn't Mean It's the Right Equipment When the Tides Change."

Have you ever done something in the workplace that didn't make sense to you simply because that was the way it had always been done? Or, have you ever failed to recognize changing conditions, and therefore didn't make the necessary adaptations to your process or equipment? If so, you are likely not alone. In the early and mid-2000s, I was primarily in Iraq, where the average engagement was within 100 meters and the vast majority of these occurred at night. Because of the circumstances, the majority of us used holographic optics that worked well for quick target acquisition. However, unless a supplemental device is used, it does not have any magnification.

In 2009, when we transitioned to Afghanistan, we learned a very hard lesson. In Afghanistan, the majority of engagements were significantly longer than 100 meters. In addition, there were a much larger number of daytime missions. However, our first deployment back to Afghanistan after our Iraq experience, the vast majority of us did not transition our optics. We did not consider the significant shift in engagements that we were likely to see.

During this deployment, we were caught in an eight-hour daytime engagement in the poppy fields and canals of southern Afghanistan. Other than our snipers, only two of us had magnified optics. As a team, we did not have the right equipment for the changing conditions, and it made that day significantly harder.

The lesson here is that, in business as in combat, conditions will change, whether it's a shift in the market, competition, technology, change in the supply chain, etc. What you have always used or what you have always done (which may have worked well in the past) may not work in the changing conditions. A proactive approach to shifts in the tide will prevent you from learning that you should have changed your optics after the fact.

Detailed *Process* Insights When THRIVING & SURVIVING

Business processes - Involve all manner of processes and practices related to managing the business. Strategy development & planning, prioritization; current situation awareness and management; business condition tracking (headwinds/tailwinds/opportunities/challenges); awareness of the organization's status in its overall life cycle; an understanding of your competition and its status, intent and direction; and an awareness of the organization's current status in its overall life cycle are all important components of your ability to thrive & survive in the ever-changing world of civilian employment.

- ★ **Strategic planning** - In civilian companies, this may be a rigorous, thorough, all-encompassing process that is effectively integrated up, down, and across all organizational levels. On the other hand, it may also be an unfamiliar, foreign process that people in positions of authority have never experienced. As with most things in life, there are infinite possible levels of strategic planning across the civilian employment community. As a general observation, though, most civilian organizations' strategic planning processes are less robust and well-integrated than what you likely experienced in the military. Depending on your role in the organization, this may/not impact your ability to successfully thrive & survive. If your expectations are for highly developed, well-integrated, robust strategic planning, and you are experiencing something less than that, use your great experience to help the company improve! Work with the relevant decision-makers to help them understand the value, and walk with them at a pace they can accept.
- ★ Processes for setting **priorities** can also vary widely. Some (much like the military's typically robust means of prioritizing) are clear, coordinated, well communicated and highly effective. Others, not so much.

BILL STORY

"Meatballs on the Wall."

During a particularly busy, hectic period, we found ourselves with far more on our plates than was reasonable, and with priorities that shifted so erratically that work felt like a giant game of "whack-a-mole." We'd get started on a particular set of priorities, expend resources, time, energy and attention, only to find that things had changed...again. I shared my concerns and the negative impact this was having on people and productivity with my boss. Knowing that it's never good to bring any boss problems without solutions, I offered a couple options, noting the one I thought best. Sadly, this all fell on relatively deaf ears. The boss then described his perspective on how to prioritize, and proceeded to espouse the "spaghetti on the wall" method. For those that may not be familiar, this includes taking a plate of spaghetti and meatballs and throwing up against the wall. You then pick a couple meatballs to focus on, and hope you get the right ones. I asked the boss, "How do I ensure I pick the right ones?" His reply? "You won't--and if you pick the wrong ones, then I've got you."

Clarity and consistency are key to prioritizing effectively. The former helps people understand what the priorities are and mitigates drama if/when things must change. The latter enables people to focus their attention on the right areas, to invest their efforts and resources with some level of confidence that what they're doing matters.

To thrive & survive over time, gain an understanding of the processes used to make priorities. If they are effective, great! Use them! If not, leverage your solid experience as a veteran to help as much as possible to evolve or emplace

processes that are clear and consistent, and help people and the organization succeed!
- ★ Multiple processes might exist to keep up with the business **situation**, **conditions**, **headwinds**, and **tailwinds**. They may vary from department to department, division to division, and function to function. They may be well aligned, or they may be unfathomably fragmented. Learn what they are, why they exist, and how they got to be what they are (for better or for worse).

> ### *BILL STORY*
>
> *"Aligning Sales Rewards."*
>
> *As is typical in many companies, our air freight company used performance bonus programs to incent high performance against key business objectives.*
>
> *One of these key business objectives was filling volume on the cargo aircraft we used. (Said simply - "fill 'em up!"). Our operations folks wanted to be sure we used every bit of airframe capacity possible. After all, we paid good money for those aircraft. Filling them up to capacity only made sense.*
>
> *Our sales team's focus was generating revenue, and more volume meant more revenue. What could possibly go wrong?*
>
> *So, our sales team sold volume! They filled those aircraft to the maximum possible extent! It was awesome!*
>
> *Meanwhile, our finance teams were monitoring business results and business conditions, attempting to identify any headwinds and tailwinds that were positively/negatively impacting business results.*
>
> *They noticed something concerning. On the upside, our revenues were at or above target; our sales teams were selling volume! On the downside, however, our profit margins were*

> *declining sharply (which is never a good thing in a for-profit company).*
>
> *Much work ensued to discover what the hell happened! Where had the cost risen so far as to materially reduce profit margins?*
>
> *It turned out that costs were essentially unchanged. What changed was the price at which sales folks were selling our airfreight service. In order hit the volume targets, to "fill 'em up," sales folks reduced prices at or below our costs, cutting into (or in some cases erasing) profit margin.*
>
> *But hey? What's the problem? They did what they were asked to do – they sold volume; they "filled 'em up."*
>
> *We had a dilemma. Our sales folks did what they were asked to do. Unfortunately, that ask was not as well coordinated nor well stated as needed to make a real, positive impact on the business.*

As you endeavor to thrive & survive, look for things that don't align or make sense. Check across borders to see if gaps or overlaps exist. If something appears wonky, say something. Get relevant subject matter experts involved. If all is good, great! If not, you've just established yourself as someone with wisdom, interest, and the courage to explore and help improve situations that are impacting the business.

★ Often, companies have few processes to rigorously assess where they are in the **organizational life cycle**. As an experienced organizational development professional, Bill has seen this unfortunate reality play out repeatedly. Many organizations are so caught up in managing current operations, and perhaps giving some attention to the mid/longer term, that focusing limited resources on this type of assessment just doesn't get much attention.

As we've described above, each stage in an organization's

life cycle has certain characteristics and expectations impacting culture, talent needs, the work environment and more. Regardless of the organization's process to keep tabs on this (or the absence thereof), your ability to thrive & survive will be enhanced if you are mindful of this evolution. Being attentive to how things are progressing (or not), where new opportunities may exist, and where more challenging situations may be emerging (e.g., there may be great opportunities in a company that overall has reached the "decline" phase), will help you make decisions and take actions that either bolster your readiness in your current role, prepare you for potential, emerging roles, or (if needed) begin the transition/job search process for your next great success. It's also important to understand that:

★ Different segments of your organization may be at different stages in their life cycle.
★ Even in mature companies, "startup" opportunities may arise.
★ Even businesses that are in decline may present fantastic job opportunities.

BILL STORY

"A Startup in a Mature Company."

The commercial goods manufacturer I worked for was clearly a mature company. One of the business segments conceived a new manufacturing process that, if successful, would revolutionize how the industry produced certain products. It would eliminate multiple steps in the manufacturing process and reduce production costs dramatically. The idea had great potential, and there was great interest and enthusiasm. Still,

SECTION 3: THRIVING & SURVIVING

> *bringing it to life and ensuring it was a repeatable, high-quality solution that delivered its hoped-for commercial value was going to be a mighty challenge. It presented a startup opportunity in this otherwise mature company. When we began to consider who should be on the team, we had to consider who held not only the right technical capabilities, but also who had the behavioral competencies fitting for this new opportunity. We were able to bring together a great team that took that new startup idea to its maximum commercial potential.*

★ Understanding **competition** is important for any business' success. Some larger, more established firms have robust processes to monitor and assess competitors and competitive pressures, emplacing countermeasures that protect or grow their markets. Some smaller, less developed organizations simply may not have the resources to do rigorous work in these areas.

Think of the military. At battalion and higher levels, they have dedicated intelligence assets available to do this work. The products of their efforts are critical to the effective prosecution of planned missions. Generally, companies and smaller units must rely on the higher headquarters' resources to gather and counter competitor information. Same concept in the civilian world, with the exception that smaller, stand alone firms don't have a higher headquarters to leverage. To successfully thrive & survive, you'll be well advised to keep an eye on your competition using whatever means are reasonably available (and legal). Read publicly available reports about your competition. Ask your customers. Keep your ears and eyes open for information available throughout your networks and so forth. If you're the person that's consistently armed with reasonably reliable competitor information and are able to understand it and take appropriate action to protect/grow the company, you're in a solid position to thrive & survive.

Job Specific Processes are important to understand if you intend to successfully thrive & survive in the long run. Being aware of current and any pending future job processes, how they align, fit, and impact each other and relevant other processes can be very helpful as you navigate your career.

* ★ **First, get clear on the expectations & deliverables required for your job.** Doing a great job in your current job is always the foundation for longer term success. Talk with your boss. Ask clearly what you are expected to deliver, what the standards are for those deliverables (time, quality, quantity, etc.). If he/she is unsure, do your level best to work together to help identify them, and then go knock them out of the park! If clarity is simply not going to happen (e.g., boss isn't willing/able to commit, situation is simply too fluid or other), then you may have to decide for yourself what the deliverables really are. To do this, reach out to others that are relevant to your job. Check with other incumbents, team members, upstream partners, customers (internal and external), etc. Get their perspective. Vet their input. Document what you think valid expectations are, then work your ass off to achieve them. It's not perfect, but it's a place to start.

    Stay mindful that the business environment is fluid and ever-changing. Things will evolve over time and this evolution may well change the expectations and deliverables of your role. Stay alert. Stay connected. Pay attention to the shifting landscape. Partner with your boss and others to ensure you are focused on and taking action on the right expectations.

* ★ **Understanding the scope/authority of your role matters.** If you're focusing too narrowly, something's going to go uncovered. If you focus too broadly, you risk inefficient

redundancies and/or stepping on others' toes (or playing in their sandbox; swimming in their ponds ... pick your metaphor).

Think of range cards, planning and identifying fields of fire, estimated ranges, priority targets, points of intersection and so forth. If you misidentify any of these (or properly identify them but then ignore them), you create a dangerous situation for you and relevant friendly forces. Over time, your scope and authority may change. Understand what these changes mean, and how you might best act upon them. If the changes are positive, enabling success with appropriate resources, great! Go forth and crush them! If, however, the changes are just scope creep, requiring broader, deeper focus and effort without additional resources, consider your situation carefully. Leverage your skills, experience, and networks to make the best of a potentially tough situation. If, on the other hand, changes to your scope and authority appear to be smaller, be sure you take a really good look at the situation – smaller isn't always a bad thing.

BILL STORY

"Why's My World Shrinking.?"

A coaching client was facing what appeared to be a negative situation in his career trajectory. He had been leading a fairly large group of people that were supporting a legacy product line. The business conditions were good, revenue was dependable, costs were under control, the people and structure were steady. He was quite happy and secure in this role. His boss came to him one day, asking him to take on a very small, very new group that was focused on commercializing an entirely new product. His first reaction was "WHY are you demoting

> *me? I had hundreds of people, and we were successful. This new gig is only about a dozen people, their budget is tiny, and nothing they're doing is proven yet!" His boss noted his concerns, then advised him to look beyond the obvious; this new assignment was supporting a top priority, strategic initiative that needed top-tier talent steering things. What's the "thrive & survive" lesson? Look beyond the obvious when considering scope and authority – smaller numbers may not really indicate your value and ability to make an impact.*

* **Defining where your job fits in the organization can also make a positive impact on your ability to thrive & survive.** This means more than just geography (the city, country) it's located in, or what areas it occupies in the plant, office, or complex, etc. It also means understanding the inputs that are required to operate (products, materials, machinery, services, etc.) and the outputs it produces (products or services). It includes understanding the sources of all inputs and the processes by which they are obtained and the uses of all products/services by the customers who purchase/consume them. All this may change as business conditions evolve over time. Be attentive to the shifting sands and be mindful of how your job fits. If the fit seems to be going in a negative direction, explore ways to position yourself for a more solid fit in the future.

* **Thriving & surviving without an effective network is damn near impossible.** As this relates to "job processes," be mindful of the interdependencies and support relationships between your job, your team, your department within and across your organization. Take note of how people interact. Observe the social norms, the communication processes and practices, how decisions are made, the level of transparency or protectionism that exists. Take reasonable action to make

the most of these to help create, nurture, and maintain networks that help you thrive & survive.

* **Finally, as you traverse your career and life journeys, remember that inputs and outputs change.** Whether they are job related (materials in and products out, contacts with people who can provide valuable insights, customers whose needs are ever-changing, etc.) or life related (e.g., changes to your family situation), the ins and outs of your experience will always be shifting. Stay situationally aware. Recognize the impact of these changes (good or bad). Consider alternate courses of action you could take to exploit the good and mitigate the bad. Always keep your career and life goals center-focus so you stay on track, moving forward towards them.

Additional thoughts:

If your organization is a startup or in the earlier stages of growth, your deliverables may be less clear. Learn to embrace the gray, add value wherever possible, be part of current success, and position yourself as a key asset to drive the organization forward to greater success.

Some jobs are easier to measure, and establishing clear expectations and deliverables is more common. A great example of this is sales – arguably the easiest, most robustly measured function in business. Whether the metric be "New Revenue Per Report Period," "Customer Retention," "New Market Penetration," "Profit Margin Above Target," or other, sales expectations and deliverables are typically pretty clear. Some other functions are a bit harder to define. Take human resources, for example. Gaining clarity on this function's expectations and deliverables can be a beast. When they are defined, they tend to focus on "process" metrics. For example: "New Training Program Delivered on Time and Under Budget;" "Employee Healthcare Benefits Programs Agreed Before XXX Date, and With No

More Than a YYY Increase in Total Cost to the Organization;" "Performance Management Reviews 100% Completed by XXX Date;" and so forth. These are not useless metrics, but often they miss the mark on accurately measuring if the job's core purpose is really being hit.

Talent Related Processes

If you want to thrive & survive in the long run, you need to understand how "talent" processes work. These may be robust, or nearly non-existent. Far too often, they are disregarded or misunderstood by the folks they impact most. This can create unexpected vulnerabilities as you continue your journey to successfully thrive & survive.

There are several talent processes that especially deserve your attention over the long run:

- ★ **Workforce Planning**
- ★ **Hiring**
- ★ **Onboarding**
- ★ **Compensation**
- ★ **Performance Management**
- ★ **Training & Development**
- ★ **Succession Planning**

Before we address these, let's revisit the "buy versus build" approaches to talent that highlight the notable differences in how the military versus civilian employers approach talent.

As we noted in the INTEGRATING section, the military has to build its talent, filling the front end of the talent pipeline with fresh, new folks and then developing them throughout their careers to fill openings at the more senior ranks. In the civilian work world, companies frequently buy their talent, reaching out to the broader employment market, other companies or maybe even their competitors.

This strategy difference drives a different talent mindset and

SECTION 3: THRIVING & SURVIVING

activities, all of which may impact your short- and long-term career success.

Workforce Planning is the process by which organizations determine how many people, with what capabilities are needed, when and where to achieve planned objectives. Further, it might address how these people are best organized for optimal efficiency and effectiveness.

The robustness and rigor of workforce planning processes in the civilian world vary wildly. Smaller, newer, startup type firms may do very little formal workforce planning, defaulting instead to the founder/leader's gut instinct about what's right. The other end of the spectrum might exist at a mature, well-operating large corporation that has sufficient resources to dedicate a team of employees who partner with its various business and functional leaders to assess business plans, business conditions, and other relevant variables to create solid workforce plans. Neither of these approaches, nor the variations between them, are inherently right or wrong, but over or under developing workforce planning processes appropriate for the business can lead to negative business readiness and reduced ability to optimize business results. For example, smaller startup companies must focus on their core business. Yes, they need to get the right people with the right capabilities on board, but emplacing large, complex, resource-heavy processes to do so is simply not good business. Conversely, large, mature, well-resourced firms who ignore or place minimal attention on workforce planning are playing a risky game on several fronts. They are less likely to have the talent capability on hand when they need it to deliver on their objectives. They risk having erratic, expensive recruiting and talent attraction activity because there's no plan. They also run the risk of high turnover (people leaving) because the people they do attract see that planning for people is not a priority. None of these are good things for the long run.

How does this apply to your ability to thrive & survive in the long run? Well, that depends. If the existing workforce planning process appears to make sense for the business situation, and you are aware of and comfortable/confident in it, then no problem! If, on the other hand, there is a disconnect, you might expect that your ability to thrive & survive will take a hit. Perhaps you will find that the company is perpetually understaffed; or that you are always overtasked with deliverables outside your scope. Or maybe you'll find inconsistent hiring practices that explode hiring during certain times of the year, only to then be followed later in the year by demoralizing layoffs. Either way, this isn't good.

Pay attention to your organization's workforce planning practices. Learn what they are. Find the positives and the opportunities for improvement. Leverage your network relationships to be part of an improvement solution.

Hiring is something you're likely familiar with; after all, you've experienced the career transition/job search process at least once before by now, and maybe more. The key here, in the context of thriving & surviving, is to understand how the internal/external hiring decisions are made so you are aware of how they might impact your ability to successfully perform today and in the future.

Some companies are highly focused on hiring from within. They see value in offering open jobs to current, qualified employees. Where this practice is common, outsiders most frequently enter the company's talent pipeline at the lower levels.

Other companies' hiring processes focus heavily on bringing outside talent onboard. There are many reasons for this. Perhaps there's a need for new expertise, new insights, or new perspective... fresh eyes to see current and future challenges and opportunities through new lenses. Perhaps the company's strategy is to take on a new business for which it has limited expertise or market presence.

Knowing and understanding the focus and process can be helpful in your efforts to thrive & survive. It can reveal the potential likelihood of you being promoted to a new opportunity. For

SECTION 3: THRIVING & SURVIVING

example, if the process is to focus heavily on internal hiring, all else being equal, it may help your odds. If, however, the hiring priority is on bringing in new talent, and the business focus is on totally new products/markets for which you have little capability, you're pretty much toast for that new role.

We covered **onboarding** in depth in the LANDING section. We mention again it here, because as you're thriving & surviving, you want to be mindful of how the current onboarding processes work. They impact how long before a new hire gets to actually join your team, their level of familiarity with the company, the team, their job; how fast they get up to speed and full productivity; their initial perception of their new work world, and a host of other things. If the onboarding process is weak, you might have to invest more time in new team members, which might take time/focus away from your core job. Be aware of the onboarding process and help optimize it where you can. Doing so will enhance your thriving & surviving effectiveness.

Compensation. We all expect to get paid! Further, we all expect to get paid fairly and equitably; to receive a fair day's wage for a fair day's work, and to receive benefits that are competitive and meet our needs.

Relative to THRIVING & SURVIVING, it's important to consider your "total compensation." Many people get laser focused on their salary or wage, and forget about the rest of their true total compensation package. As we showed in the LANDING Section, this typically includes several key components:

"TOTAL" Compensation *(It's about far more than money.)*

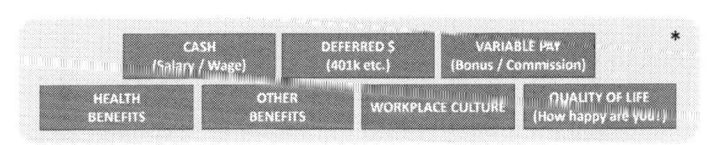

CASH (Salary / Wage)	DEFERRED $ (401k etc.)	VARIABLE PAY (Bonus / Commission)
HEALTH BENEFITS	OTHER BENEFITS	WORKPLACE CULTURE	QUALITY OF LIFE (How happy are you!)

* - *Typical components. Many details & variations in each.*

- ★ Cash Compensation - Base salary or wage
- ★ Deferred Compensation (Retirement Plans)
- ★ Variable Compensation (Bonus/Commission)
- ★ Health Benefits
- ★ Other Benefits (relocation, flextime, training/growth opportunities, vacation, etc.)
- ★ Workplace Culture
- ★ Quality of Life

Common Compensation Process Insights:

- ★ *Compensation and benefits are expenses.* All organizations, whether for-profit or nonprofit, seek to reduce expenses – either to improve their profitability (for-profits) or to enable greater delivery or services for their benefactors (nonprofits). Thus, employers seek to provide the least possible compensation to obtain the talent capability they need.
- ★ *Compensation levels are not arbitrary.* Expanding on the point above, most employers do some level of research to understand the employment market, typical pay and benefit levels, and the ranges that are common for jobs, industries, and markets. Said another way, few employers just throw darts at the wall to set compensation levels.
- ★ *"Equity" is a focal point for compensation decisions.* Basically, this is determined by answering the question, "Is the company providing compensation that is fair and reasonable for similarly situated people inside and outside the company?" The external equity question is pretty easy to understand – if we aren't providing compensation that is substantially similar to other employers, we won't attract great talent. Internal equity reviews help minimize concerns between employees that similarly situated people are paid similarly. This doesn't mean everyone gets exactly the same pay; far from it! More experience, a greater record of success, broader, deeper

SECTION 3: THRIVING & SURVIVING

expertise in one's field, a robust, value-adding network with key players in the market—hell, even a great relationship with the boss—may be reasons one's compensation may be more than another.

★ *Benefits are a significant part of total compensation.* On the benefits side, again competitive concerns are important. If another employer in your area is offering benefits that the employment market values and you aren't, you're at risk of losing current employees and not attracting new employees to fill your ranks. Further, it's important to realize that benefits (especially healthcare benefits) are costly to employers, often equating to upwards of 30% of wages and salaries. This cost is always a consideration when employers are seeking to attract and retain top tier talent.

★ *Not all benefits are required by law.* In fact, many are not. Retirement programs, vacation, medical insurance and so forth are not legally mandated everywhere. They exist because of the competitive pressures in the employment market. That said, where benefit programs are offered, the terms and conditions and how to's of each program are highly regulated to protect both the employees and employers. These regulations are often at federal and state levels, which can create some interesting situations for multi-state companies.

★ *Compensation and benefit programs are typically reviewed periodically.* In larger, more sophisticated companies, this may be annually. In smaller, newer companies the reviews may be less rigorous and more or less frequent.

★ *Bonus, incentive, or "pay at risk" programs can be designed just about any way the employer chooses (as long as they don't run afoul of financial, non-discrimination, or other similar laws).* Typically, they are pretty straight forward, with stated targets, an assessment of performance against those targets, and calculation of payout based on performance against target.

- ☆ The targets may be individual, team, or organizational. They may be a combination of these. Many variable compensation programs include all three.
- ☆ These programs are often separate from individual performance management processes (which further makes those less relevant, leading some people to think "Hey, I got my bonus, why should I care what my performance review says?")

Compensation can also look different depending on what phase of your business's life cycle it is in, and the organization's legal structure (for profit, nonprofit, Limited Liability Company, "S" Corporation, or other). A couple of examples:

- ★ Startups may offer vested stock options (a form of deferred compensation whereby you are paid with a certain number of ownership shares). The upside of this is that if the stock value skyrockets, you make more money. The risk is that if the stock value tanks, it may become worthless. The reasons companies offer this is to incent you to perform well and help drive the stock value up.
- ★ An S Corporation could pass through earnings into an employee stock ownership plan or ESOP.
- ★ Executive-level leaders' compensation may be more heavily weighted toward variable and deferred compensation rather than cash comp, and their other benefits packages may be notably different than lower-level positions.

Understanding these, how businesses generally decide what to provide, and how they align with your needs, wants, and expectations can directly affect your wallet, materially adding to/detracting from your thriving & surviving success.

BILL STORY

"Show Me the Money."

I like money. But if money is your main focus as you are attempting to thrive & survive throughout your career, you're missing the big picture.

I've talked with many transitioned veterans who landed well-paying gigs and were miserable. Guess what? They are looking to transition again.

I've done it more than once (apparently, I'm a slow learner). Got the big bucks, but didn't fit in the workplace culture; I wasn't even close to happy, and the quality of life was miserable.

On one occasion, I simply made a bad decision. I ignored my gut instinct (and my wife's insight), and chased the money. After a very short time, I left. I was in transition again, by my own choice.

On another occasion, the job started off great! Met all my expectations. I was happy. Then the company evolved. The culture changed. The benefits changed. The money changed. Things were not good. I stayed far longer than I should have as my quality of life plummeted. My happy meter bottomed out. Eventually, I left. I was in transition AGAIN.

Over time, I learned. I managed to find roles that met every need in my "Total Compensation" equation.

DAVE STORY

"Taking a Pay Cut on Purpose."

As we stated when talking about total compensation, money is just part of the equation. For most, one thing is almost certain: money doesn't equal happiness. Pulitzer Prize winning historian David McCullough once said, "Real success is finding your lifework in the work that you love." When working for the insurance firm, I was making pretty good money, but had the opportunity to make really good money. Many of the senior executives in the region were getting ready to retire, and they were getting ready to pass on their client portfolios in the next couple of years. The earning potential was enormous.

However, there was something missing. I just didn't feel like I was making the impact I could be. I didn't feel challenged. I knew that I would not feel happy or fulfilled long term if I stayed, regardless of the money that I could make in the future. When the opportunity at the VA presented itself, I was willing to take a pretty substantial pay cut (over 25%) in order to try and explore a career that filled that void. I didn't necessarily find it at the VA, but life is a journey and that was just one necessary stop on the way to finding a career that ultimately did. When we talk about total compensation, do not forget that your own personal happiness is perhaps the most important component of that equation.

Each of us must make the "balance decision" that is best for us—in the moment, and for the future. Therein lies the challenge. Work to keep everything in balance. Assess and understand the cost – benefit of every opportunity.

As you consider your future, do yourself a favor—look at the big picture. Make decisions that align with more than just your wallet.

BILL STORY

"Rental Agreements."

When it comes to thriving & surviving in the work world, I've long held that the relationship between employer and

SECTION 3: THRIVING & SURVIVING

> *employee is a bit of a "rental" agreement. The employer is renting the employee's business behavior, to accomplish certain things in certain ways. The employee agrees to this based on the terms and conditions the employer provides. If either party in this "rental agreement" decides that the situation is no longer attractive, they have the option to renegotiate and/ or end the agreement.*

Understand the situation. Define your expectations (and make sure they are reasonable). Be mindful of how the winds are blowing and go make good things happen!

As we've noted earlier, **performance management** in the civilian work world is often far different than in the military. Understanding how it works, why it's designed the way it is, and what it's used for can be helpful as you navigate your thrive & survive journey.

Typical steps in a robust performance management process include:

- ★ Goal setting and alignment
- ★ Ongoing performance feedback
- ★ Performance evaluation
- ★ Development planning
- ★ Evaluation discussion
- ★ Application of evaluation results to relevant, other processes (compensation, training, succession planning, etc.)

There are as many variations and applications of this process as you can imagine; after all, each organization exists in a unique space and they have to do what's best for them.

Unfortunately, companies frequently don't leverage the full power of a robust performance management process. Maybe their goal setting is lacking (or totally absent). Maybe there's little/no feedback to help employees optimize performance. Maybe there's no focus on development to improve performance gaps or prepare people for future successes. Maybe the evaluation discussions never happen. Maybe, maybe, maybe....

BILL STORY

"The Only Thing Performance Reviews Do is Feed the Compensation Beast."

One of the companies I joined had a pretty robust performance management process—on paper. There were goal setting steps, requirements for recurring feedback, even some expectation that managers would address development needs and plans for their employees. On paper, it looked pretty good. But in practice, people simply didn't do it all. Some raters just didn't know how to do it (which is inexcusable). Others were perpetually "too busy" to do it all (also inexcusable). The end result of all this was that the overall rating (a number) was the only thing that was consistently documented—although it wound up being quite meaningless to the employees in the cases where managers actually provided feedback. Imagine how inspiring it is to learn that you scored a rating or 3.74 on a five-point scale...how does one even interpret that? Given these considerations, why did the overall rating get documented? Because it was the number that was plugged into compensation calculations that determined what, if any, increase an employee might receive. I suppose there could be a redeeming aspect to this if these ratings actually made a distinction between people's levels of performance; the only problem was that they didn't. (e.g., the pay difference between a 3.74 and a 4.3 might be less than 1-2%; or the lower rated employee might get a bigger bonus because bonuses are often discretionary and employers often have lots of latitude). The net effect was that rockstar performers' calculated increases

> *were substantially similar to others' who were barely getting by. And then, the management teams could make independent adjustments as they saw fit (and as budgets allowed). Needless to say, most folks thought the performance management process was a joke, and it surely didn't help drive business, team, or individual success.*

As a military veteran, you are likely used to a fairly robust performance management process. If you land with an organization that is lacking in this area, you may be disheartened. If so, don't make a knee jerk reaction. Do your job to the best of your ability. Professionally share your observations for improvement. Use your experience to help improve things. We get it. We've lived it. Bill has built robust global programs that replace sub-par processes. If things simply won't change, decide what you're going to do. Can you perform well in the current situation? Can you discern appropriate goals even if they're not documented? Is the informal feedback enough to satisfy you? If you're good to go, keep going! If you're not, however, start considering your options in another role, another organization, or maybe even another industry.

Training & Development

Some may say this is one of the military's greatest strengths. From basic training to initial job training, to professional development and beyond, the military does training & development differently and better than the vast majority of civilian organizations.

The difference is a product of the "buy versus build" talent mentality addressed above. After all, if I can go buy capable talent, why would I spend the money to train and develop people?

Another factor playing into this is the difference in how most civilian businesses operate. As we mentioned in the LANDING section, unlike the military with its familiar "train, deploy, refit, repeat" cycle, businesses are "deployed" all the time. They are on production working hard to provide their products/services all the time. Time, money, and other resources that distract from this get scrutinized carefully to ensure the decision-makers are convinced they are investments that make sense (and will generate more revenue and profit than they cost).

> ## *BILL STORY*
>
> *"Budget Cuts - Training Cuts."*
>
> *Most of the companies I worked for primarily viewed training and development as a "nice to have" expense rather than a value-adding investment in the future of the company and its people. This being the case, when times got tight, revenue and/or profit plans were not achieved, and money had to be saved, one of the very first things to get cut was the training budget. Usually not all of it; mandatory compliance, safety and other "keep us out of jail" training usually continued as planned/budgeted. It was frustrating. Various people in positions of authority (Leaders?) had spoken passionately about the need for training to optimize our current capabilities and development to prepare folks for future success. It was important! That said, it often wasn't urgent, and thus, decisions were made to cut the budget, suspend the programs and hope that future business conditions improved so training investments could be re-instated. If challenging business headwinds continued, headcount reductions in the training team were always an option of first resort. To a degree, this makes sense. If you have to cut heads to save money, do you cut the folks who are making the products, or do you cut the staff that supports them? Unfortunately, this can become a*

vicious cycle. Business conditions cause training cuts; thus, people aren't well trained, which reduces their ability to consistently deliver at high quality levels, which contributes to lower sales... round and round it goes.

As military veterans, experienced in the military's outstanding training and development processes, your expectations might be very different than your civilian colleagues'. If there's a disconnect between your expectations and the realities of your work world, consider it wisely. Assess the root cause(s). Explore the breadth and depth of the circumstance. Professionally offer your insights and attempt to help improve things. You may or may not be successful, but by taking a thoughtful, professional tact, you will present yourself as a focused, value-adding team member, and that's always a good thing when it comes to thriving & surviving.

DAVE STORY

"There Are Many Ways to Train Your People."

In the military, as we talk about in this section, there are many plugged-in professional development opportunities for both you and your team. These opportunities may not be as obvious in the civilian sector, but that does not mean they do not exist. Your company may be well-resourced and emphasize professional development, or it may not. As a leader who is invested in your team, if you do not emphasize this growth (again, for the sake of both yourself and your team), it is much easier to become stagnant as opportunities and schooling are not as commonly inserted into the growth pipeline as they are in the military.

> *What does this mean then for you? Communicate with your management team about your growth plan for your team. You may have to be more deliberate with budgeting for these professional development opportunities. Budget time for internal training, because remember, you are likely always in production, so finding this time will be more difficult. Think of board meetings, planning meetings, etc. as training opportunities for your team. What external opportunities exist, and how can you leverage internal or external money to fund these? It may be more necessary to communicate the return on investment of these opportunities to your management team. The point is, it will likely be more difficult to plan, find time for, and resource training. But if you don't do it, it is likely that no one else will either. If you are an individual contributor, seek out professional development opportunities for yourself and be your own best advocate.*

Succession Planning & Career Management

Succession planning and career management in the civilian work world are not the same as the military. With nearly three decades of combined experience in this world, we've simply not seen an organization that does career management as robustly or as well as the military.

Career paths, career plans, promotional pathways, succession plans, and all the related processes, practices, norms, structures, and systems vary as widely as you can imagine.

The E1/W1/O1 start point, with well known, well communicated, and well executed progression through logical steps to terminal, top-tier E9/W5/O10 levels are nothing like most civilian companies' practices.

There are many possible reasons for this difference. We suggest three root causes:

SECTION 3: THRIVING & SURVIVING

- ★ The "buy versus build" talent mentality.
- ★ A general lack of appreciation for the investment value of providing robust succession planning and career management.
- ★ The pace and variability of civilian business.

Buying talent rather than building it often reduces the perceived need for succession planning and career management, the thought being, "Why would I spend precious resources on those things when I'm just going to look outside when an opening arises?"

As logical as that perspective might seem on the surface, it creates an unfortunate, broader, more general lack of appreciation for the great value that investing in succession planning and career management can bring to the organization's current and longer-term success. After all, people (and organizations) point their money (and other resources) where their priorities are. In this case, investing in recruiting services for new talent is often the default rather than directing those funds toward succession planning and career management.

We've also seen that the fluid, ever-changing, and sometimes unpredictable nature of civilian business can be a compelling factor to avoid succession planning and career management investment. After all, why would we spend tons of time, money, and other resources on processes and systems that build for a future we can't reliably predict?

Lest this all sound like bad news, let us assure you, it isn't. It is very different than that with which you are accustomed, but different doesn't always mean "bad."

This less structured environment provides a level of freedom and opportunity that the military never could. If you have a good idea of where you want to be, what you want to do, and are willing/able to take charge of your career, there's a good chance you'll get there.

THRIVING & SURVIVING in this regard involves a few basic concepts:

- *Keep your eyes/ears open for opportunity.* These may be within the same company or at other, different organizations. Remember the lessons you learned in your career transition. Network with a broad variety of people. Be mindful of your purpose. Do the work that keeps opportunities on the horizon.
- *Make your aspirations known.* Specific career path steps may not be in place, but letting relevant others know what you aspire to enables their ability to be part of your success!
- *Demonstrate your "5 A's" - Aspiration, Ability, Availability, Agility, and Action.* Bill covers these in his first book, as key characteristics employers look for in new job candidates. They are also focal points employers consider when seeking people to fill new, different, larger roles. If you want to thrive & survive, demonstrate your "5 A's" through your career, and not just when you're between successes.

Succession planning is where past, present, performance, and potential collide. Its purpose is to ensure the organization has a pipeline of qualified talent ready to perform successfully in key roles in the future. The need is forward-focused; what will be needed, and people's potential to fill those needs. Since no one has a crystal ball, one's past and present performance are considered.

Career Management focuses on how careers are aligned and how people might progress through their time with the company. As noted earlier, few companies emplace processes anywhere near as robust and rigorous as the military's. No matter the process particulars, there are two typical lanes in this space that you'd do well to understand: Career Pathing and Career Planning.

- Career Pathing is organization-focused, and deals primarily with assessing, understanding, and documenting how jobs best relate to one another and how they progress throughout and across the organization.

- ★ Career Planning is individual focused, dealing primarily with helping individual employees plan their course from where they are today to where they want to be in the future.

To thrive & survive in the long run, you'll have to own your journey; working with relevant staff and leaders to understand potential career paths (even if there's nothing clearly defined by the organization) and to chart your own career plan. Having these in place gives you a framework for progression and is especially helpful when unexpected changes in business conditions arise. Bastardizing a concept from our field artillery friends, it's always best to have a target list, and when things change, to shift from a known point.

DAVE STORY

"Capable, Credible, Perspective, and Preparation."

I had just retired from the Army and was networking my ass off. During the process, I was fortunate enough to get introduced to the CEO of a major healthcare center in the region. Let me set the stage...

I had been told during my transition that as a leader in the Special Operations community, a job was going to just fall in my lap. Come up with a value proposition, build a translatable resume, buy a shiny new suit, and voila; I was ready to get hired as the next senior VP of Operations. I had all the training and experience I needed to run operations in an industry that I knew nothing about, because hey, I was an experienced leader. Now, am I saying that I couldn't learn it? Not at all. I am sure I could have learned it. However, I needed to get some experience in the industry before 1) I could be an effective leader in operations in the healthcare field, and 2) I needed to learn the language of business.

So, I went into the meeting with the CEO full of vim and

> *vigor, ready to articulate the value I could bring to the healthcare system. We had a great conversation, and afterwards he told me, "I'm not exactly sure where you can fit in but let me have my VP of HR give you a call." A couple of days later, she called and one of her first questions was, "What do you want to do?" Pretty simple question, but it stumped me. What do you mean what do I want to do? I want to be a leader in your organization. So, I asked her "What is there?" What a boneheaded thought process that was. I learned a ton from that phone call, and she actually ended up on my board later, so we shared a good laugh. The point is, no one can answer that question but you. Where you go and what you do needs to be an integral part of your career and life planning journey, and the best person to do that is in the mirror.*

Problem Solving Process – Not part of our model, but an important part of THRIVING & SURVIVING

Business conditions are fluid, ever-changing in the face of challenges and opportunities that present innumerable decision points and problems. Understanding how problems get solved is an impactful part of thriving & surviving. If your approach is notably different than the organization's, you may be facing a long haul.

Three realities seem to lie at the core of how businesses approach problem-solving:

- ★ Focus on current execution and results.
- ★ Limited strategic planning and less than effective integration of strategy throughout the organization.
- ★ Lack of standardized problem-solving practices across the organization.

SECTION 3: THRIVING & SURVIVING

Many companies focus on the short term. Execute today. Get the job done. If the results are good, keep going. If a problem erupts, deal with it in the most expedient manner possible. Problem solving models are often no more complex than "See it. Fix it. Forget it." AARs (after action reviews) as you knew them in the military rarely exist, and the concept is not broadly understood. This is unfortunate because the value of continuous learning and continuous improvement on future success is lost.

When it comes to strategic planning and integrating strategy across the company, there are a wide variety of approaches. Certainly, some companies do solid planning, formulating a meaningful strategy, translating that into valuable operational plans, and enabling successful tactical execution. But in our experience, these organizations are the exception.

Some don't build strategies at all. Some build them and then shelve them. Few robustly walk the planning dog top to bottom, start to finish, concept to execution. This lack of coordination throughout the ranks and from start to finish can create real problems that eventually will need to be solved.

> ## *BILL STORY*
>
> ### *"Weak Link in the Chain."*
>
> *My company's top team got together to build their strategy. They brought in a world-class strategy development consultant team to advise them. The results of this expensive work were quite robust. It recognized probable industry and market headwinds and tailwinds, clearly identified strategic objectives, defined supporting objectives, and so on. At a top level, it made good sense. So far, so good. Each member of the top team was tasked with rolling this strategy out to his/her*

> *direct report team and sharing the strategic objectives, and defined supporting objectives. The expectation was that they would all build a corresponding strategy within their areas of responsibility, narrowing down the objectives to the appropriate scope, and establishing operational goals and tactical targets for their teams and people that brought the strategy to action. These were reasonable and relevant expectations. The problem was that not every top team member knew how to do this work, and some simply didn't find it to be an urgent priority. Yes, they knew it was important, but they had urgent fires they had to deal with first! The impact of this was significant. Those that understood the concept embraced it, and took action to bring strategies to life that performed better over time. The ones that dismissed the strategy coordination work often found themselves floundering, wondering why their people and teams were running off different priorities that may or may not have had much to do with the company's top-level strategy, and then spending much time and energy problem-solving their various challenges.*

The lack of standardized problem-solving practices also can create challenges for people and the organization. Imagine this scenario. You're working as an operations leader in a manufacturing plant with highly developed and broadly understood problem-solving practices. You all know how to handle problems when they arise, identifying them, assessing them, performing root-cause analysis, defining and assessing alternative courses of action, selecting the best one, and implementing it. Now, let's imagine you and your team are working on a new project with the advanced engineering team, exploring ways to overcome problems by bringing some great new product to market. If that great, smart, creative team solves problems in a different way, you all may be in for a challenging time.

If you want to thrive & survive in the long run, understand how problems are solved in your organization. Discover what factors are

SECTION 3: THRIVING & SURVIVING

contributing to the existence of problems in the first place. Do your best to leverage your solid problem-solving capabilities to improve the situation.

> ## BILL STORY
>
> *"Obeya Room."*
>
> *First, a little background. The overarching philosophy behind obeya comes from Lean. (The general concept of this is that ultimately, everything must focus on how the final product – the result of different specialists working together – creates value for the customer.) Toyota first created obeya rooms during production of the Prius in the 1990s. You might think of an obeya room as a "war room," a command center that draws together leaders from across departments to manage strategy, programs, projects, and more. Obeya rooms can help break down silos by putting key leaders in a room together and interlocking their efforts into a cohesive, successful whole. It enables the alignment of goals, streamlining of efforts, leveraging of expertise, and problem-solving across borders. This occurs by providing every player with a complete view of everything from top-level strategy to the various departments' goals, metrics, KPIs (key performance indicators), current status, opportunities, and challenges. An obeya room gives leaders a clear view of what everyone is working on, as well as why and how. They also can see how their own efforts support or hinder others, and the overall strategy or project.*
>
> *The first job of an obeya room is to determine the goal for the strategy or project. This is important because you must know what success will look like before you get started. Goals are then defined for each department involved. This being done, problems are documented, analyzed, and action plans are put in place. Charts and graphs are used to provide a visual*

display of progress and challenges. All information is available to everyone all the time. It's important to note that obeya rooms are meant more for debating and discussing big picture issues and for enabling understanding of how all departments are working together toward a single, customer-focused end goal. It also serves to develop teamwork at the management level and keep everyone focused on accomplishing strategy.

Now, for the story ... Several years ago, the company I was with was dealing with some complex customer-focused issues that required dedicated, integrated work between and across various departments. The situation was business critical, in that failing to achieve our overall goal would have a material negative impact on the company. We had an outstanding business leader who suggested the obeya approach as the best path toward success. One of my peer functional leaders took the reins. He did a great job setting things up and getting the ball rolling. The concept was pretty new to most of the participants, so there was a bit of training along the way to help set a solid baseline of understanding. Things were humming along quite well until some point where they began to derail. Department heads became less collegial. Rather than offer constructive feedback and improvement ideas, they began sniping others. Progress updates were less useful. Problems were getting whitewashed and minimized. Overall, the pieces and processes were in place, but they were not being used well. To this point I was a casual observer of this process. As a member of the senior management team, it wasn't my place to be an active participant. Think about the Assistant Division Commander – Support (ADC-S) coming into Brigade staff meetings and being a regular participant... yeah, it just doesn't work like that. At one point, I approached my peer (who had set this up) and our boss, offering my assessment of how things were going. They agreed progress

> *was off track, and asked for a solution. We agreed that I would attend these meetings and offer real-time feedback on how I saw the process unfolding. I stayed out of the technical kibbles and bits and focused specifically on how people were interacting and behaving in the sessions. At first there was some resistance...those that were misbehaving knew it, and they didn't like being called out. Some of them improved. We had to move a couple of them out to other, less critical roles.*

So, why tell this story here? It goes to the heart of how problem-solving processes can impact your ability to thrive & survive. The company had to try something new so it could thrive & survive. That meant people had to learn something new, and beyond that, they actually had to buy in and use what they learned. This story also points out that no matter your role, you may have great insights, and be able to offer value-adding capability beyond the obvious.

Product/Service

Introduction

Every business or organization whether for-profit, nonprofit, privately held, or publicly traded, offers some manner of product or service to the market and the world. These products or services are provided as answers to customer needs, and as solutions to the company's business objectives (be that profitability, or servicing benefactors of their nonprofit mission).

YOU are also a "product" that provides a "service" to the business and its stakeholders. Understanding YOU is an important part of thriving & surviving.

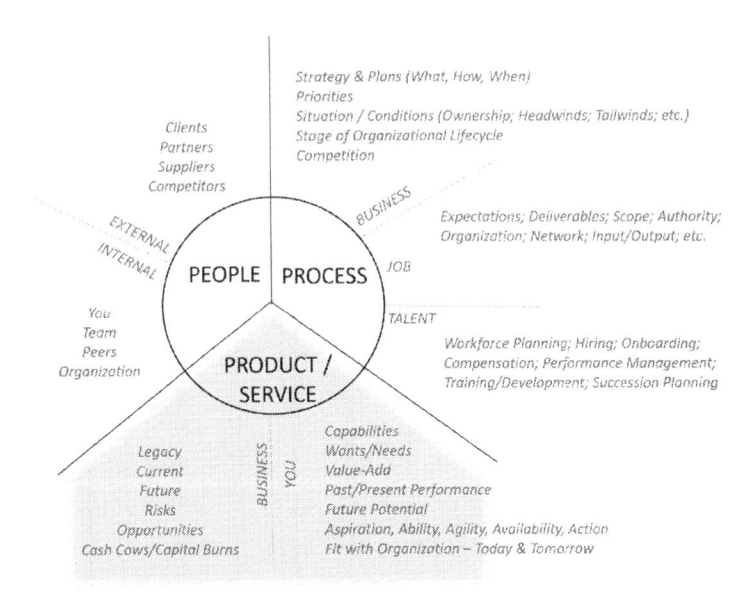

THE 3P MODEL – PRODUCT/SERVICE

Strategy & Plans (What, How, When)
Priorities
Situation / Conditions (Ownership; Headwinds; Tailwinds; etc.)
Stage of Organizational Lifecycle
Competition

Clients
Partners
Suppliers
Competitors

BUSINESS

Expectations; Deliverables; Scope; Authority;
Organization; Network; Input/Output; etc.

EXTERNAL
INTERNAL

PEOPLE | PROCESS

JOB

You
Team
Peers
Organization

PRODUCT / SERVICE

TALENT

Workforce Planning; Hiring; Onboarding;
Compensation; Performance Management;
Training/Development; Succession Planning

Legacy
Current
Future
Risks
Opportunities
Cash Cows/Capital Burns

BUSINESS   *YOU*

Capabilities
Wants/Needs
Value-Add
Past/Present Performance
Future Potential
Aspiration, Ability, Agility, Availability, Action
Fit with Organization – Today & Tomorrow

General *Product/Service* Insights When THRIVING & SURVIVING

Make sure products/services you provide are the very best they can be – delivering on customer expectations reliably and predictably. People want to know that they are getting what they expect – every time they purchase the product/service.

Customer wants and needs shift over time. Products and services that once were successful might simply fall out of favor and become irrelevant. Does anyone remember VHS and Betamax video tapes? Rotary dial home telephones? Gas station attendants (Who pumped your gas, checked your oil and tires, and even washed your windows!) To thrive & survive throughout your career, you'll do well to pay attention to how attractive the products/services you support are to your customers. If they are rock solid, great! But be mindful that they may run the risk of becoming commoditized, barely distinguishable from your competitors' offerings, and more susceptible to pricing pressures (all of which makes it harder to operate profitably).

Never forget that YOU are a product, providing a service to your employer. Just like other products/services, distinctive advantages can erode over time, and become less valuable to your customers. To thrive & survive, you must also be mindful of your distinctive advantage(s) so you don't become just another option in a very full world of other talented people. This should not be a foreign concept for our military veterans. You've likely spent much of your career discovering what training, assignments, and experiences are most likely to make you a top-tier candidate for the spots you seek on your career journey. Similar here in the civilian world. As you travel your career journey, seek out the experiences, education, assignments and so forth that make you attractive to employers, and a sought-out candidate rather than just another warm body. If you're not sure what those are, lean on your network. Engaging a career coach, advisor, or mentor would be a great option here.

Detailed *Product/Service* Insights When THRIVING & SURVIVING

Let's begin by discussing "Business" products.

To thrive & survive well, you really need to understand what your business/organization provides the world. What are the products it offers? What services does it provide? How do these offerings help make the world (or at least a part of it) a better place? Without this understanding it's difficult to understand how you and your role fit in the big picture. Understanding business products and leveraging that understanding can help you position yourself for success today, and in the future.

> ## *BILL STORY*
>
> *"Hitching Yourself to the Wrong Star."*
>
> *I had a coaching client who was a high performer, high potential employee with a solid track record of success and a broad portfolio of capabilities. He was savvy in his approach to managing his career, and mindful that thriving & surviving in the long run is a task we each need to own.*
>
> *The company he was in was quite large, with a diverse set of product lines for an array of customers in various industries.*
>
> *At one point, he had the wonderful opportunity to select his next role from several different internal options. We discussed a variety of topics, including the products each opportunity supported.*
>
> *He clearly had more familiarity with one product line. He had worked in/around that business for a few years, and was quite comfortable with it. He knew the product's history, its capabilities and limitations, and the value it brought to customers.*
>
> *One of the other opportunities was focused on a different product line, one with which my client was not quite so familiar. He had the technical and educational chops to qualify for the open role, but he hadn't worked as closely with this product line.*
>
> *At first blush, the obvious choice was to go with the option related to the more familiar products.*
>
> *While I understood his position, I pressed a bit. I suggested he re-frame his analysis and consider the future potential for each product line. Which was more likely to*

grow? Which was more likely to be in the customers' sights for the future? Which offered more opportunity to positively impact the company in the future?

He did his due diligence and discovered the product line he was most familiar with had somewhat different (and less) potential for the future. It was a legacy product that met past and current customer needs very well, was proven reliable, and was appropriately profitable. But it was also just about to the end of its potential for product improvement. Said simply, it did what it did quite well, and no manner of improvement was going to make it notably more capable, effective, efficient, or profitable. In addition, it was a component on an end-product that has been on the market for decades.

The other, less-familiar product line focused on cutting-edge technology. It supported emerging market trends, and while not as established, it had huge potential upside in terms of revenue, profitability, customer satisfaction, and more.

We discussed the situation, focusing on my client's long-term goals. What did thriving & surviving look like to him? Was working steadily on an established product, making incremental improvements on something that supported a customer's 80-year-old end product attractive? Was diving into something new and emerging, with less knowledge/experience, a risk proposition that he desired? Which one did he consider best aligned with his desired future? Which one was likely to meet his preferences for work/life balance? The questions went on and on.

In the end, my client decided that taking on the newer, less familiar product line option was the way to go. He recognized the risks and opportunities and understood the impact on quality of life. Though he had a bit of a learning curve at first—working his ass off and experiencing a bit of work/life imbalance— he's knocking it out of the park now.

As we've described previously, there are various types of business products/services. Leveraging your awareness of them to enhance your thriving & surviving success is time well spent.

- ★ **Legacy**
- ★ **Current**
- ★ **Future**
- ★ **Risks**
- ★ **Opportunities**
- ★ **Cash Cows & Capital Burns**

Legacy products/services are those that have been around for some time. Understanding their history is important and provides context about how they got to where they are today. Understanding legacy products/services' relevance and value to customers is an important leverage point for your ability to thrive & survive. If the legacy product/service's relevance to your customers is waning, the survivability of your company and/or your job may be at risk. Think of photographic film. Kodak and other companies successfully provided film to various markets for decades. The advent of digital camera technology changed all that. Yes, there is still some demand for film, but the markets have shifted significantly to digital. If your job was in the film industry, thriving & surviving took on a whole different set of challenges as this product shift arose.

As we mentioned in the LANDING section, some products/services answer a **current** need. We highlighted the fidget spinner example, which was a fad that arose quickly and burned out nearly as fast. If your job was directly tied to these items, you likely had a helluva good short-term run, and then found yourself wondering what came next. When it comes to thriving & surviving, there's nothing wrong with working on products/services that answer current needs, but always be aware of the future. Look at where things are likely going, and take actions to position yourself for continued success with them, or other paths to success if they wither.

Future focused products/services target an emerging need. This product space can be exciting and risky. Market swings, customer market preference shifts, competitive pressures, and other issues all may impact how realistic it is that the need for these products/services will exist in the future. Costs of commercializing the product/service may turn out to be prohibitive. The technology to bring them to market may be incredibly complex. The list of variables is nearly endless. That said, a couple of core business questions to consider include: does this make economic sense given today's realities? Does the potential upside outweigh the potential challenges? The nature of some jobs is to focus in this space. Research and development, advanced engineering, product development are some examples. If that's where your passion and capabilities lie, great! Just be aware that your ability to thrive & survive long term in this space may require you to consider your options if the new products/services don't successfully come to fruition.

Some products/services are **cash cows**. They generate lots of revenue and lots of profit. Other products/services **burn tons of capital**. They require a lot of money and other resources to become realities. Both can be important pieces of a business portfolio. Cash cows can provide relatively dependable sources of money that can be used for other purposes, while those that burn lots of capital can represent necessary investments into expanding current markets or establishing new ones. As they relate to successfully thriving & surviving in your career, it's worth your time and energy to understand what's what, the general direction they are heading, and how that may impact your career.

Whether the products/services your company provides are legacies, serve a current or future need, or are cash cows or capital burners, they all come with inherent levels of **risk and opportunity**. Thriving & surviving in the long run requires awareness of these risks, assessment of them against your career and life plans, and definitive action to mitigate the risks and optimize the opportunities. Be attentive. Consider things clearly. Act decisively. And you will thrive & survive well!

BILL STORY

"A Tale of Two Successes."

One of my very good friends has a career in advanced engineering. He loves being at the front end of ideas and figuring out the engineering solutions to bring them to life, so they can answer customer needs in a way that makes commercial sense for his employer. Often, doing this type of work can burn through a lot of capital. He's contributed to numerous successful new products and has also been involved in some that just didn't fly. He's fine with that. He knows that failed new products may be risky to his career, and he has changed jobs and employers. But overall, he's done a great job of building a robust network of key players, and a stellar reputation as a professional. He celebrates the wins, learns from the losses, and is energized by the inherent risks. He is living the definition of thriving & surviving.

Another good friend of mine has worked in the same small manufacturing company for nearly forty years. The company has a short list of clients that have predictable, profitable product needs. There may be small variations over time in terms of volume and/or specifications, but generally things keep rolling along in very similar patterns. Their customer list includes a large portion of legacy products that are cash cows. He loves his job and has been successfully thriving & surviving for decades!

The point here is that despite the specific product or service, and despite their nature, successfully thriving & surviving is a very individual thing. Success to one may be misery to another (neither of my two friends above would thrive & survive in the other's shoes).

SECTION 3: THRIVING & SURVIVING

No matter the nature of the products/services related to your career, there will always be associated risks and opportunities. Legacy products/services may continue to be anchors in the industry, or they may become less desirable over time. Products/services targeting current opportunities may grow into long term staples of your business, or they may fizzle fast. New products/services that are being developed for anticipated future needs may be spot on; or they may turn out to be colossal commercial flops.

I know what you may be thinking: "This is some abstract silly stuff, that only concerns some high-flying C-suite executives and over-paid analysts." *Au contraire, mon frère.* This is exactly the stuff that drives business decisions, and that shapes the battlefield in which you choose to operate. They have a direct impact on your ability to thrive & survive. You don't have to be an expert in all of these, but ignore them at your own peril. Don't just do your job; stay aware of the situation, and consider your options for forward progress, however you define that.

BILL STORY

"Drive Shafts and Electric Motors."

A large employer had been in business for decades. It was a leading provider of parts to name brand automotive manufactures. Its products were known for their quality and durability. Some of these products had been manufactured and sold for many years with only minor, incremental changes to meet evolving customer needs. The products were profitable, and work related to them was core to overall business success. As always happens in business, new ideas, trends, technologies, and needs began to emerge — in this case, around electrification. New market possibilities were on the horizon for companies that were early to wrangle the opportunities. As

> *you might imagine, the crossover of experience and expertise between our legacy products and the new opportunities was minimal. After all, designing and manufacturing mechanical components didn't generally include a heavy need for electrical-based technology. The business leaders recognized the opportunity, and initiated strategies to become a top tier player in the electrification space. This was definitely a good thing for the company, but it also forced some difficult decisions to be made. How much focus, effort, and resources should be shifted from legacy, profitable products to this new electrification opportunity? What are the risks of changing focus? What are the risks of not changing focus? What type of talent capability was needed? These and so many more questions arose. The leadership team did an outstanding job of threading some pretty delicate needles to set a sound strategy. That said, some individual employees faced some tough situations. If their skill sets, experience, capabilities, and preferences were not aligned to the new direction, their ability to thrive & survive in their current roles and with that company was at risk. Some were capable, but unwilling to change. They loved what they had been doing, and weren't about to shift gears—understandably, their journey got rocky. Others had capability gaps that were just too wide to bridge. These folks either found new roles within the company or moved on to other employers. In the end, diligent work went into creating the best teams possible to successfully continue the legacy product work, and to establish the new electrification business.*

YOU As a Product

Managing your career is your job. As we've mentioned, no one cares more about your career than you do. Considering yourself as a "product" that you must manage and market can be a valuable approach to successfully thriving & surviving in the long run. Understanding your capabilities, wants, needs, value-add, past and present performance, future potential, aspiration, ability, agility, availability, and actions are all important to accurately and robustly assessing your fit with organization today and tomorrow. Awareness of how your employer perceives your fit is also important.

So, what's the point to all this?

Things change. Sometimes in ways that are right up your alley; sometimes in totally different ways. These changes may cause you to consider whether to stick in place or to jump off to another opportunity.

When that time comes, being ready is always better than winging it.

- ★ Know yourself, your career plan, and your life plan.
- ★ Know the situation.
- ★ Understand your options and their likely risks and rewards.
- ★ Make the decisions you believe are best for your ability to thrive & survive.
- ★ Then, attack that next step vigorously!

THRIVING & SURVIVING SUMMARY

One does not thrive & survive without effort. Be mindful and continually assess whether or not your career aligns with your life journey. If so, great! Keep on keepin' on! If not, look closely at how you might adjust your current situation, or if need be, to make another transition. You only get one shot at life, do yourself a solid - pay attention to how things are going, and make adjustments where needed.

FINAL THOUGHTS

Congratulations! Having made it to this point in the book, you've invested a fair amount of time, effort, and attention in yourself. You've taken an important step to prepare yourself for a future where your career and life journeys align to bring success, however you define it.

We hope that you've found value already from this investment.

We are confident that by putting these insights to action, you will realize even more value.

Further, we hope that we've inspired hope in you.

Hope that keeps you moving forward to optimize the great, exciting days ahead.

Hope that helps you successfully traverse the challenging days that befall us all.

Hope that your career and life journeys are long, rewarding, and full of joy.

Be well our friends. Keep up the fire.

KEY INSIGHT SUMMARY

LANDING

General

1. LANDING is about identifying the people, processes, products/services that are relevant to your job.
2. Doing the hard work to land the job merely gets you to the starting line. It is critically important to get off the blocks strong, get a good start. Making the right impression on this new team will largely be dependent on how you shape your actions relative to the people, processes, and product/service at your new company.
3. Ensure that your new job aligns with your overall life plan

People

4. Employers also want to see their new employees land well.
5. Quickly connect with your co-workers and new teammates beyond the name and job title. Build a deliberate plan to do so.
6. Don't overcomplicate things; identifying the "Who's Who" and the "What's What" is the key in the LANDING phase.
7. Employers don't speak "mil-speak" or "veteran-ese." Learn their language, just like you would expect them to learn yours if they joined the military.
8. Listen more than you speak.
9. There may be biases or pre-conceived notions about veterans. Be you; biases are broken by positive action and results.

10. No one wears their resume on their chest in the civilian workplace. Understanding the landscape of both your co-worker population and external stakeholders is still doable. It may just take a little background work.
11. INTERNAL
    - *You* - First impressions matter. Be on time, dress appropriately, be attentive, listen actively, speak clearly, engage eagerly, be open to learning, identify how you and your position fit within the bigger picture.
    - *Your Team* - Identify what positions exist on your team, what they do, and how they fit.
    - *Peers* - Peers can be great resources to you when you land. Identify who your peers are. Explore the nature of their relationships. Discover points of positive potential and discern negative consequences.
    - *Other Organizational Members* - Identify the organizational architecture and who does what; keep your eyes and ears open.
12. EXTERNAL
    - *Clients* - People and organizations outside your company with whom you work, who bring certain knowledge, expertise, capability, or connections that better enable you and your company to achieve success, and that derive some manner of success for themselves.
    - *Suppliers* - Suppliers are individuals or companies that provide a product or service, for a fee, that you need to successfully complete your mission.
    - *Competitors* - Competitors are entities that are competing in the same market space with either a similar product/service, a replacement product/service, or a product/service that eliminates the need for your product/service.

Process

13. Every company does things a little differently, so it is essential to identify overall business processes, the processes related to your job, and talent-related processes.
14. Identifying existing process maps can be very helpful.
15. Organizations' processes likely have been in place long before your time at the company. The fastest way to "be that guy" is to start pumping in suggestions before understanding how all of the pieces interact with each other.
16. Most civilian companies are "deployed"—on production—all the time! Standing down for any reason takes away from revenue potential, and thus is not often a preferred approach.
17. Training is frequently viewed in the civilian workforce as a cost rather than an investment, and costs are not good for the bottom line.
18. There may be some ambiguity when you first join a new company, and there may not be a field manual for everything (or anything)! But even in the absence of policy (SOPs) there likely will be common practices. Discover what these are, so that you can begin to conduct business in a manner similar to what the organization is familiar with.
19. BUSINESS PROCESSES
    - ★ *Strategy, Plans, And Priorities* - Identify what your company's strategic plan is and how your role fits within this strategy. Identify what early indicators are relevant to your new role, and the processes related to tracking them.
    - ★ *Stage Of Organization's Life Cycle* - Businesses tend to follow a life cycle from Launch/Startup to Growth/Expansion, then Shakeout/Stability, Maturity, and Decline. Simply identifying roughly where the organization is in its life cycle is sufficient when landing.

- *Competition* - Defining competition, and the processes by which it comes to life will help drive your interactions with competitors and clients, and result in achieving competitive advantage rather than losing it.

20. JOB SPECIFIC PROCESSES
    - *Expectations* - Know exactly what the expectations of your role are. Do the work you were hired to do, demonstrate capability, build credibility, and your opportunities to do more, different things will grow.
    - *Deliverables* - How often? What quality? To which customers? Are there any constraints? What are the reporting procedures? How do different deliverables interact with each other? Are they complimentary? Do they conflict? What products or processes depend on your deliverables, and what do you depend on?
    - *Scope and Authority* - Identify who owns the decision-making authority for decisions that impact your position, and how broad/deep these authorities extend.
    - *Organization* - Organizations may be broken down by functional areas such as marketing, operations, finance, sales, engineering and others, or it may be broken down by product line or project. Global companies will likely have divisions based on geography.
    - *Network* - Don't stop networking just because you got hired.
    - *Input/Output* - Knowing what your input/outputs are helps you identify where reliable, dependable, repeatable processes may be replicated, and a general sense of the 'direction' of your workflows.

21. TALENT RELATED PROCESSES
    - *Workforce Planning* - How the company manages its

workforce planning will be a good indicator of its overall talent strategy.
- ★ *Hiring* - Knowing the hiring process will help you understand where to prioritize your efforts and how you can add value right out of the gate, setting yourself up for future success.
- ★ *Compensation* - Think "total compensation" and not just what goes directly into your bank account in the form of a paycheck.
- ★ *Performance Management* - At this phase, knowing what is being used and what your expectations are in the process will be adequate.
- ★ *Training/Development* - You are your own biggest advocate. Training and development are more decentralized and self-driven than in the military.
- ★ *Succession Planning* - When you are landing, succession planning may not be at the top of your priority list; however, keep your eyes and ears open to get a basic level of awareness about how it is addressed. Knowing how succession planning is handled at your organization may give you an initial impression about how this process might impact you later.
- ★ *Onboarding* – In the civilian workplace, onboarding will rarely be as rigorous as the military. Be present for the experience. Look beyond the surface when things aren't what you expected. Remember that the gaps you experience may only be gaps from your perspective. There are likely history, background, context and constraints of which you are not aware. When asked, offer positive feedback that might help improve the onboarding process. Be part of the solution, not the cause of headaches right out of the gate

Product/Service

22. When first landing, it's important to start identifying your business' products/services. After all, your job exists to help deliver the best possible product/service at the least possible costs.
23. Remember that YOU are a product that provides services to the employer, and you need to ensure your ability to do so is well maintained and developed.
24. By growing your capability, your credibility, and thus your "brand," you can grow your ability to help the company deliver their products and services.
25. Employers' business mission, product/service are as important to them as your military mission was to you.
26. Bottom line: employers have work to do, and need people who fit well on their team.
27. Sometimes business conditions change. The good news is that when business conditions change and it impacts your landing, extreme examples are rare, and most employers are empathetic enough to do their very best with you.
28. YOU AS THE PRODUCT OR SERVICE
    - ★ When the employer extended an offer for you to join their team, they saw capability in you to do the work they need done and to fit well on their team.
    - ★ If you have capabilities beyond the current job, keep them in your toolbox, close at hand. You never know when the chance may arise for you to demonstrate these also!
    - ★ We all have wants and needs. When landing, it's wise to be mindful of yours; to vet how well this new gig aligns with them.
    - ★ A disconnect between reality and your wants/needs will likely create some challenges over time.

KEY INSIGHT SUMMARY

- ☆ If things are going well, drive on! If there are some concerns/red flags, build in time as you land to vet them, make decisions, and take appropriate actions.

29. BUSINESS PRODUCTS AND SERVICES
    - ★ Legacy products/services are those that have been around for a while; perhaps years or decades.
    - ★ Some products/services answer a current need. Identifying products/services in this category provides insights as to the lay of the land, especially in regard to potential product/service offering changes that may be on the horizon.
    - ★ Identifying the risks and opportunities of the products/services most closely related to your role can be time well spent when landing.
    - ★ Some products/services are cash cows. They generate lots of revenue and lots of profit. Other products/services burn tons of capital.

INTEGRATING

General

30. During the INTEGRATING phase, you are moving past the formalities of the onboarding process, learning how things really operate, and establishing your place in the organization.
31. The INTEGRATING phase is time to start successfully doing the work that needs to be done, while fitting in with and adding value to the team.
32. "Capable" and "Credible" are two different things.

- ★ "Capability" is evidenced by past success.
- ★ "Credibility" speaks to potential and relevance.

33. Once your capability becomes credible to the employer, you are on your way to integration success!
34. To integrate well, you need to add value — as the employer measures it.
    - ★ Get clear on expectations. Learn why they are important, and how they are measured.
    - ★ Understand how you fit and add value to each of them, and how the boss needs to hear about progress.
    - ★ Go forth and deliver to the very best of your ability.
35. Money drives business. You better have at least a cursory understanding of business accounting and cash flow through the company.
36. You Can Do it. Don't fall prey to the "oh shits." Be confident; you've done tough stuff before, and you can do this.
37. Your new organization is what it is. It's not the one you came from.
38. The military must "build" its talent; in the civilian world employers often "buy" talent. This impacts how leadership and career development are understood and managed.
39. Leadership means very different things in the civilian world. It rarely is as robustly understood as it is in the military. Investing in leadership development is unfortunately rare.
40. Innovation is a funny thing. It is a huge priority for some companies, but for others it is a necessary evil.
41. Learn when to lean on and leverage your military experience directly and when to be more subtle.
42. Pay attention to the culture. It's the work world you're going to be living in.
43. Integrating can take energy. Be resilient. Keep a positive perspective.
44. Be assertive without being aggressive. Press on, but know

when to get off the gas and coast for a while to let the journey evolve.
45. Your focus greatly impacts your success. Yes, we need to remember our past, but we must focus forward.
46. Integrating well requires a certain amount of vulnerability. This is the antithesis of everything we learned and became in the military. Reframe the definition. Consider appropriate, helpful vulnerability as being open, honest, transparent, and exposed to others, new ideas, new processes, and new products/services that are inherent in your new work world.
47. Integrating well also requires solid conflict resolution capabilities. Understand the situation, apply appropriate interventions, and do your level best to find the "win-win."
48. Networking wasn't just for transition. To integrate well, you're going to need a solid network. Get out and meet people.
49. Be you.

People

50. Whether internal or external, people are your "stakeholders."
51. Know what you know, acknowledge there's far more you don't know, and learn how you fit.
52. INTERNAL
    * *You* – Understanding yourself, your capabilities, preferences, pet peeves, aspirations, and your "Why, How, and What" are foundational to integrating well. Being self-aware will help you assess and respond to various situations in a way that stays true to you without over- or underreacting.
    * *Your Team* - Integrating well with your direct teammates makes a real difference in your overall success.

Understand your team and their professional interests and aspirations.
- ★ *Peers* – Peers are those folks with relatively similar roles at relatively similar levels in the company, with whom you may or may not have regular interaction, and who are working in different departments, divisions, units, or functions of the organization. You'll need to learn how to effectively interact with your peers to accomplish your mission.
- ★ *Organization* – There will always be people in the broader organization that have seemingly zero relevance to your job. It's still worth your time and effort to keep your eyes/ears open to who these folks are, how they fit, what value they bring, and so on. You never know when an unexpected opportunity may arise that changes your assignment and puts you in direct contact with these good folks.

53. EXTERNAL
    - ★ No job or business exists in a vacuum. There are many other people outside the company that impact and are impacted by you and your business. They, too, have specific perspectives, interests, challenges, opportunities, expectations, and timing.
    - ★ *Clients* – These are your source of revenue (in a for-profit company) and the community you serve (in a nonprofit company). Without their demand for your products/services, the organization (and your job) go away. Learning and understanding who they are, why they are buying/consuming your product/service, what their priorities are, and the challenges, opportunities, constraints, future plans, and other factors affecting them makes you a more valuable employee.
    - ★ *Partners* - Partners are people/organizations outside your company that have established partnership

KEY INSIGHT SUMMARY

agreements beneficial to them and your company. Learning and understanding who your business' partners are, how they operate, and their unique areas of excellence can provide invaluable insight as you integrate, and add to your individual value proposition.

★ *Suppliers* – Those people/organizations from whom you/your company purchases goods/services that enable your business to operate. Learning and understanding them and their goals, business models, and constraints is important to your ability to negotiate service agreements that are a win-win.

★ *Competitors* – Other organizations that are competing with your firm for market share. Much like the military, it is important to know your competitors. What is their value proposition? Their strategy? What does their supply chain look like? Their pricing models? And so much more.

Process

54. Business Processes - Learning and understanding the following categories of business processes can place you in a strong position to integrate broadly and deeply, and to add real value to the organization.
    ★ *Strategy, Plans & Priorities*
    ★ *Scope & Authority*
    ★ *Organization*
    ★ *Network*
    ★ *Input/Output*
55. Talent Related Processes - Integrating well includes learning about the talent-related processes that impact you, your current performance, and your potential future pathway. Learn all you can about them along the way.
    ★ *Workforce Planning*
    ★ *Hiring*

- *Onboarding*
- *Compensation*
- *Performance Management*
- *Training/Development*
- *Succession Planning*

Product/Service

56. Once you know the products or services that the company offers and the strategy behind it, the key to integrating well is to figure out how you can add value to them. Organizations produce/provide certain products/services for a reason. No matter the reason, to help you integrate well, it's a good idea to dig below the surface, to really understand the who, what, when, why, and how behind the products/services. Few products/services exist forever without change.
57. Integrating well depends on you always being mindful that YOU are a product providing a service to your employer. Don't ever lose track of your responsibility to lead and manage your own career journey. Be diligent in assessing and understanding your value as a "product" to the employment market for today and for tomorrow.

THRIVING & SURVIVING

General

58. To thrive & survive in the long run:
    - Be keenly aware of your surroundings.
    - Stay well informed and knowledgeable as broadly and deeply as possible.

- ★ Always keep a dual focus on today and tomorrow.
- ★ Seek balance in all things.
59. Success is what you define it to be. YOU have to define your success.
60. The civilian work world is fluid. Many variables impact your work world.
61. You'll be faced with challenges and opportunities, and may have to make decisions about whether to stay, go, or attempt to adjust your employment situation.
62. Thriving & surviving is all about leveraging your capabilities, skills, experiences, and your understanding of and relationships with the people, processes, and products/services that surround you.
63. "Leveraging" means working positively with and through others to overcome challenges, optimize opportunities, and achieve individual and organizational success today and tomorrow. It DOES NOT mean taking advantage of or using others for negative or self-serving purposes.
64. As it relates to your life journey, thriving & surviving is all about situational awareness, and ensuring your situation aligns with your overall life plan. Are you getting closer to your career destination? If YES – leverage it to optimize current and future success. If NO - reassess to confirm, define better next steps, and take professional action.
65. To thrive & survive over the long term, you need to look out for yourself, and do what's right for you, your current success, and your future. Strike and maintain a very careful balance between being a team player and being your own Chief Marketing Officer.
66. Balance technical and soft skills; leverage your intangible skills to achieve tangible results.
67. No matter how "big" you are, how much you enjoy your current gig, or what you think is next in your career plan, sometimes things happen. Uncontrollable forces invade

your reality and create changes that are unexpected. These may be great, positive surprises, or they may be the last thing on earth you'd ever want.
68. As your time with an organization grows, so does your capability. To keep the great role you have, and/or to grow your career over time, you must also continually expand your credibility.
69. Do the best work you can do. Be the best team player you can be. Learn all you can learn. Build the best network possible. Then let the chips fall where they may.
70. Business conditions change. Leadership teams change. The winners in the thrive & survive game are those that adjust to both and that build credibility no matter the headwinds/tailwinds.
71. Organizations have a life cycle. They are where they are. It impacts how they operate – and how well you might thrive & survive. There are great opportunities and challenges in every phase of this life cycle. Be aware of where the winds are blowing and how that is impacting your role as well as the people, processes, and products/services around you.
72. Shit happens. No matter your capability, your experience, your style, your leadership, your professionalism, your dedication, or anything else, there are times when uncontrollable, nonsensical factors carry the day. Don't live in fear of the negative potential, but always have a PACE plan in case the unexpected arises.
73. Understanding risk, its impact, and how it is handled in your new industry, company, or job can be a huge benefit to your ability to thrive & survive. Do your level best to know and experience as much as possible as deeply and broadly as you can. Get comfortable knowing that you'll never know everything, and that those unknowns can have real impact.

People

74. INTERNAL
    - ★ To thrive & survive, you need to continue to broaden and deepen your understanding not only of the people, but also how you build and leverage relationships that help you, them, and the organization succeed.
    - ★ Stakeholders will always be part of your journey to thrive & survive.
    - ★ In business you will find team members playing a variety of roles. Some are defined by the job: the operator, the supervisor, the accountant, the IT specialist, your HR partner, and so on. Beyond these, people bring other, less tangible team member roles, including:
        - ✭ *Sounding Boards*
        - ✭ *Blind Faithful*
        - ✭ *Naysayers/Devil's Advocates*
        - ✭ *Technical Experts*
        - ✭ *Sage Purveyors of Wisdom*
        - ✭ *Fresh New Players*
    - ★ You are always in a much more powerful position to thrive & survive if you know who you are, what you bring to the party, how you define success, where you are, where you're going, and how you plan to get there, rather than wondering about it all and hoping the winds of change might randomly blow you some great place.
    - ★ The sense of team in the civilian work world often looks quite different than it does in the military. That said, success rarely comes to those who don't know, understand, respect, regard, and play well with team members.

- ★ Team members play a variety of roles. Identify, learn and leverage your team members to bring out the best in them, and to benefit from the value they bring!
- ★ Peers can make or break your thriving & surviving success.
- ★ Peers will have their own priorities, motivators, agendas, relationships, egos, abilities, etc. Some will be great colleagues. Others will simply co-exist in your orbit. Others still will be thorns in your side.
- ★ There will always be some number of other folks in the organization with whom you need to interact to make progress, knock down doors, etc.
- ★ People really are the key to success. Know yourself. Understand your team and your peers. Build and nurture a quality network throughout the organization. Leverage the positive relationships, and improve the challenging ones where you can. You'll be glad you did.

75. EXTERNAL
    - ★ Finding and engaging with partners who cover your blind spots, who bring the needed expertise you lack, or who otherwise help you move forward to success is smart.
    - ★ To thrive & survive think beyond the transactional. Seek to build business relationships that are win-wins.
    - ★ Don't slip into the negative world of slamming your competitors. Be better than they are.

76. Each stage in an organization's life cycle has certain characteristics and expectations that impact culture, talent needs, and the work environment.
    - ★ Different segments of your organization may be at different stages.
    - ★ Even in mature companies, startup opportunities may arise.

KEY INSIGHT SUMMARY 283

- ★ Even businesses that are in decline my present fantastic job opportunities.

Process

77. Processes Evolve. To thrive & survive in the long run, you'll need to not only know, understand and be able to use existing processes, you'll also need to be situationally aware, noticing the tides of change and the impact those changes are having on the processes that are part of your world.
78. Look for opportunities to improve processes. Having a mindset of continuous improvement will always be beneficial to your long-term success. Changes may be a slow evolution, where the impact is barely perceptible. They may also come from sudden, major changes that arise out of nowhere.
79. Don't get stuck in the "we've always done it this way" mindset.
80. Business processes may span the entire business and will likely cross department or functional lines.
81. Most civilian organizations' strategic planning processes are less robust and well-integrated than what you likely experienced in the military. Work with relevant decision-makers to help them understand the value, and walk with them at a pace they can accept
82. To thrive & survive over time, gain an understanding of the processes used to make priorities. If they are effective, great! Use them! If not, leverage your solid experience as a veteran to help as much as possible to evolve or emplace processes that are clear and consistent, and help people and the organization succeed.
83. Understanding competition is important to the success of any business.

84. Job Processes are important to understand if you intend to successfully thrive & survive in the long run.
    - ★ Get clear on the expectations & deliverables required for your job.
    - ★ Understand the scope/authority of your role.
    - ★ Over time, your scope and authority may change. If changes to your scope and authority appear to be smaller, be sure you take a really good look at the situation – smaller isn't always a bad thing.
    - ★ Defining where your job fits in the organization can also make a positive impact on your ability to thrive & survive.
    - ★ Thriving & surviving without an effective network is damn near impossible. Inputs and outputs change. Whether job or life related, the ins and outs of your experience will always be shifting. Always keep your career and life goals center-focus so you stay on track, moving forward toward them.
85. Talent Processes - These may be robust or nearly non-existent.
    - ★ "Buy versus build" strategy differences drive a different talent mindset in the civilian world, which may impact your short- and long-term career success.
    - ★ Workforce planning - Pay attention to your organization's workforce planning practices. Learn what they are. Find the positives and the opportunities for improvement. Hiring, in the context of thriving & surviving, is to understand how the internal/external hiring decisions are made so you are aware of how they might impact your ability to successfully perform today and in the future.
    - ★ Compensation - Relative to thriving & surviving, it's important to consider your "total compensation." Many people get laser focused on their salary or wage, and

KEY INSIGHT SUMMARY

forget about the other factors contributing to the rest of their "total compensation package."

★ Performance Management in the civilian work world is often far different than in the military.
  ☆ There are as many variations and applications of this process as you can imagine. Understanding how it works, why it's designed the way it is, and what it's used for can be helpful as you navigate your thrive & survive journey.
  ☆ If you land with an organization that is lacking in this area, you may be disheartened. If so, don't make a knee jerk reaction. Do your job to the best of your ability. Professionally share your observations for improvement. Use your experience to help improve things.

★ Training & Development - The military does training & development differently—and better—than the vast majority of civilian organizations.
  ☆ The difference is a product of the "buy versus build" talent mentality addressed above. Afterall, if I can go buy capable talent, why would I spend the money to train and develop people?
  ☆ Unlike the military, with its familiar "train, deploy, refit, repeat" cycle, businesses are "deployed" all the time. They are "on production," working hard to provide their products/services all the time. Time, money and other resources that distract from this get scrutinized carefully to ensure the decision-makers are convinced they are investments that make sense (and will generate more revenue and profit than they cost).

★ Succession Planning & Career Management in the civilian work world are not the same as the military. The reasons for this include:

- ☆ The "buy versus build" talent mentality
- ☆ A general lack of appreciation for the investment value of providing robust succession planning and career management
- ☆ The pace and variability of civilian business

86. Career Pathing is organization-focused.
87. Career Planning is individual-focused.
88. To thrive & survive in the long run, you'll have to own your journey; working with relevant staff and leaders to understand potential career paths (even if there's nothing clearly defined by the organization) and chart your own career plan.
89. Problem Solving Process -To thrive & survive in the long run, understand how problems are solved in your organization. Discover what factors are contributing to the existence of problems in the first place. Do your best to leverage your solid problem-solving capabilities to improve the situation.

Product/Service

90. Make sure products/services you provide are the very best they can be – delivering on customer expectations reliably and predictably.
91. Customer wants and needs shift over time.
92. Never forget that YOU are a product, providing a service to your employer.
93. "Business" Products/Services - To thrive & survive well, you really need to understand what your business/organization provides the world.
94. Future focused products/services target an emerging need. Consider your options if the new products/services don't successfully come to fruition.

KEY INSIGHT SUMMARY 287

95. Some products/services are cash cows, while others burn capital (money). Understand what's what, the general direction in which they are heading, and how that may impact your career.
96. All products/services come with inherent levels of risk and opportunity. Be aware of these risks, assess them against your career and life plans, and take definitive action to mitigate the risks and optimize the opportunities. Be attentive. Consider things clearly. Act decisively.
97. Never forget that YOU are a product, providing a service to your employer. Managing your career is your job. When opportunity arises, being ready is always better than winging it.

ABOUT THE AUTHORS

BILL KIEFFER

https://www.linkedin.com/in/williamkieffer

Bill has coached, advised, mentored, and worked with hundreds of service members, veterans, and others around the globe regarding career transition, leadership development, and performance improvement throughout his career.

He is the author of *Military Career Transition: Insights from the Employer Side of the Desk, which* was released in July 2021 as the #1 New Release in Amazon's Job Hunting category.

He is President & Chief Advisor of Kieffer & Associates Limited, an advisory firm specializing in Military Veteran Career Transition, Leadership Coaching, Strategic Talent Management, and Professional Speaking and Facilitation services.

He is also:

- ★ Coach, coach advisory board member, and faculty member for The Honor Foundation, a nonprofit group

providing career transition services to the special operations community.
- ★ Master trainer for Ranger for Life's *A More Elite Transition program*, serving the U.S. Army's 75th Ranger Regiment.
- ★ A Member of the Board of Advisors for Law Enforcement Connect, which provides career transition services to members of the law enforcement community.

Bill is a senior human resources executive with more than 22 years of professional experience in multiple large, complex, global companies. His broad-ranging work includes full spectrum human resources and talent management, and coaching/advising individual leaders and teams, from the C-suite to the shop floor.

Prior to these experiences, Bill served nearly 12 years active duty as a U.S. Army officer in a variety of command and staff positions. He is a veteran of Operation Restore Hope in Somalia, supported Operation Just Cause (the Panama invasion), operations in Central America, and Hurricane Andrew relief operations. During Bill's assignment with the U.S. Army Logistics Management College, he was selected as their Instructor of the Year. A Distinguished Military Graduate from the University of Toledo ROTC program, Bill later went on to earn the U.S. Army Ordnance Center's Herbert W. Alden Award, as the outstanding honor graduate of the Ordnance Officer Advanced Course. He was the recipient of several awards and decorations and earned both Airborne and Air Assault qualifications.

Active in his community, Bill was twice appointed and thrice elected to public office, and serves with several veteran-related organizations.

Bill was honored to present "Investing in the Middle" at TEDx Toledo in 2017. He has worked in and traveled to 33 countries — he's set foot on every continent except Antarctica.

His education background includes:
- ★ Strategic Human Resources Program - Harvard Business School

- ★ Leadership Education Program - Harvard University's John F. Kennedy School of Government.
- ★ Master of Science, Administration degree - Central Michigan University
- ★ Bachelor of Business Administration degree - the University of Toledo
- ★ Numerous other military and professional development courses

Bill is a certified coach via Marshall Goldsmith and the WHY Institute.

As for his personal life, he is married with five grown kids. In his free time, Bill loves riding his Harley.

DAVE WHITE

https://www.linkedin.com/in/davidmwhite1

David is an 18-year veteran of the Army's Special Operations Command. He deployed fourteen times in support of the Global War on Terror; four times to Iraq, and ten times to Afghanistan. He medically retired in 2020 after suffering from a gunshot wound sustained in 2018. David is the recipient of five Bronze Star Awards (2 for

Valor), the Purple Heart, and numerous other military awards. He has attended and graduated from a multitude of military schools throughout his career.

Currently, he serves as the Director of Firelands Forward, a three-county workforce collaborative in Northern Ohio. Under his leadership, Firelands Forward was awarded the top award for Talent Development and Retention from the International Economic Development Council, and the community impact award from the Childcare Resource Center. His published work consists of the "Workforce Hierarchy of Needs" in the Scientific Research Institute's Journal of Business and Management.

David also:
- Serves as a mentor for the Three Rangers Foundation
- Serves on several local and regional workforce and economic development boards
- Is an Adjunct Professor of Business at Bowling Green State University

His education background includes:
- Leadership Decision Making Program - Harvard Kennedy School of Government
- Executive Master of Business Administration degree – Ohio State University's Fisher College of Business
- Bachelor of Sports and Health Science degree - American Public University
- Lean Six Sigma – Black Belt Level II
- Graduate of numerous other military and professional development courses

David is married to his wife Libby, and they have two children: Sawyer and Leo.

Made in the USA
Monee, IL
25 June 2023